f GRACE

by Dave Brosha

Foreword by Viktoria Haack

First Edition

For information on purchasing bulk quantities of this book, or to obtain media excerpts or invite the author to speak at an event, please visit rmbooks.com and select the "Contact" tab.

RMB | Rocky Mountain Books Ltd.
rmbooks.com
@rmbooks
facebook.com/rmbooks

Cataloguing data available from Library and Archives Canada
ISBN 9781771605861 (hardcover)
ISBN 9781771605878 (electronic)

All photographs are by Dave Brosha unless otherwise noted.

Design by Colin Parks
Cover photo: Sand dunes in low light are always a photographic "win," but these unique formations in the Gobi Desert in Mongolia took my breath away with their layered symmetry. It almost looks like two people lying on their sides. (Location: Khongoryn Els, Gobi Gurvansaikhan National Park, Mongolia.)

Printed and bound in China

We would like to also take this opportunity to acknowledge the traditional territories upon which we live and work. In Calgary, Alberta, we acknowledge the Niitsítapi (Blackfoot) and the people of the Treaty 7 region in Southern Alberta, which includes the Siksika, the Piikuni, the Kainai, the Tsuut'ina, and the Stoney Nakoda First Nations, including Chiniki, Bearpaw, and Wesley First Nations. The City of Calgary is also home to Métis Nation of Alberta, Region III. In Victoria, British Columbia, we acknowledge the traditional territories of the Lkwungen (Esquimalt and Songhees), Malahat, Pacheedaht, Scia'new, T'Sou-ke, and W̱SÁNEĆ (Pauquachin, Tsartlip, Tsawout, Tseycum) peoples.

We acknowledge the financial support of the Government of Canada through the Canada Book Fund and the Canada Council for the Arts, and of the province of British Columbia through the British Columbia Arts Council and the Book Publishing Tax Credit.

TONES of GRACE

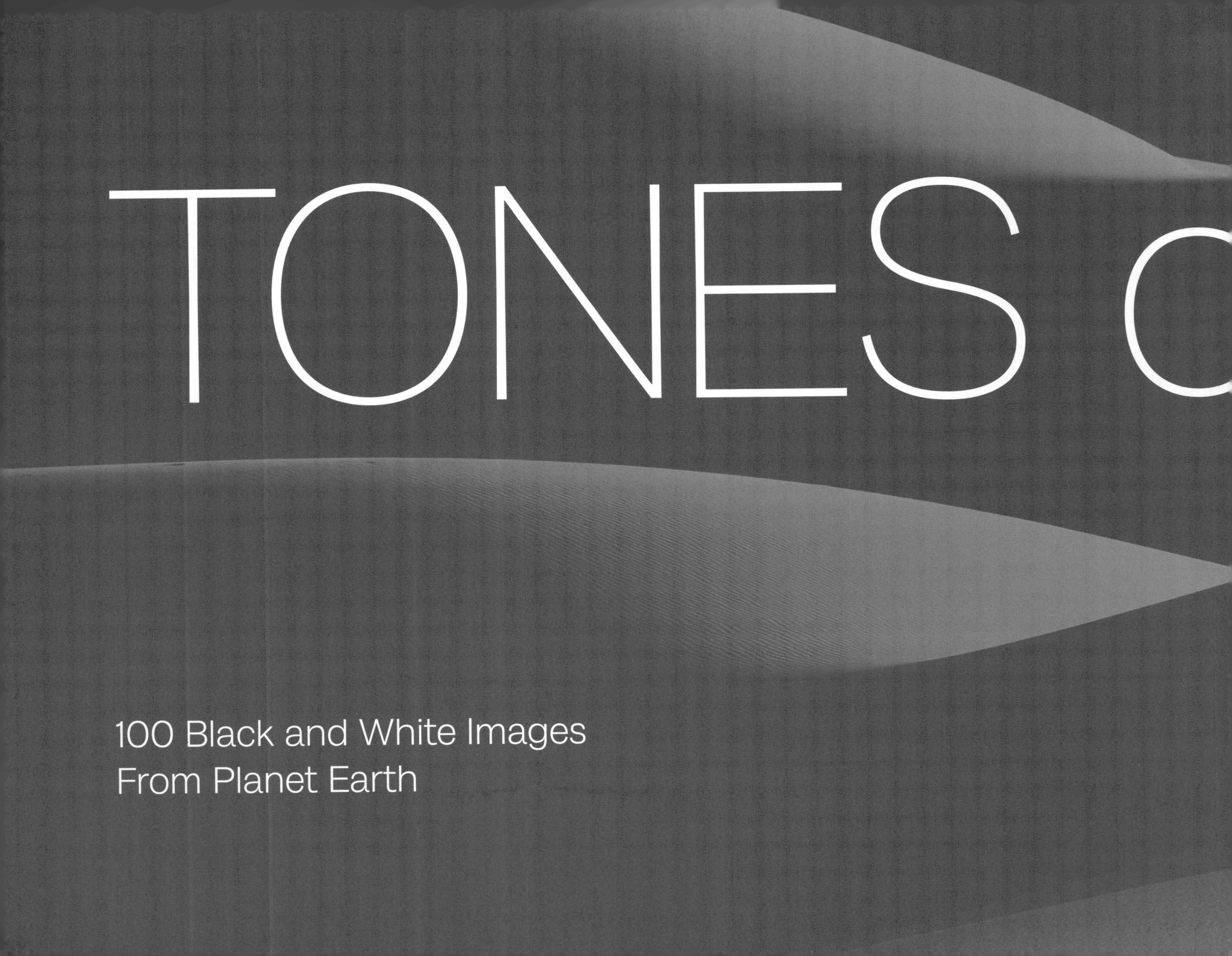

TONES O

100 Black and White Images
From Planet Earth

Contents

Dedication

With this, my third collection of images, I am no less grateful now than I was when I typed out the words for my initial body of work, *Northern Light*.

An artist's life isn't always easy, and it takes a lot of hard work and dedication to remain present within this space. A lot of the journey is internal, to be certain, but the *external* has an oversized influence on the health of your path. People drop into your life, and many of them stay. Some you know, and they know that they have helped you. You tell them, in person. Others help you more than they'll ever know, even if they've never met you. They're inspirations from afar, but no less important. The known, and those you've never met – they help shape your world view and your existence. Their impact is large, and both categories deserve to be thanked.

First and foremost, I want to thank my children: Lily, Liam and Luke. You are the smile in the course of a day. You are the light. You are the colour.

To Amy. You helped me in countless ways in the creation of this collection, and in life.

Viktoria Haack, you are an inspiration, and a photographic wizard. Your view of the world is one we should all treasure. Your words I will forever cherish.

To Don and the team at RMB. Thank you for believing in me.

To the creatives and artistic souls who have influenced me and the images within this book: the world needs your light. You never know when you click a shutter to capture an image that you might change someone's life in the process, but you've done that. You've changed me. Within the pages of this book, I list a number of influences and I am offering a heartfelt thanks to them all, but I'll single out Sebastião Salgado here. Your dedication and craft have altered my path in dramatic ways. I found a new road to travel because of you.

To Erin, thank you for your gift – it sparked a passion. And thank you for all the good you have brought to my life. It cannot be quantified.

Foreword

by Viktoria Haack

It appears to me that many of the good deeds that come from the direction of Dave Brosha arrive with a sentence like this one: "So, random question...would you have any interest in...?"

When I think of Dave, I immediately envision his beautiful imagery, but I cannot think of him as a photographer alone; his personality and kindness are inseparable from his work. I think of him not only as a very talented creative with a unique personal vision of the world but also as an optimist, a mentor, someone who consistently raises up and encourages others and, most importantly, a father who cares for and is deeply committed to his family.

I moved to Canada from the UK in 2007. It wasn't long before I discovered Dave's work.

I can remember the very first photograph of his that caught my eye: an incredible image of a Mi'kmaq warrior reflected in a pool of water. It was photographed at sunrise with beautiful lighting – yet it was the overall mood that was so fascinating. He not only captured an intriguing portrait – he captured a sense of a foreign northern land that I had never experienced and now wanted to visit.

From there, I recall searching out more of his images and being fascinated by the breadth of his work and its quiet beauty: portraits that draw you in not just by virtue of captured personality and emotion but also through their use of environment. It is easy to see why Dave is not a fan of labels, as his work fluidly crosses genres. His love of nature and the landscape seeps into his portrait work and vice versa. For me, evoking mood in portraits can be a challenge, but often feels easier to accomplish than in a landscape or nature image. We are already working with a vessel filled with human emotion, but to relay a sense of mood in the landscape is another thing. Dave's non-human subjects are also mood filled and highly evocative. They offer us a clear sense of what it's like to be in that place, and something of Dave himself: how he experienced it, what he was *feeling*. As a generalist photographer myself, I understand how Dave's worlds flow into each other. There is no defined line between portraits and landscapes: he is captivated by the beauty of existence in all its varied forms.

Let's go back to the start. Dave sent me a message via social media that started with the words above: "So, random question

Viktoria...would you have any interest at all in being one of my 2019 Land and See speakers?"

Land and See is Dave's brainchild: a creative gathering and conference combining landscape and portrait genres, bringing together a diverse group of artists, photographers, musicians, comedians and storytellers, held in a beautiful barn on beautiful Prince Edward Island. I was both surprised and flattered to be asked to present. The invitation didn't come without some trepidation, however: anyone who knows me knows that public speaking is my nemesis and something that has long been a fear for me. In university days, for example, I would prepare for weeks leading up to the date of a seminar presentation. I would know my subject and material inside and out, but on the day I was to present, my nerves would get the better of me and I would opt to stay home rather than give the seminar. At school, I was always the kid at the back of the class who desperately wanted to ask or answer the question but just couldn't find a voice, fearful that what I might say would fall short or wouldn't be eloquent enough. For most of my life, I have continued to struggle with confidently expressing my opinions and thoughts on a wider stage. As a result, to some extent, my photography has been an outlet for this expression.

The unexpected invitation from Dave to present at Land and See was extremely flattering but also incredibly daunting and something I fretted about for weeks beforehand. I felt as though I needed to face my fear once and for all, so before I could change my mind, I said yes!

The barn and property on Prince Edward Island immediately felt familiar: a little like returning home to my roots in England. No clinical conference hall for this event, but instead a beautiful old barn set on Dave's former rural property. My fellow presenters couldn't have been more welcoming. Some were returning presenters and some were nervous and new to public speaking (like me). For many of the attendees, this event was a familiar one on their calendar, one they have returned to over and over. Dave has essentially created an environment of camaraderie, friendship, creativity and support. In short, there couldn't have been a better situation for me to attack my fear head on. During the few days of the workshop, I felt myself relax, begin to focus less on myself and my own nerves, and fully embrace the creative experience. I can honestly credit Dave with being instrumental in helping me find my voice and begin to overcome my greatest long-standing fear. Mine is just one example of the many times I've witnessed Dave encourage and support his fellow artists.

Dave is well known in the photography world for his generosity of spirit; as his own career has flourished, he has lifted others up in the process, regularly bringing little-known artists and quieter voices to the fore and supporting them in their own creative journeys. So, when I think of Dave, it is not only as an extremely talented and accomplished creative but, just as, or even more importantly, as a beautiful and kind human being.

These days, many of our relationships are formed online. Eventually meeting that person can sometimes lead to disappointment if they don't quite match up to their online persona. Having met Dave first online, I can attest to his being just as genuine in person as he is in the online world. I've asked a few people to give me their opinions of him and the words that have consistently come up are deeply artistic, creative and sensitive. Driven, ambitious and passionate.

The photographs on these pages reflect the artist: I can feel Dave's sensitive and thoughtful personality. He takes us with him on a journey across the globe, into a world of light and shadow. This is not a postcard collection of places; this is a personal response to moments in time. For some it is enough to capture how a place looks, but here we are experiencing not just how it looks but how it looks and *feels* to the artist. A lifetime of experiences is captured in the moment when he presses the shutter. Dave is often in the role of leader, mentor and "rallier of troops"...but to me, these images represent the quiet, contemplative, almost introspective man.

Most of us experience the world in colour. There is no colour in these images to romance and intoxicate us, and with it removed, we are left with the visceral elements of composition, texture, shape, light and shadow. They feel honest and straightforward and yet they are so much more than just a documentation. Dave takes us beyond what others might see, into the deeper scene. These photographs are filled with stories and emotion.

We journey across the globe in the pages of this book, into a world of light and shadow. From Botswana to Antarctica and beyond, diverse continents united by Dave's unique vision. Snapshots of times and places, familiar and yet unfamiliar as the medium of black and white helps us transcend reality into a realm that isn't abstraction but is beyond our normal experience. The world seems simplified, more focused. Small moments in time become works of art: a tiny tree framed by cloud or mist in Bhutan, sheep gazing into the lens against the brooding landscape of the Faroe Islands. By documenting the places he experiences, perhaps he will lead us to care a little more about protecting them. We look at our familiar world – but framed in a different way – through the sum of Dave's life experiences, in this, *Tones of Grace*: timeless, moody and otherworldly.

Beginnings

My monochromatic journey started on a cozy Christmas morning several years ago.

Before that moment, I had photographed black and white images, to be certain, but never with much intention. A moment here and there would be seen and captured in colour, and later – in the editing suite – the thought would strike me that there might be a possible monochrome image there, if only I could see beyond the colour. I would hold my breath, strip out the colour and pray the end result was something with power – similar to images I'd seen in publications like *Life* magazine, or the street and landscape photographs from such masters as Henri Cartier-Bresson or Ansel Adams. My attempts sometimes hit the mark, but often they failed. Black and white was an art form, but one I hadn't given enough dedication to. I was far from creating a body of work with power and impact. I instinctually knew it would take more effort; half-hearted attempts rarely prove successful in life. I knew I wanted to become a better black and white artist, but I wasn't sure what, exactly, that looked like for me. I didn't know the *how*.

That Christmas morning changed everything: I just didn't know it yet. As I watched my young children open their presents with joy permeating the air, a gift was pushed toward me. I ignored it at first, content to take in the excitement in my "littles'" eyes, listen to the sound of their happiness and take in the smell of the wood stove that warmed the room. Eventually, I couldn't ignore the present any longer. It was big, and heavy. I had the feeling it was a book, but wow, if it was a book I had never received a book this heavy before. *What is this?* Taking off the bow and peeling back the paper, I saw the mystery reveal itself. *GENESIS*, by Sebastião Salgado. *Incredible*, I thought, as I cracked the spine to this massive tome. *This looks incredible*. I said my thank-yous as I quickly gave the book a scan. Image upon image of the planet's beauty. All in black and white. I'd heard of Sebastião Salgado and was roughly aware of his work, but had never studied it, or acquired any of his books. *This is a really beautiful book. Truly. Thank you.* I set the book down to continue watching my children. I knew I would pick it up again, soon.

My black and white journey truly started that afternoon, after all the discarded gift wrap was cleaned up and put away. After I made a big brunch for everyone. After a coffee or two was poured (perhaps spiked by a little Baileys). I finally sat down, sipping on yet another steamy beverage, and opened *GENESIS* once again.

Photo books, for me, are a religious experience. They open my mind and heart to new ways of looking at the world around me. It's not simply "looking at pretty pictures." It's allowing yourself to be impacted by a different perspective, a new vantage point, a learning earned from someone who has walked a different path. Not only have these photographers physically been to different places, geographically, than you, they've put their entire life experience into the images they created and presented. I know when I look at an image from a photographer I admire that I'm not simply seeing that singular capture. I'm seeing the years and countless thousands of exposures they made until that point that formed their vision, nurtured their art and developed their world view. Opening *GENESIS*, which is essentially Salgado's black and white love letter to the natural world, and taking in page after page of the planet's beauty, I was not only seeing some interesting locales and fantastic compositions through an artist's eyes, I was – in that moment – in the starting phase of transforming my own perspective of the world around me. A grand statement? Perhaps. But the truth of the matter is that big changes in a person's life often come from the simplest, and humblest, of origins.

....

A gentle thud. I closed the book after soaking in the last page, and stared off into space. An idea was brewing, even if it wasn't fully formed. Ideas are numerous in my mental space; acting on those ideas is a different story. I find if I don't capture an idea – if I don't jot down a note or tell someone immediately about it – I lose that idea to the ether. Ideas require action. As this idea bounced around my head, I took out my phone, and opened my "Notes" app. *Goal: an entire year, starting January 1st, shooting entirely in black and white...*

Could I do it? Seriously do it? Was this idea crazy? Could I willingly give up colour photography for a year? Did I really want to commit to that? The next day, I made it semi-official. I wrote a post on my Facebook wall, indicating my plan. It was hard to back down now, which was precisely the point.

The year started with optimism and excitement for my monochromatic journey ahead. Almost every year I set myself a goal in photography, a nudge to move myself along, from both a technical skill set and artistic growth perspective. This was simply the most ambitious goal I had ever given myself. A year is a long time, but I was excited at the prospect of trying. Within that goal, I gave myself some parameters, and some flexibility. I still had client work to do, and not all my clients would be excited about receiving black and white images, so I would allow myself to shoot colour imagery for clients. My own personal work, however, was to be in black and white. Whatever creative work I embarked upon would be with this goal, this objective in mind. Why? Because for me, my strongest growth always tends to come out of immersing myself in a subject. I need to live and breathe it – to always have it at the forefront of my mind for a period of time. I knew if I stuck to this lofty goal I would emerge a much stronger black and white artist. It was inevitable. I wanted *that*, so badly. Growth is fuel. For an artist, and for a person.

The year ahead held a lot of promise, and a lot of travel. Just as Salgado's work in *GENESIS* spanned the globe, my black and white year promised much of the same: I had journeys booked to Antarctica, the Faroe Islands and Namibia. Destinations known for colour and vibrancy. I was asked to join a series of expedition cruises to Antarctica as photographer-in-residence, sharing my expertise on photography with others who'd signed up to the expedition. In the Faroes and Namibia, I would be co-leading my own photographic tours, alongside business partner and extremely talented photographer Paul Zizka. The opportunities for unique visuals would be numerous; the question would be if I could stick to my goal and continually push forward my vision over the year.

As much as the year started with a great deal of optimism, that fuel was short-lived. Despite all my plans, all my good intentions, I broke my promise to myself...almost immediately. After a week of sticking exclusively to black and white photography as the New Year rolled around, I found myself on the shores of the Falkland Islands, approximately 480 km off the tip of South America. As excited as I was for this monochrome journey, I was seduced by the colours around me: the green lushness of the place and the vibrancy of the rockhopper and king penguins I encountered – my first ever penguin sightings. Almost on instinct I turned my camera from monochrome mode back to colour, and over the next week I primarily remained there. As I journeyed from the Falkland Islands to South Georgia to Antarctica, I photographed beautiful cyan and cobalt icebergs, coral and magenta sunrises, and the vast, brilliantly colourful characteristics of the various species of wildlife I encountered along the way. I wasn't angry at myself for this; it was my first time in these new lands, and I was experiencing them purely and instinctually. But, *still*. This wasn't what I'd set out to do.

I was fortunate, that year, however. I was booked to travel to Antarctica not just for the one journey, but for three. I would cross back and forth across the notorious Drake Passage from the southern tip of Argentina to Antarctica, and back again, three times. This meant, in practical artistic terms, that I had three "kicks at the can." Where I failed, initially, I eventually returned to my goal. I stood on the deck of the ship and set my camera to monochrome mode. It remained there for the bulk of the remaining two journeys, and for most of the next four or five months.

I didn't spend a year shooting exclusively in black and white, but over the course of those months I lived, ate and breathed monochrome photography in a way I had never dedicated myself before. Hundreds and thousands of frames. Tens of thousands, actually. Within that focused time, within that period of intention, something remarkable happened – predictably, I suppose – but I grew as a black and white photographer in *dramatic* ways. I learned more about the craft in that period of five months than over the previous 15 years as a photographer. I started seeing in black and white. I could gaze upon the world and know, instinctually, what monochromatic tone a colour would take on and how different brightness values of light would represent themselves. I started to understand what would make a great black and white subject, and what subjects or scenes wouldn't lend themselves as strongly to monochrome. During this period I learned quickly, and I learned with excitement – and there was a lesson within the learning process itself. Because of this black and white experience, I will now *always* preach to anyone wanting to learn something new to immerse yourself in a subject – to focus your attention by restricting yourself. Photography has thousands of "components" within it. Countless gear choices. It can be overwhelming to learn, to be sure. You can't possibly learn all these components at once, no more than a person learning guitar can take in the fretboard, barre chords, fingerpicking and strum patterns all at once, starting out.

But if you pick one piece of the puzzle and "live" in that world? It's remarkable how quickly it all starts to make sense.

In the years since that less-than-graceful start, my knowledge and appreciation of black and white photography has only deepened. I am (unironically) a visual learner, and one of the ways I learn best is by studying the photographs of others. My education in the years since I've embraced monochromatic photography has revolved around "doing," certainly (being in the field shooting countless frames), but an essential part of my process has been to study and analyze the photographs of others that have caught my attention – the images that have taken my breath away. The deeply personal family photographs of Sally Mann. The exquisite street photographs of Alan Schaller. The mysteries of Vivian Maier. The long-exposure mastery of Marc Koegel. The lively and historical photos of Tanuma Takeyoshi. The masters I mentioned previously: Ansel Adams and Sebastião Salgado. My list of influences is much longer than these photographers, of course, but these are some of the most poignant for me. I continue to be influenced daily, for the very premise of being a photographer is to keep your eyes open to the world around you. Whether it's a new, younger artist I stumble upon on social media, or a random photo book I find on the dusty shelves of a used bookstore, one of the things I love most is discovering a new collection, or a new image, that captures my attention – that makes me pause. Inspiration is the lifeblood of photography – of all artistic pursuits, actually – and being inspired by "the world out there." This collection depicts landscapes, placescapes and our planet's wild creatures. You won't find many people in this collection; maybe someday I'll publish a book of my favourite monochromatic portraits (of which I have many). Every collection of images needs some degree of focus, and my parameter for this collection – my guiding light – was "scenes that depicted the world at large." A broad stroke, to be certain, but I wanted to show that the world is many things. There's beauty in the curve of a fallen log, a fox peering over a hill, or the perfect symmetry of a bridge from beneath. There's poetry in the way mist lies gently within a valley, the joy of children jumping and in the gaze of a lion. There's quiet contemplation in the fall of water, how sheep roam and the shape of a sand dune. The world is all of this, and so much more.

The images you'll find within these pages are my story and my interpretation of the world around me. I never pretend to be the best at anything I do, or even good for that matter. That's up to others to decide, should they choose. I create because I have to – I really have no other choice. Those who know this, and can relate to the need to create, *know*. When you catch an artistic bug, you *must* follow that bug. It's a calling, and it's a necessity. It's an itch you have to scratch, and when you fully embrace your artistic self, it becomes a fire within that you have to let burn. When I capture an image or a collection of images I am inherently proud of, sharing them becomes the *release* of that fire. I don't look to the impact an image has on anyone else. Why? Because I can't control that – I can only determine, before sharing, if it has caught my *own* attention. If it has made *me* excited. Is it a strong enough moment – within a life of many moments – that I want to remember, and preserve? Will it become part of my own story? We curate our moments, and selectively remember the bits and pieces of our lives. The images I choose to share become my own curated version – for myself, to be sure, but for my children as well. Not that I want to impress them, or anyone else for that matter. I do want to inspire, however. If the only result of my photography is that they, and others, look upon the world and try to understand its many facets and possibilities – to see the beauty in light and shadow and form – and want to go see it for themselves? To pause a little longer in the world, "out there," and truly consider all the gifts the world has to offer? I will consider that a success, and that is all I need from this photographic journey.

Sebastião Salgado once said, "I don't believe a person has a style. What people have is a way of photographing what is inside them. What is there comes out." These images, this collection, is a part of what is inside of me; a cross-section. It is not all that is within me, of course, but it is representative of my heart and soul and visual musings. It is a collection of moments in my story to this point. It is a monochromatic perspective from a life, lived. These images are representative of my passion, and they embody my own introspection on the conditions, the visuals, the slices of time that have been presented to me. I don't know what "style" they fit within, or if there's a box that holds them. The language of my photography is light, lines, observations, creative interpretations and moments. These images, these tones of grace, are the expression of that language.

This is my own personal monochromatic genesis story. I hope, truly, that you enjoy – and may you tell your own stories, in whatever medium calls your own name.

Dave Brosha, January 2022.

THE JOURNEY

100 BLACK AND WHITE IMAGES FROM PLANET EARTH

TITLE

The Faroese Feeling

Of all the images I've photographed in the Faroes, this one to me best represents the North Atlantic archipelago. Sheep, dramatic hills and even more dramatic weather.

Location: Gjógv, Faroe Islands

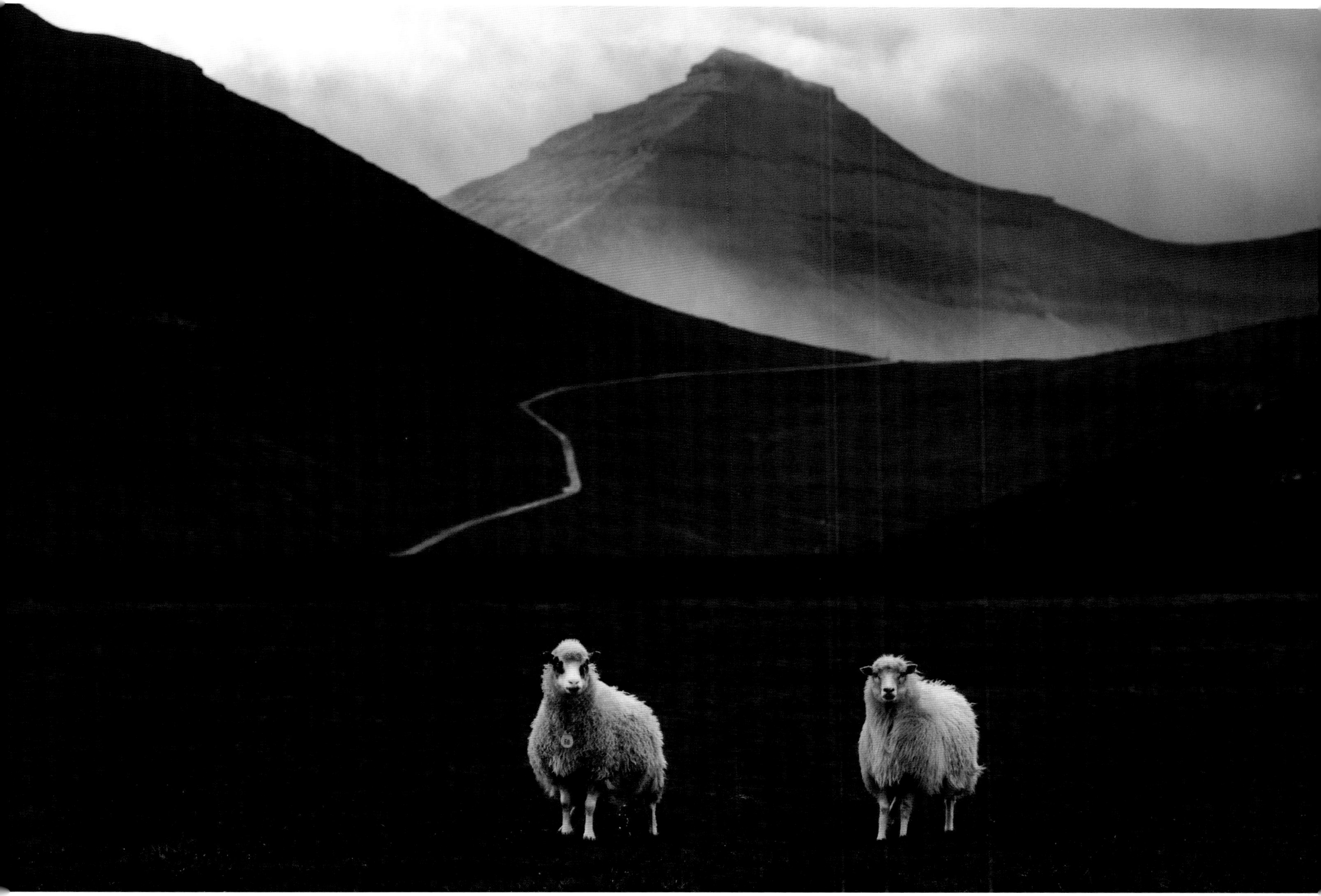

TITLE

Mountain Mood

High above the incredible Kluane Ranges in the Saint Elias Mountains, which span Alaska, the Yukon and the northwestern part of British Columbia.

Location: Kluane National Park and Reserve, Yukon, Canada

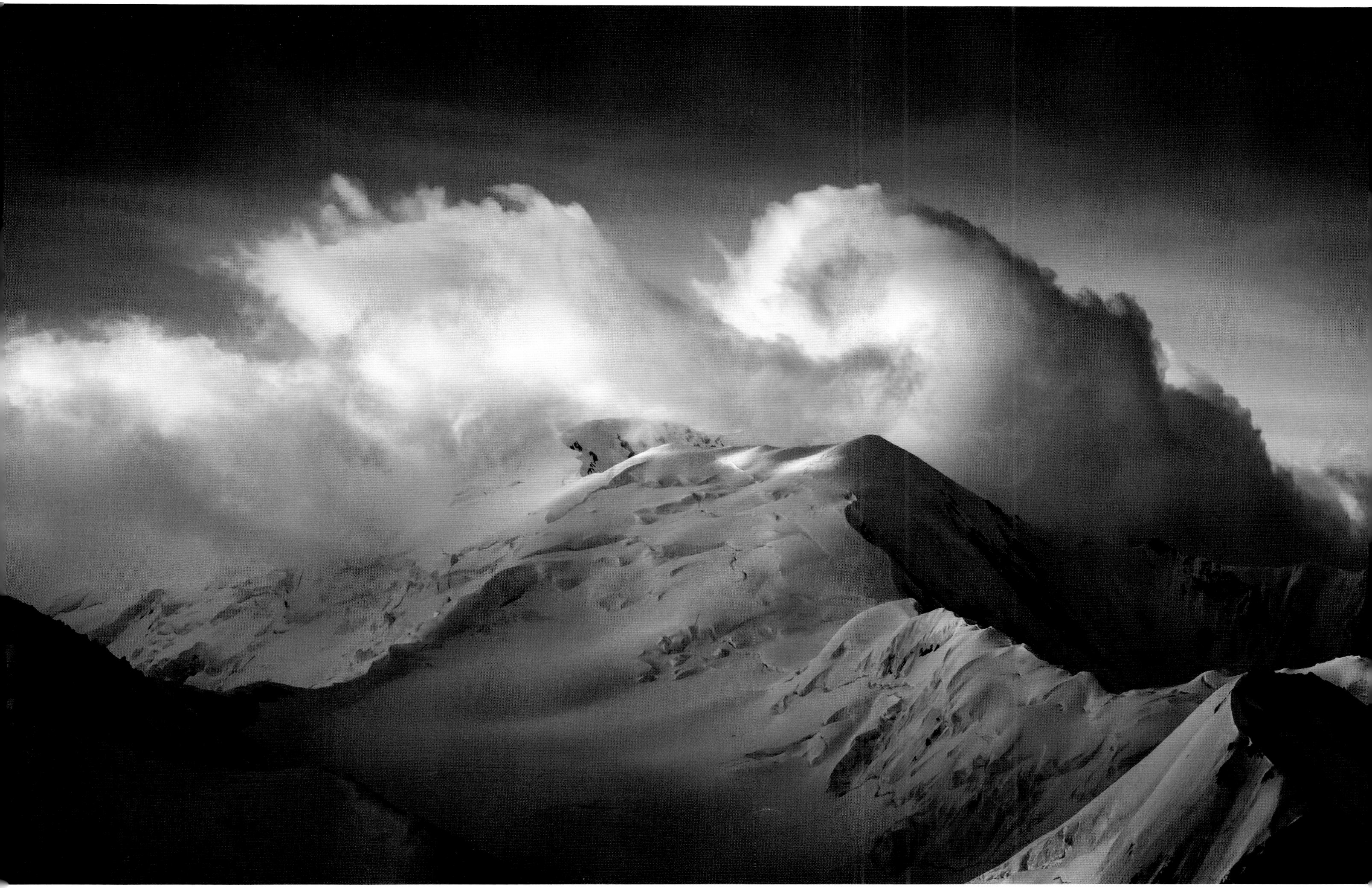

TITLE

Eyes of the Arctic

On patrol with the Canadian Rangers on Ward Hunt Island, in the Canadian High Arctic. The Canadian Rangers are the "eyes and ears of the Arctic," and are a valuable part of the Canadian Armed Forces.

Location: Ward Hunt Island, Nunavut, Canada

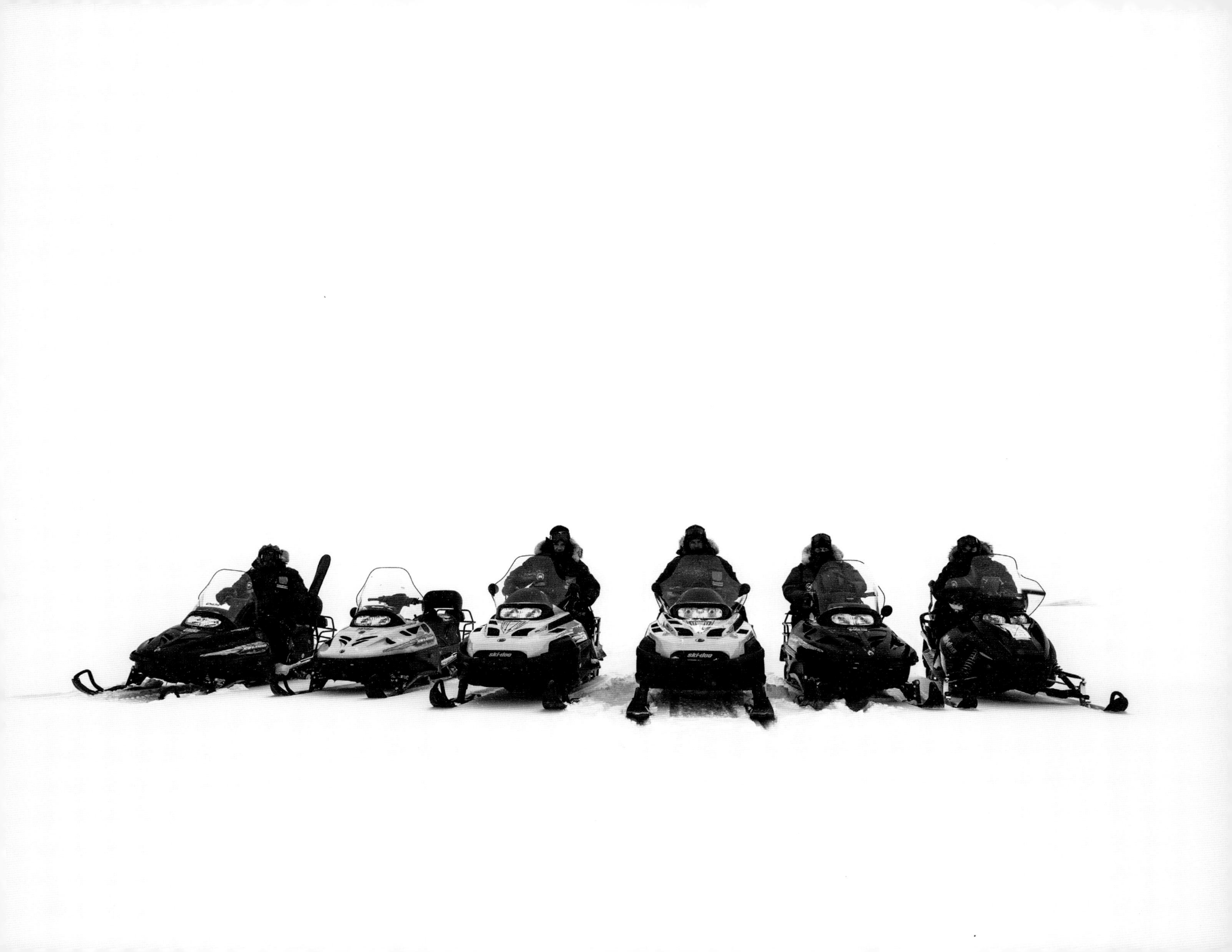
ski-doo
ski-doo

TITLE

Island Gaze

My home province of Prince Edward Island is unique because it has no “large” land-based wildlife, like deer, moose or bears. Foxes and coyotes, however, steal the show from a wildlife photography perspective and always capture my interest with their unique beauty.

Location: Brackley Beach, Prince Edward Island, Canada

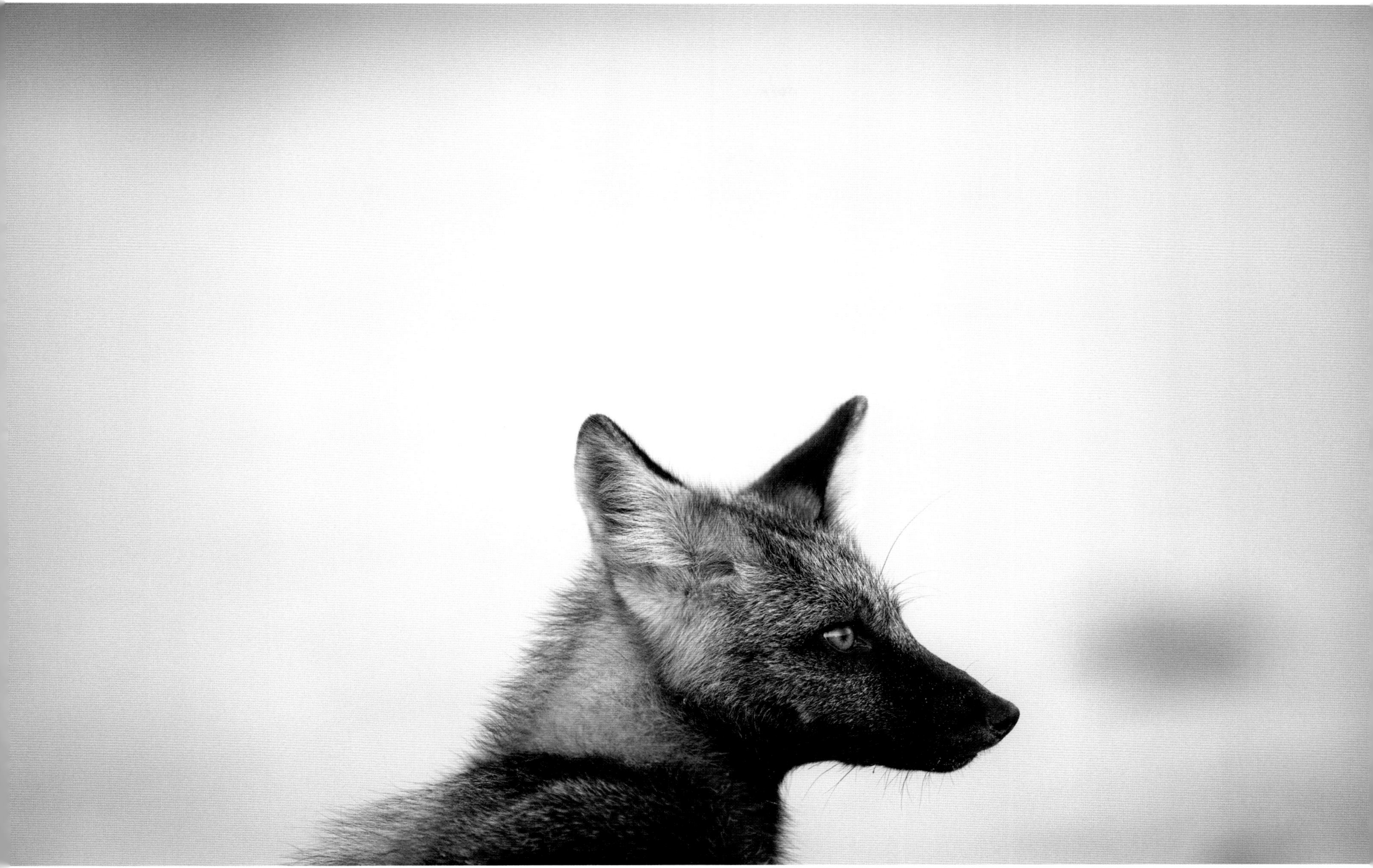

TITLE

Curves

Sand dunes in low light are always a photographic "win," but these unique formations in the Gobi Desert in Mongolia took my breath away with their layered symmetry. It almost looks like two people lying on their sides.

Location: Khongoryn Els, Gobi Gurvansaikhan National Park, Mongolia

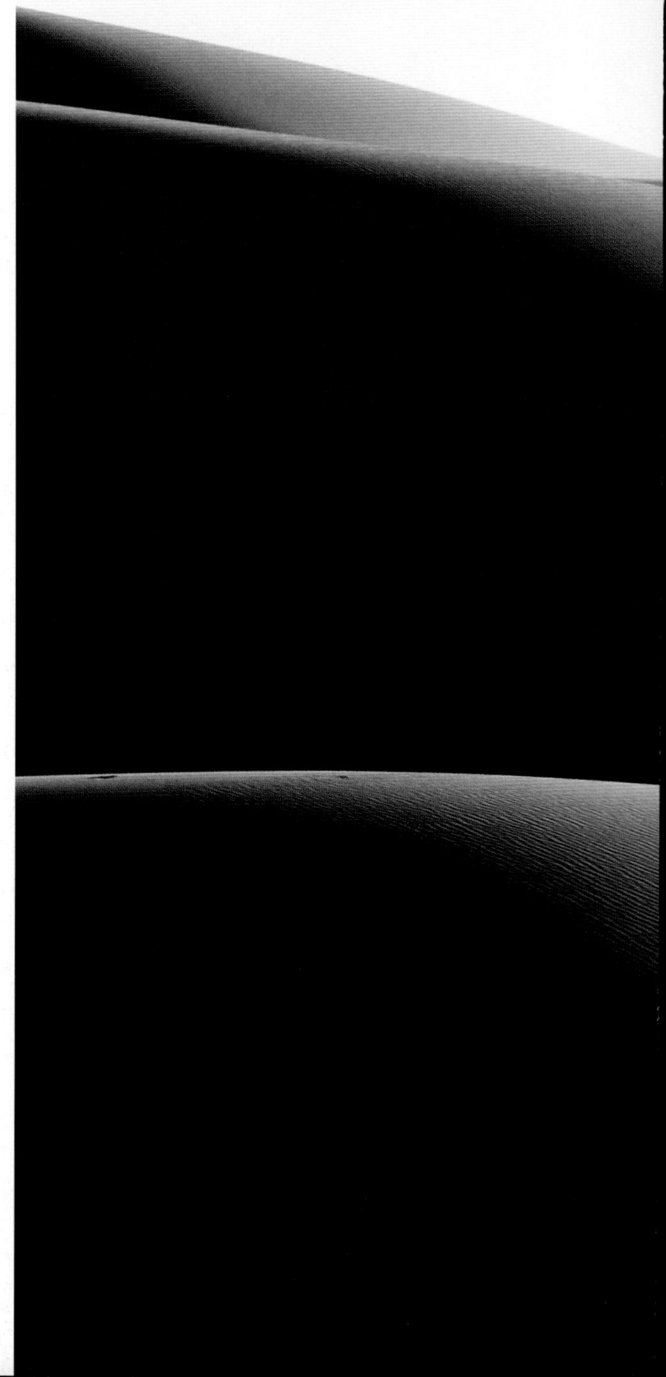

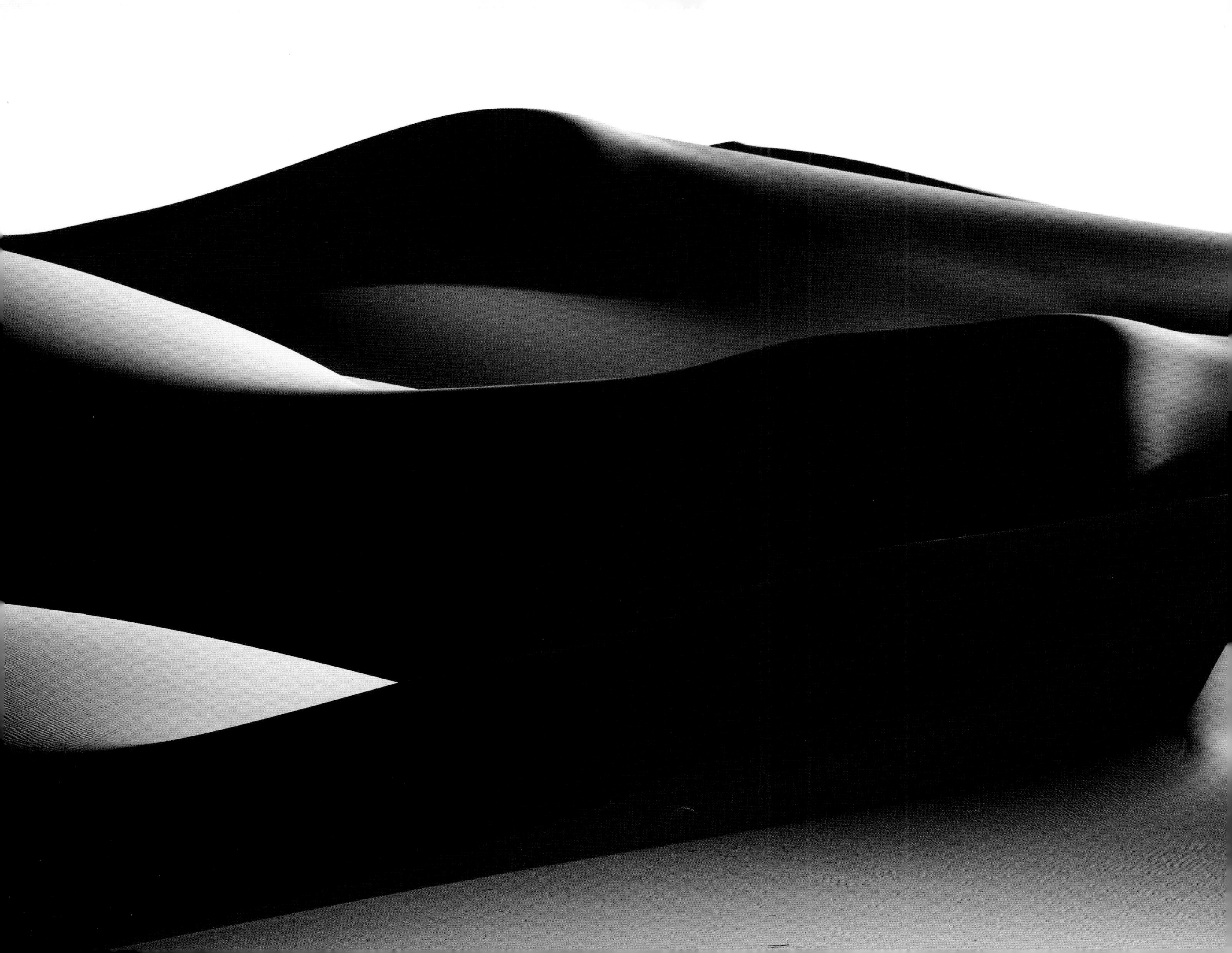

TITLE

Pride of a Nation

Any time you're on an African safari and come across a lion, your heart hits an extra beat. They are truly one of the most magnificent animals on the planet. Of all the times I have personally encountered lions, this was the most memorable experience, and he unwittingly gave our group a show as he lazily ignored us while hiding from the hot African sun.

Location: Chobe National Park, Botswana

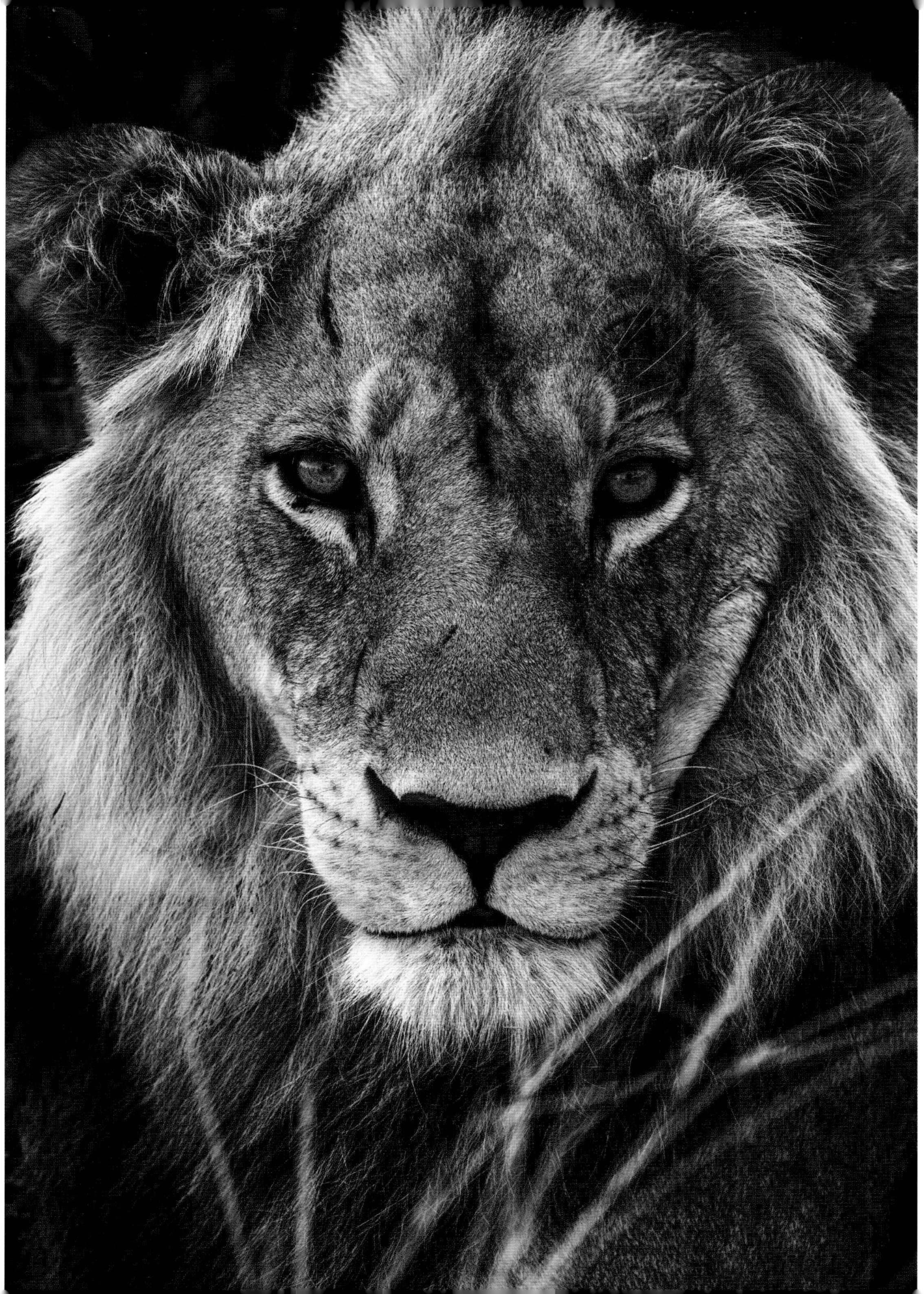

TITLE

The Streets

This is one of the first street photographs – and one of the first black and white images – that I ever made that I liked, near the beginning of my career. Days later, I would start an incredible journey to Mount Everest.

Location: Kathmandu, Nepal

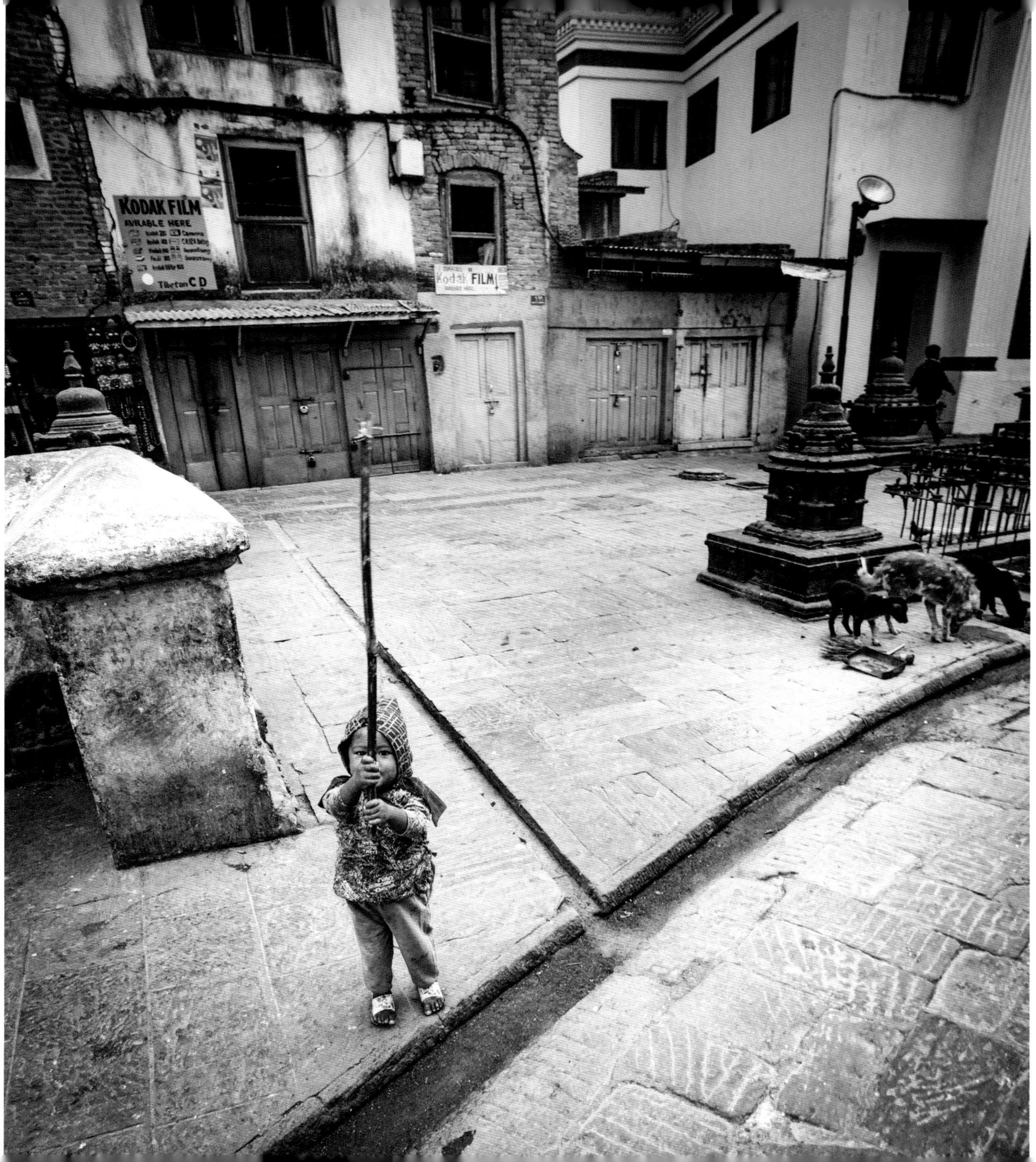
KODAK FILM
AVILABLE HERE
Camera
Tibetan C D
Kodak FILM

TITLE

Moondance

When I can't sleep, I'm one of those weird people who sometimes gives up and goes out for a drive or a walk. This image was photographed on an insomnia-laced evening in eastern Québec, and the beauty of the night quickly eliminated any frustration with the lack of sleep.

Location: Lac-Témiscouata, Parc national du Lac-Témiscouata, Québec, Canada

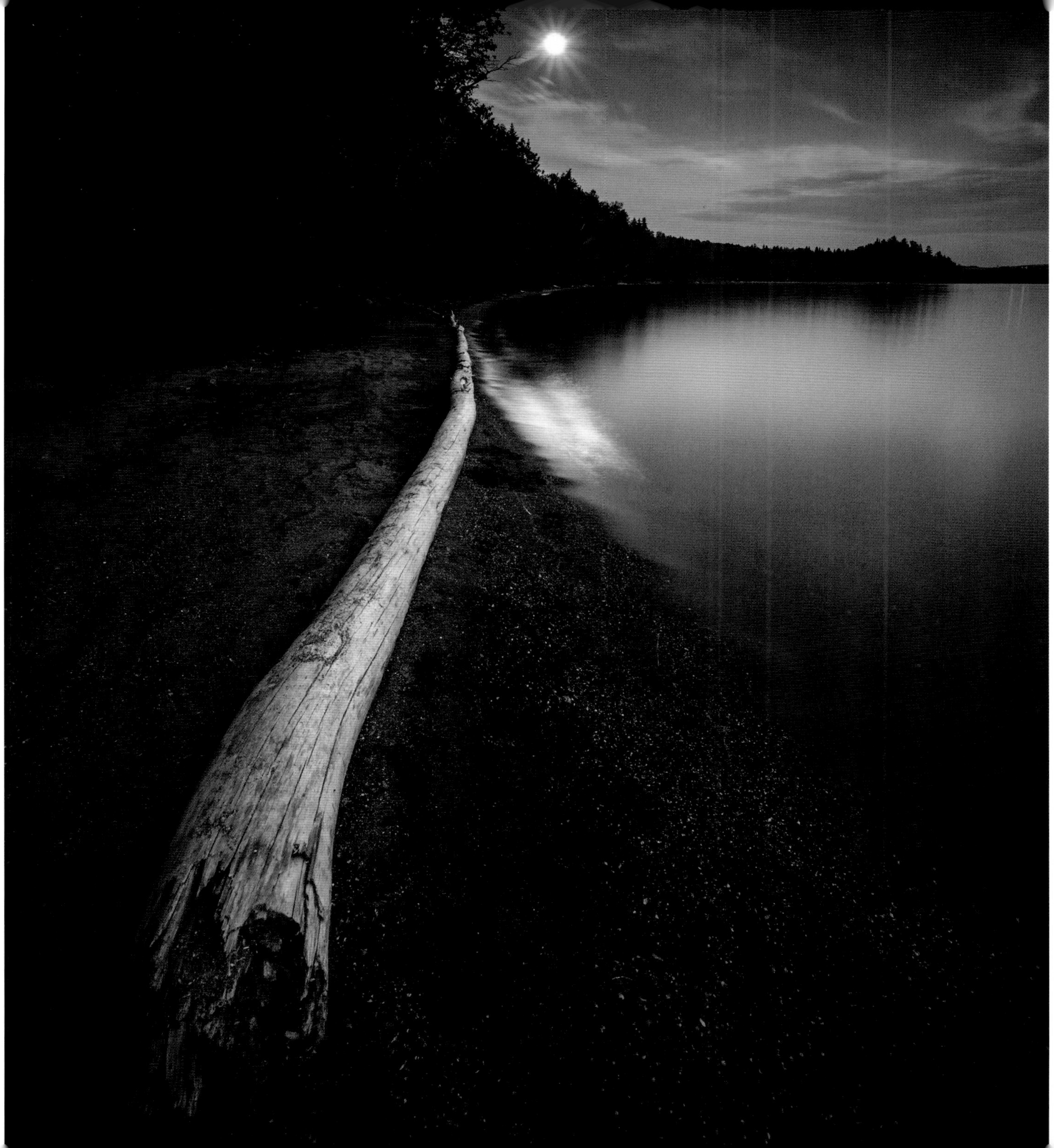

TITLE

They Might Be Giants

My commercial work has brought me to countless fascinating places, and going to these places many will never see always makes me appreciate the creative career I have chosen. This image is from a day spent documenting remediation efforts at the infamous Giant Mine in Yellowknife, Northwest Territories.

Location: Yellowknife, Northwest Territories, Canada

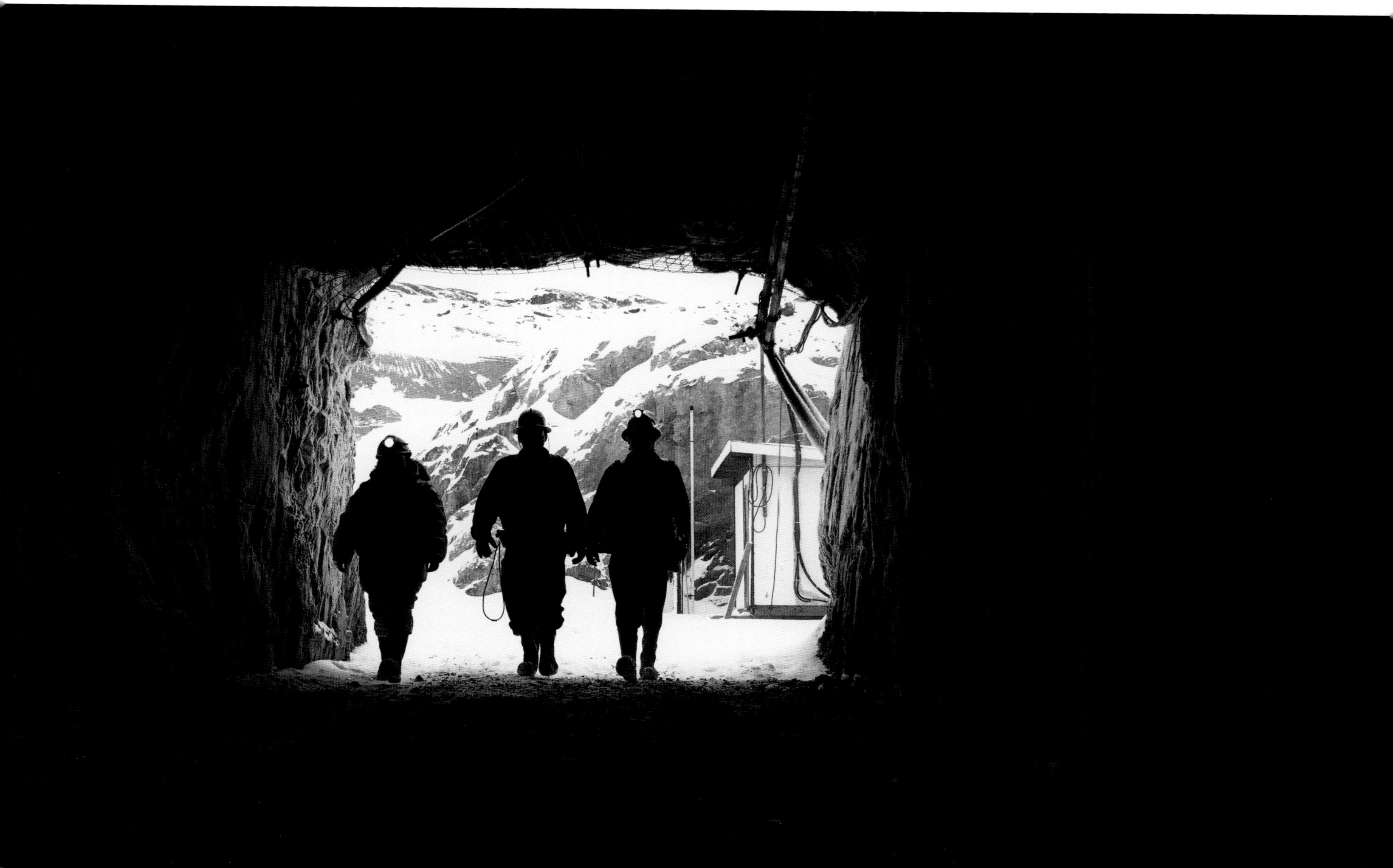

TITLE

The Bridge

I love looking for symmetry, both in the natural and human-made world, and this scene called my name. The Rosedale Suspension Bridge, which crosses the Red Deer River along the Hoodoo Trail in southern Alberta. Early morning, 2012.

Location: Drumheller, Alberta, Canada

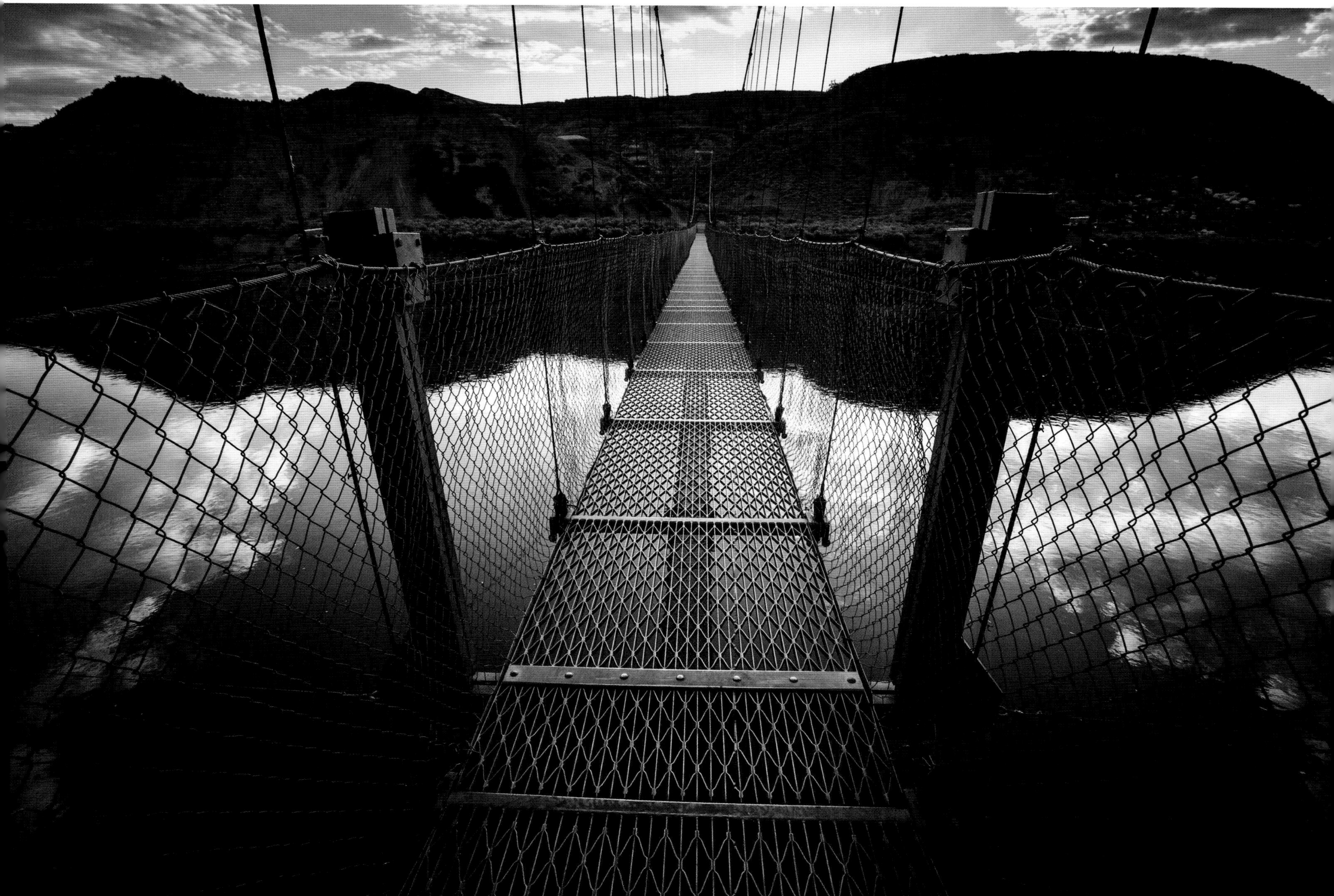

TITLE

The Fury

The Múlafossur waterfall in the extremely picturesque village of Gásadalur is one of the most iconic places to photograph in the Faroe Islands. The Faroes are one of the greenest places on earth, and usually this plummeting waterfall is depicted surrounded in colour. After capturing it the "traditional" way, we decided to return on one of the stormiest days I've encountered in the Faroes, and the moody conditions were perfect for one of my all-time favourite images.

Location: Gásadalur, Faroe Islands

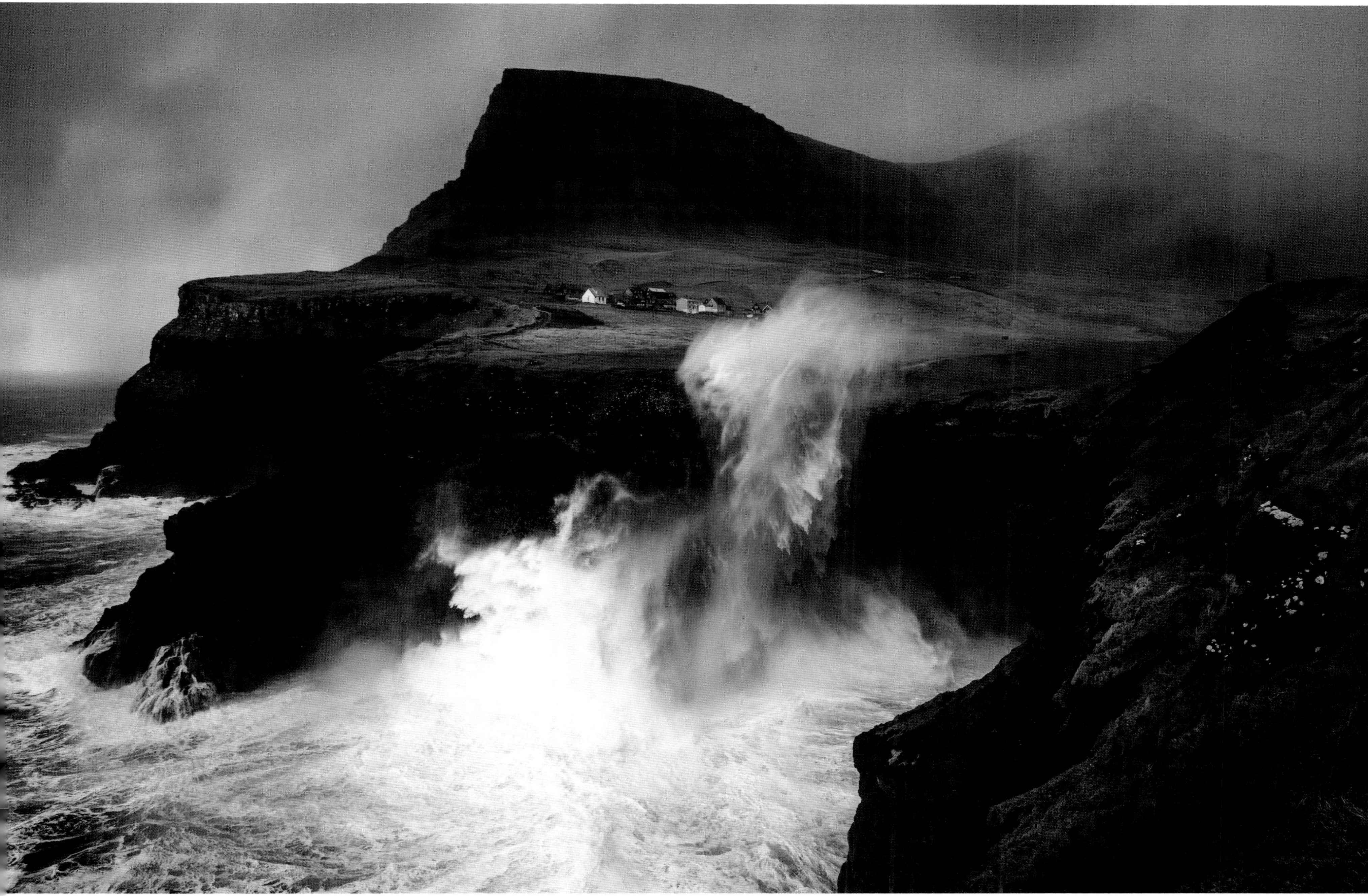

TITLE

Stand Tall

The formidable Cape buffalo, also known as the African buffalo. Beautiful photographic subjects, to be sure, but one of the animals I have the healthiest respect for, as they are known to be quite dangerous to humans. Give them plenty of space, however, and they'll make for incredibly stoic subjects.

Location: Chobe River, Chobe National Park, Botswana

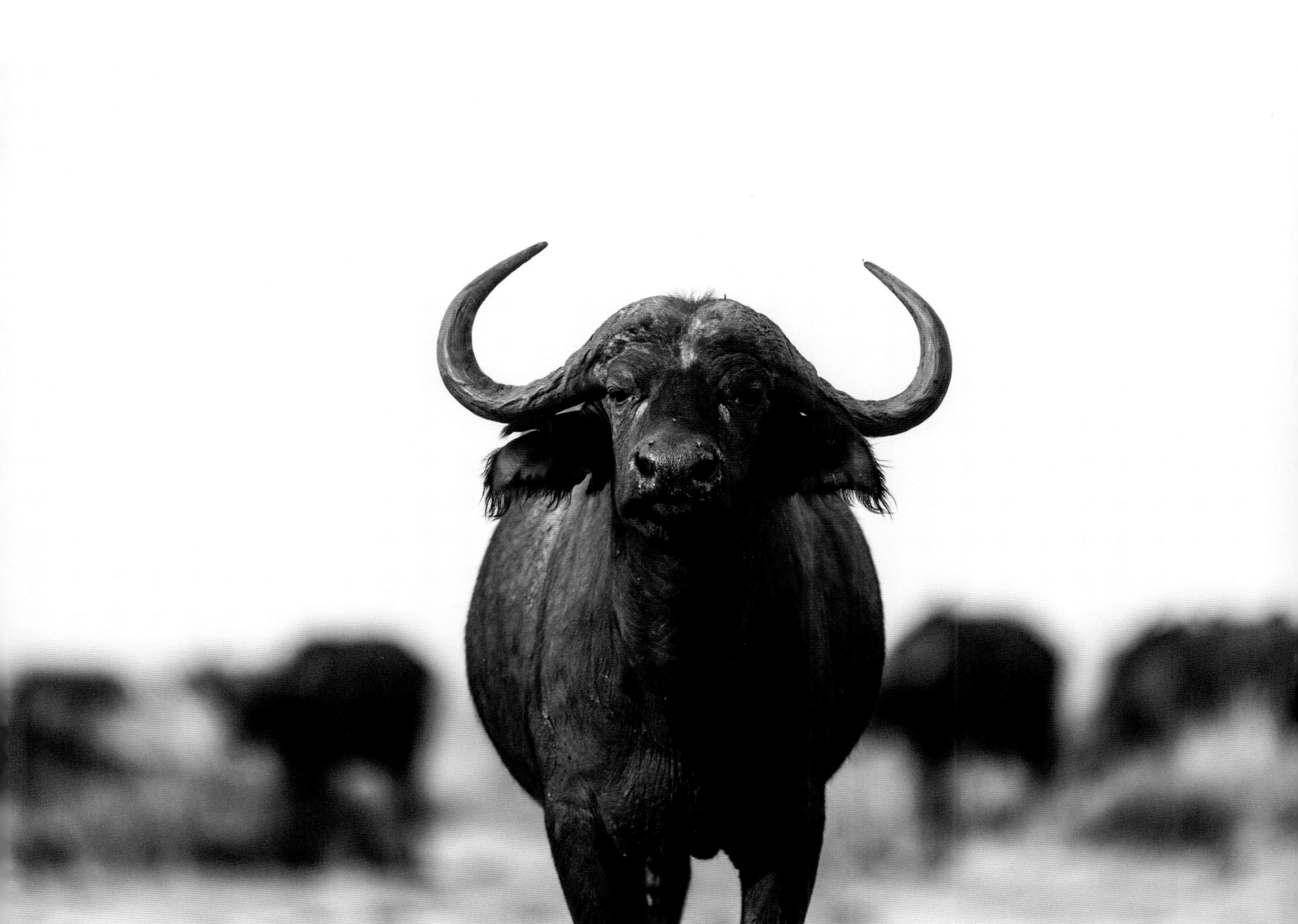

TITLE

Into The Wild

Auyuittuq National Park is home to some of the most spectacular mountains in Canada, and most Canadians aren't even aware of its existence. Located on Baffin Island, in the Canadian Arctic, this park covers an incredible 21,470 square kilometres and is full of granite peaks, glaciers and endless beauty. It's also home to one of the most memorable treks of my life, a two-week adventure with friends Sam and Robbie (pictured here). We truly went into the wild during this July journey.

Location: Auyuittuq National Park, Nunavut, Canada

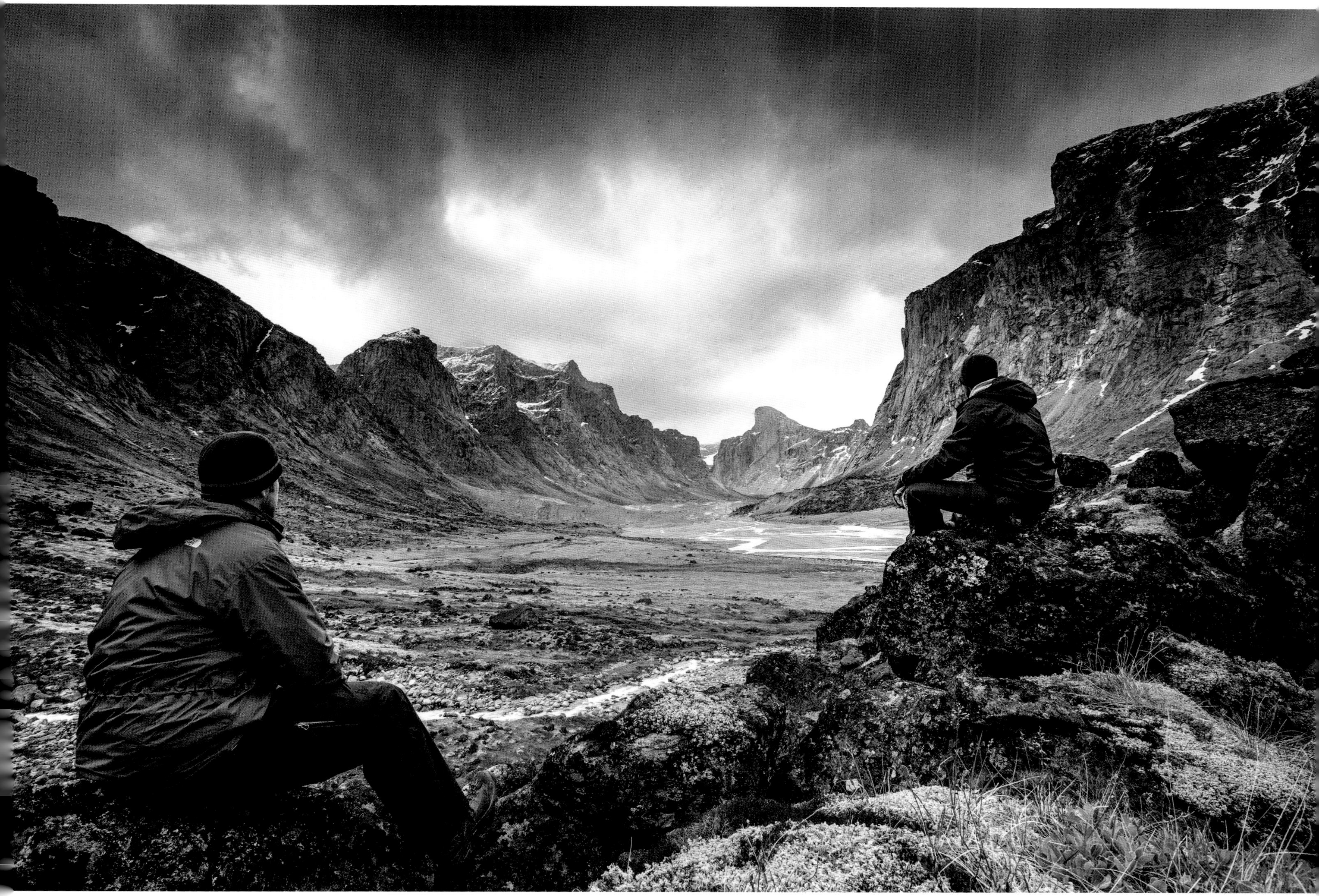

TITLE

We're All in This Together

For me, great wildlife photography isn't so much about capturing an animal with excellent sharpness or technical perfection but capturing some essence of their personality or interaction with their surroundings. I look for the moments, and when they happen I feel I've done my job well. This is one such moment, featuring chinstrap penguins in Antarctica, and it took a lot of patience to wait for it to reveal itself to me.

Location: Antarctic Peninsula

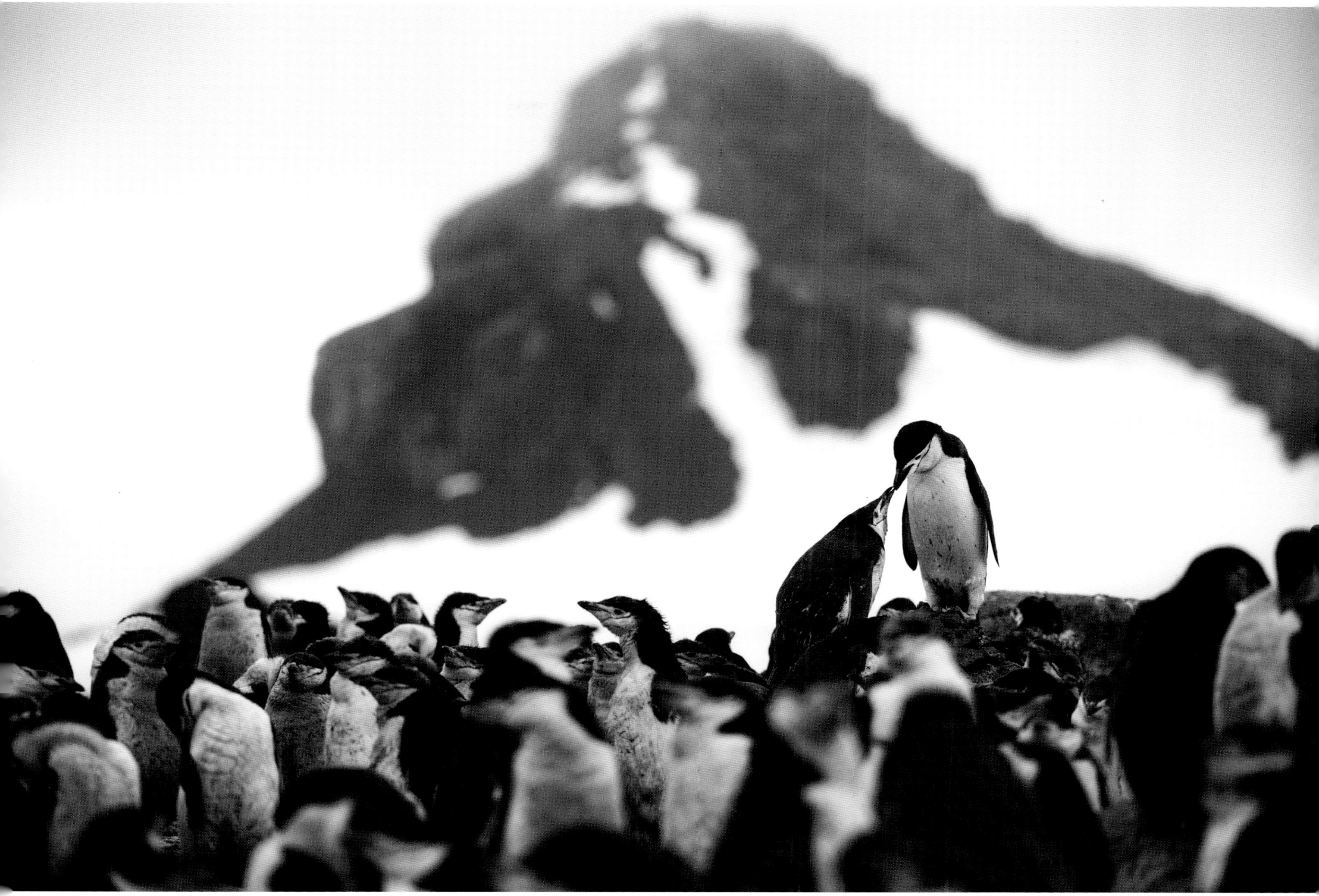

TITLE

Fallen

One aspect of nature photography that makes me happiest is that it immerses you in your surroundings and makes you more “present” than we, unfortunately, often find ourselves. You see, smell and hear the world around you. You look for the quiet beauty. You often look beyond the obvious. You seek, and sometimes you’re lucky enough to see it.

Location: Banff National Park, Alberta, Canada

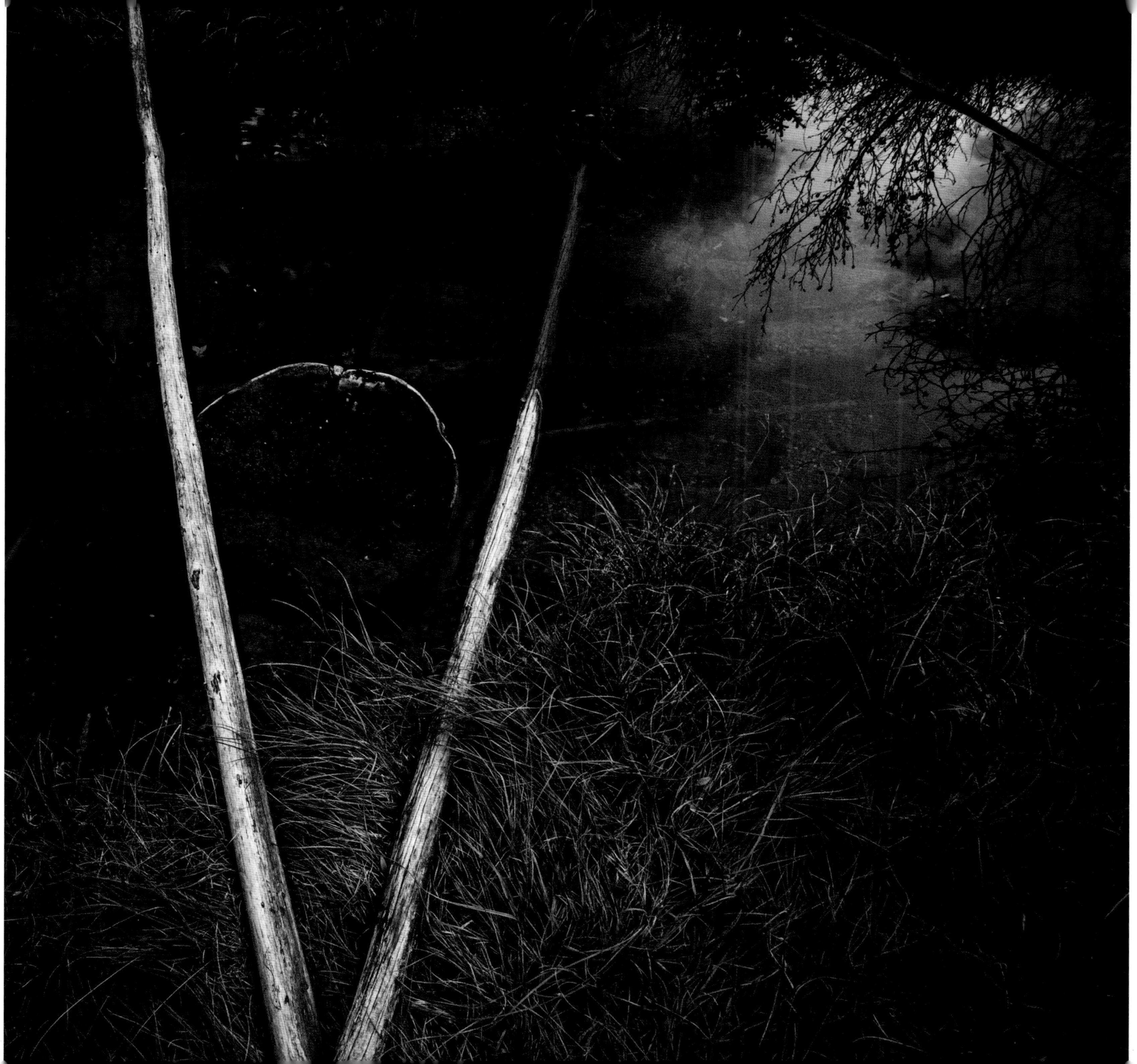

TITLE

The Hill Walkers

A recurring theme in my Faroese photography is to shun its incredible greenness (almost the entirety of the archipelago is covered in grass) and embrace its monochromatic beauty. Moody weather often makes for prime black and white photography, and I suppose this draws me in, in ways I can't quite explain.

Location: Streymoy, Faroe Islands

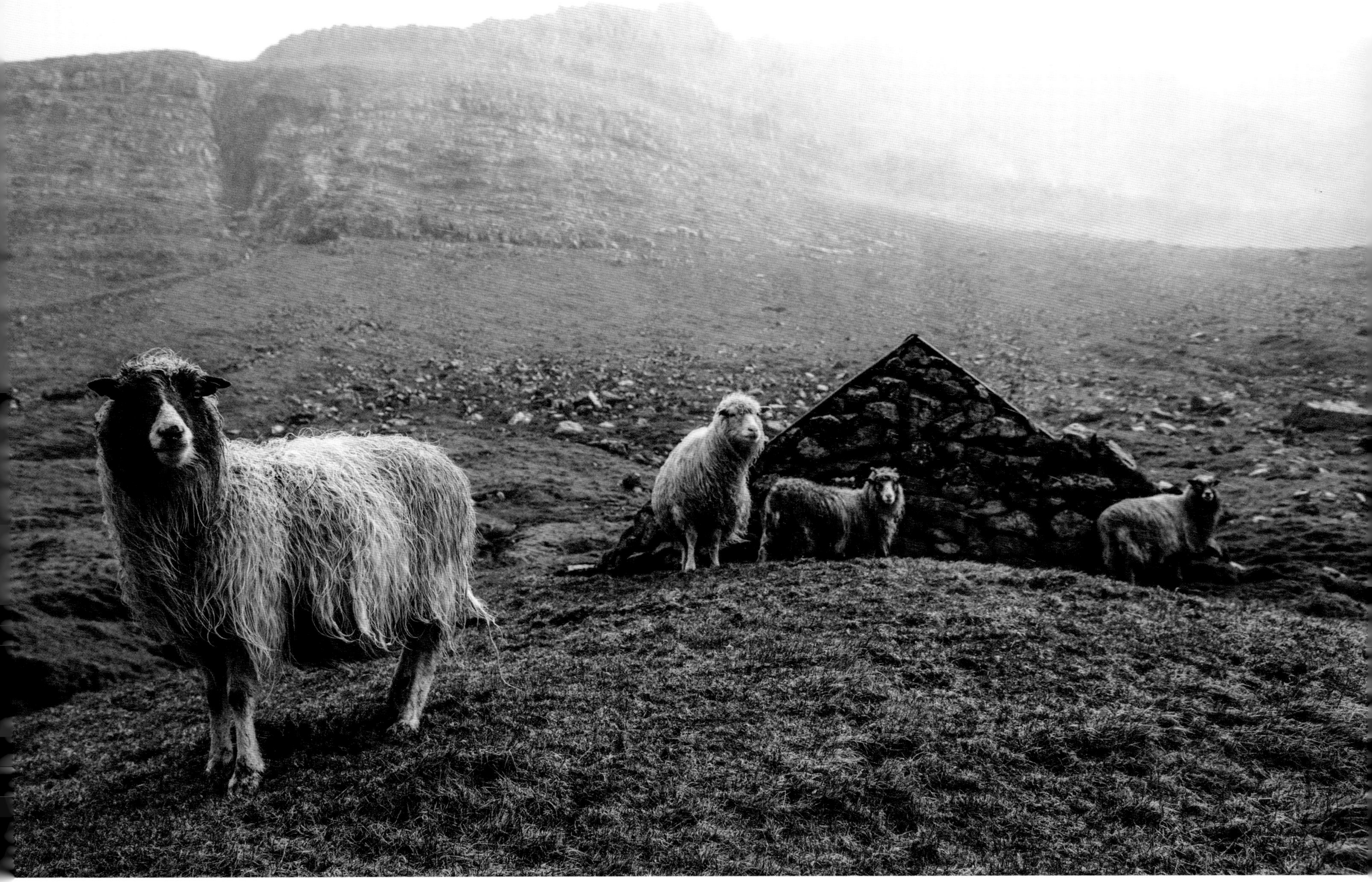

TITLE

The Wanderer

There are images from around the world contained within these pages, but it's a simple beach right down the road from me here on Prince Edward Island that captures my heart like no other place. Here, you'll find me wandering.

Location: Canoe Cove, Prince Edward Island, Canada

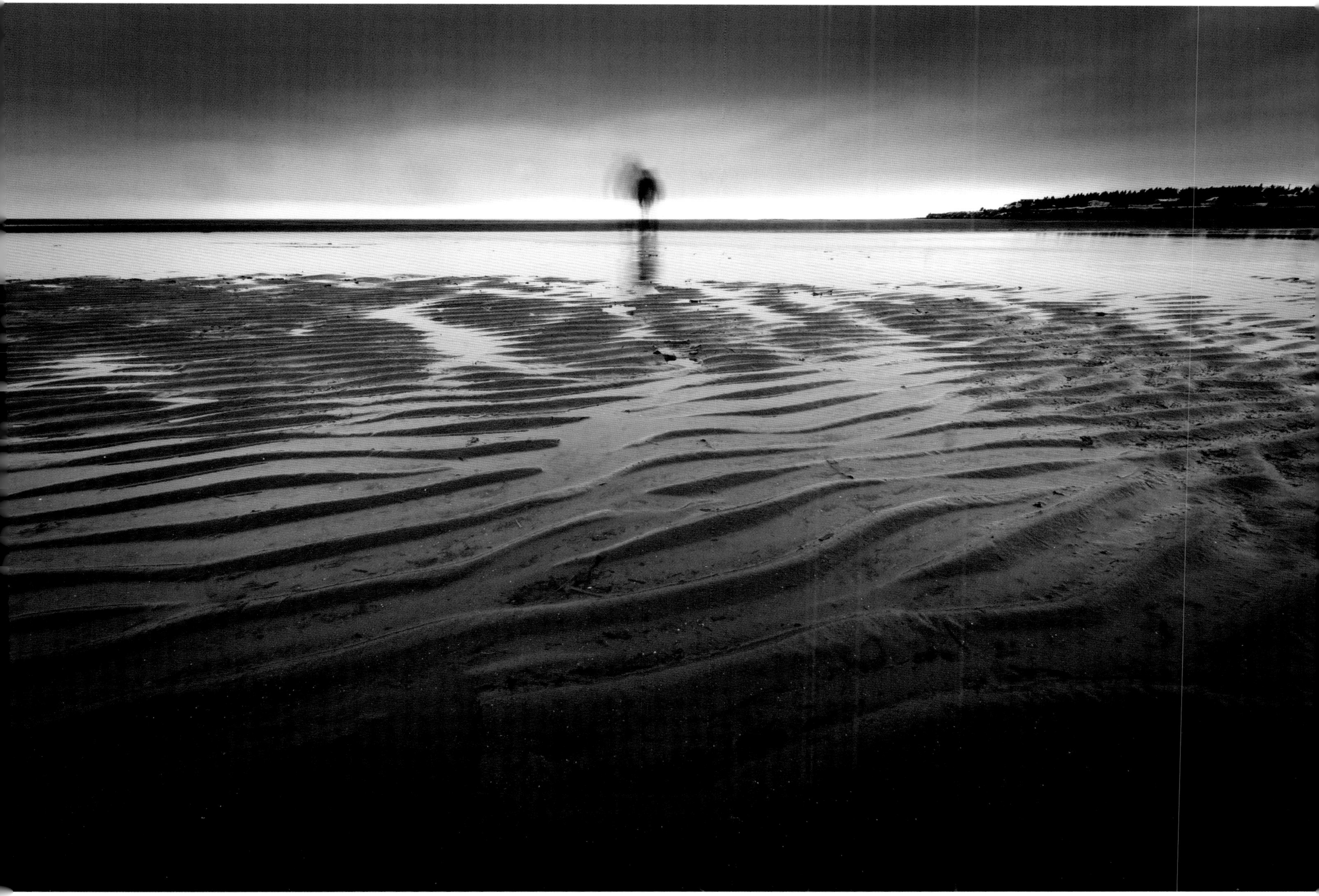

TITLE

King of the Hill

Witnessing death and the circle of life in the natural world is never a "fun" experience that brings you joy, but it is the inevitable truth of nature, and an important subject as a photographer to capture in order to present a full and complete story. Here, a lion stands over a Cape buffalo he recently downed. The moment almost seems tender, but we know what's in store.

Location: Okavango, Botswana

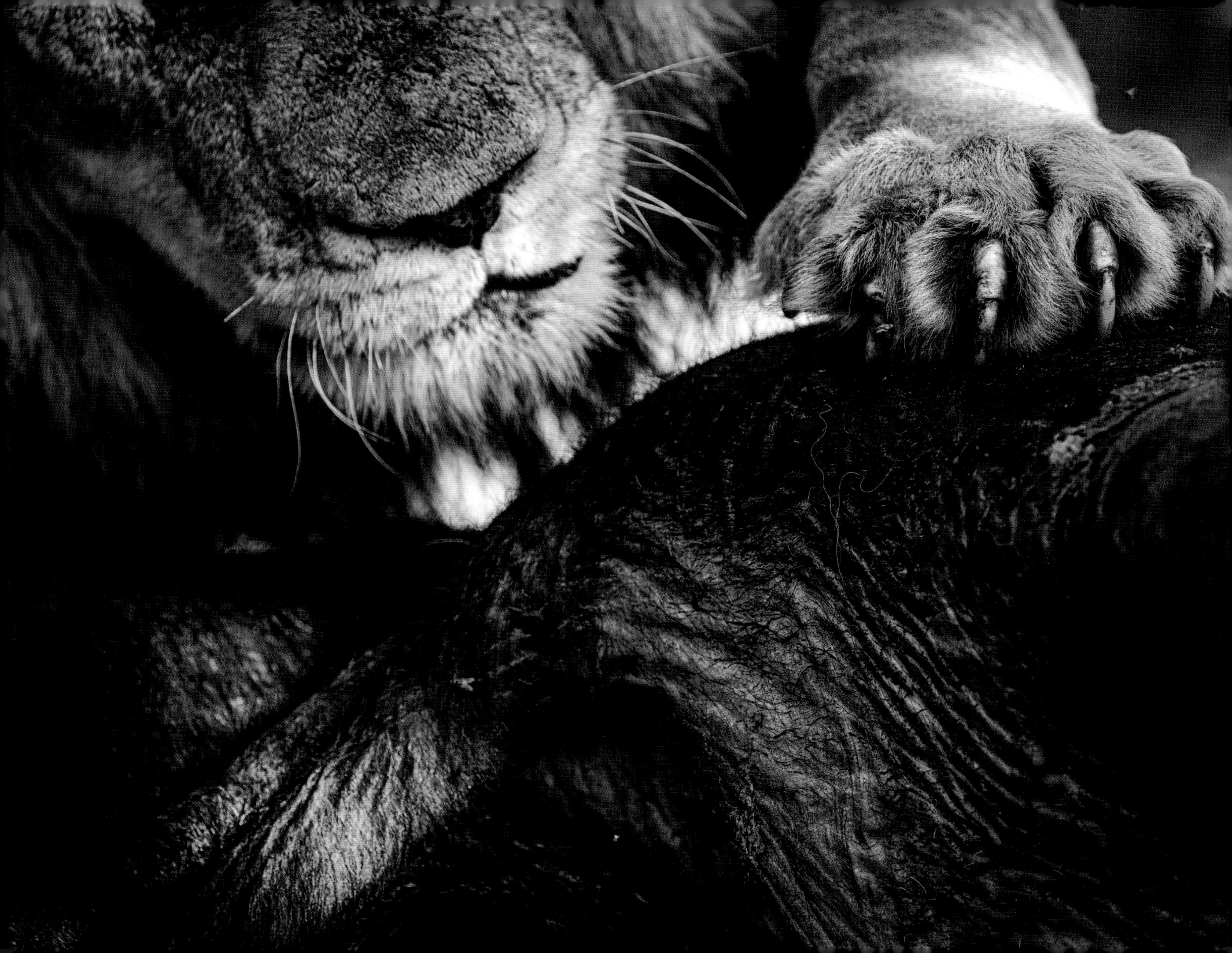

TITLE

Emergence

One of the reasons why mountains are so intriguing to nature photographers is that they're an endless symphony of light – an ever-shifting dance of light and shadow. Moment over moment your entire field of view can change as clouds shift, light rises or drops and your own perspective changes. I'll never tire of mountains.

Location: Kluane National Park and Reserve, Yukon, Canada

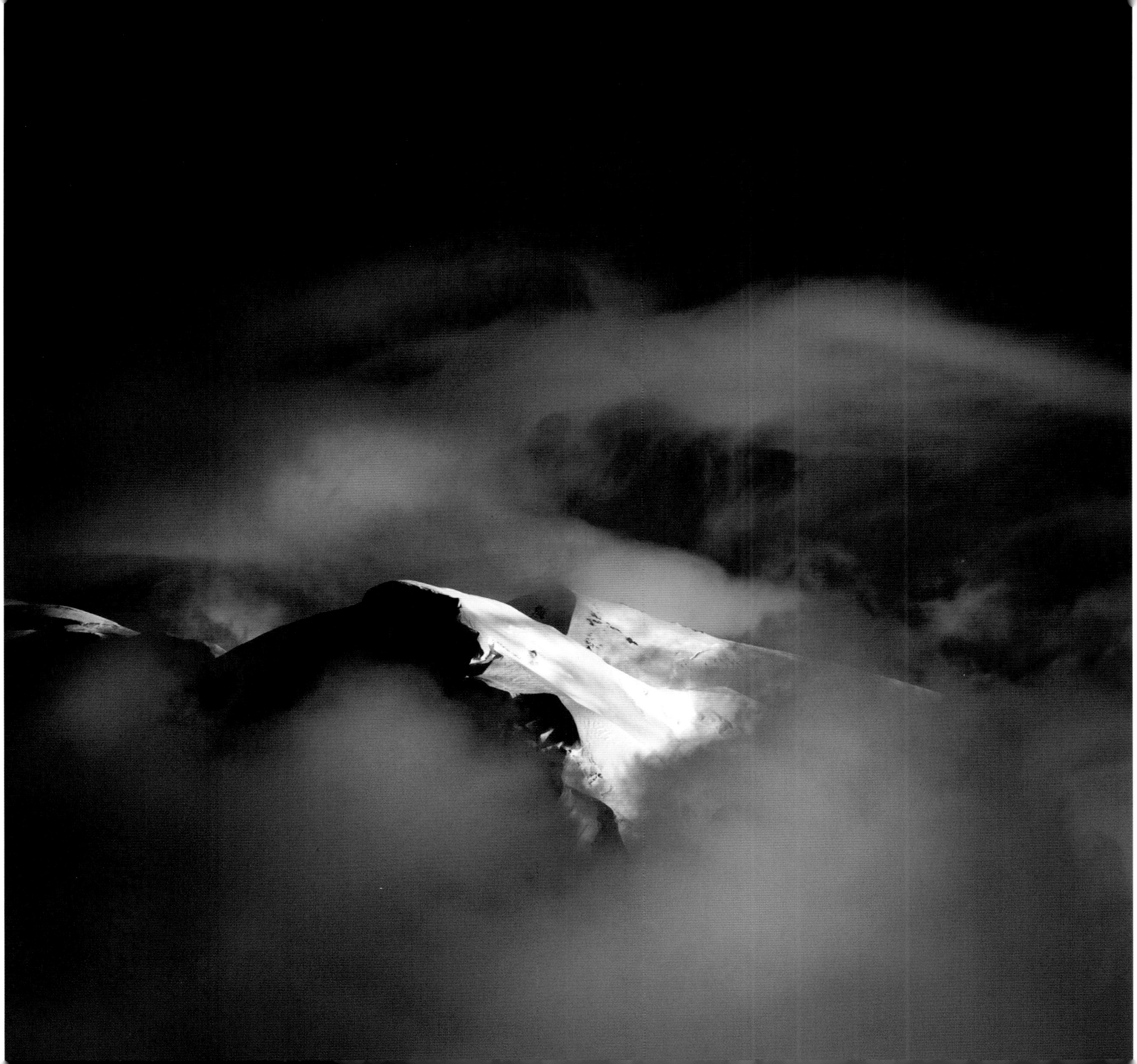

TITLE

Silent Beauty

Many foxes in Prince Edward Island have, sadly, become habituated to humans and often barely acknowledge your presence if you approach at a safe distance to photograph them. It makes for great photographic opportunities, but it often makes me think about the human impact on wildlife and our relationship to our wild partners in this world.

Location: Brackley, Prince Edward Island, Canada

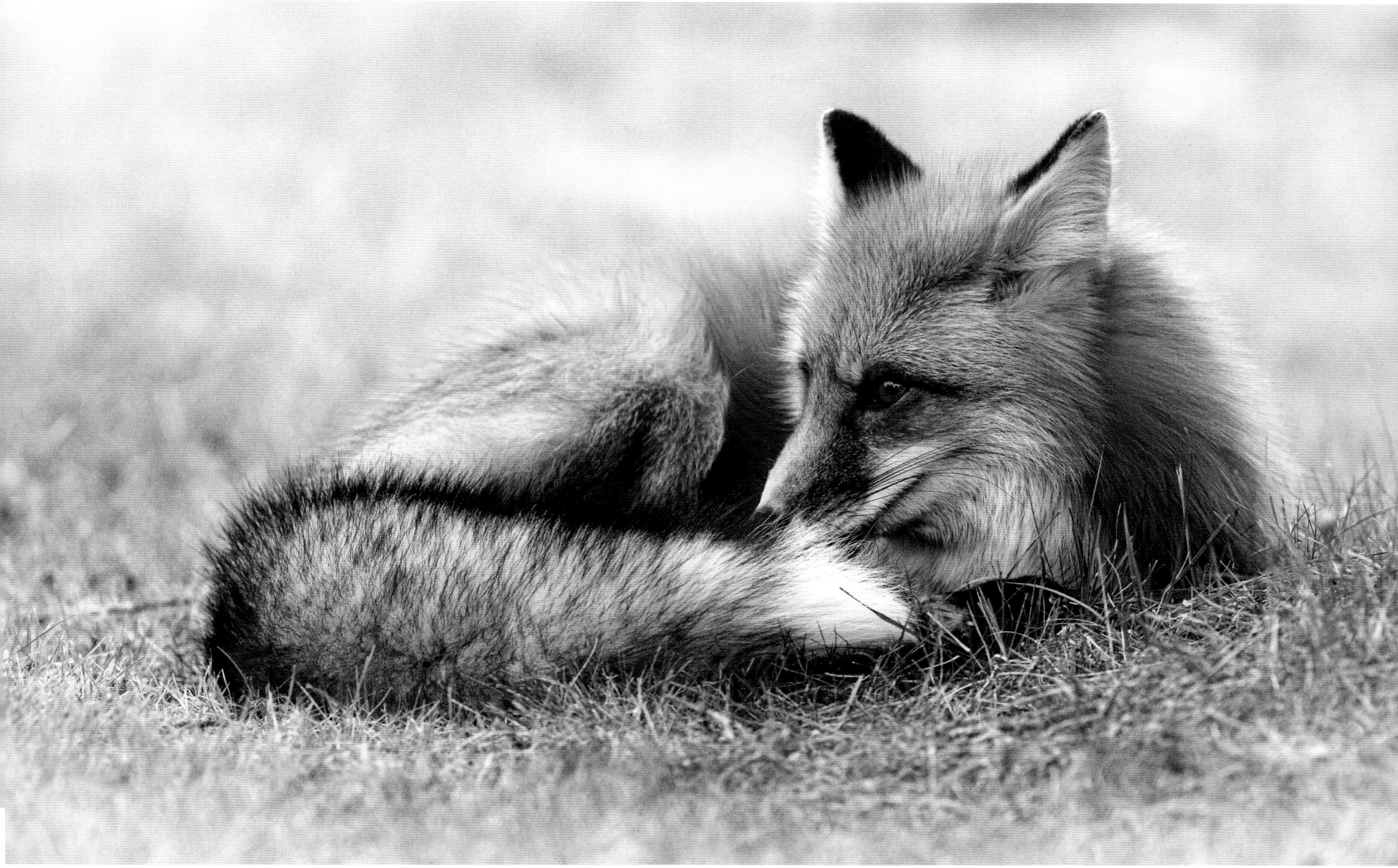

TITLE

The Road Warrior

I'm always looking for an opportunity to get creative – to try to create a story in my images, even if there isn't one on first glance. While many of my images are "photojournalistic" in nature (what you see is what I saw), sometimes I have fun out there. Here, I asked my travelling companion, Paul Zizka, to head up a trafficless, foggy road in the Yukon to create this pre-visualized image.

Location: Kluane National Park and Reserve, Yukon, Canada

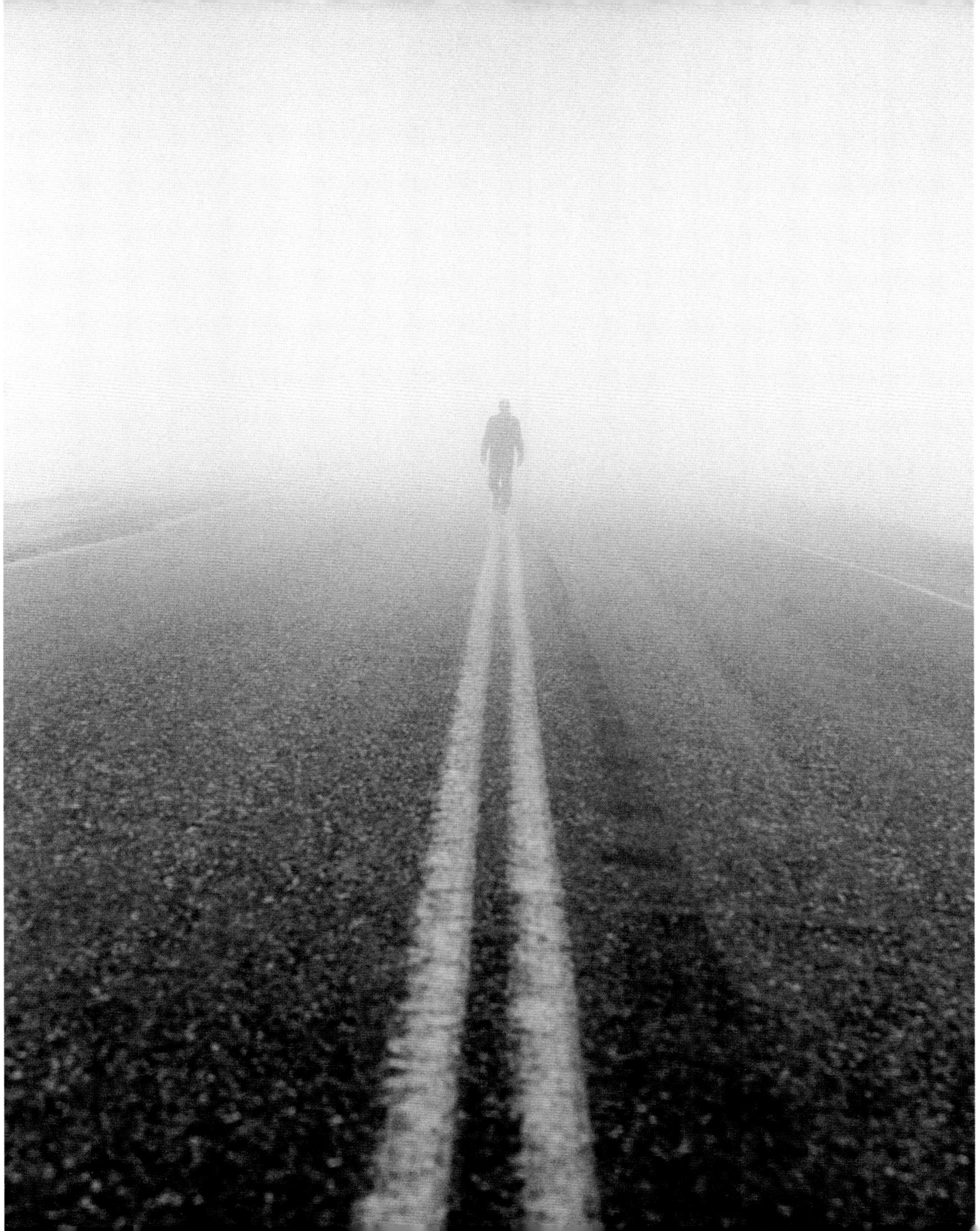

TITLE

The Sleepwalker

This was photographed shortly past 4:00 a.m. I awoke in my tent, chilled to the bone, and couldn't sleep and decided to hike to the far side of Lake O'Hara and spend some time playing in the Seven Veils Falls. Wet, cold and incredible.

Location: Yoho National Park, British Columbia, Canada

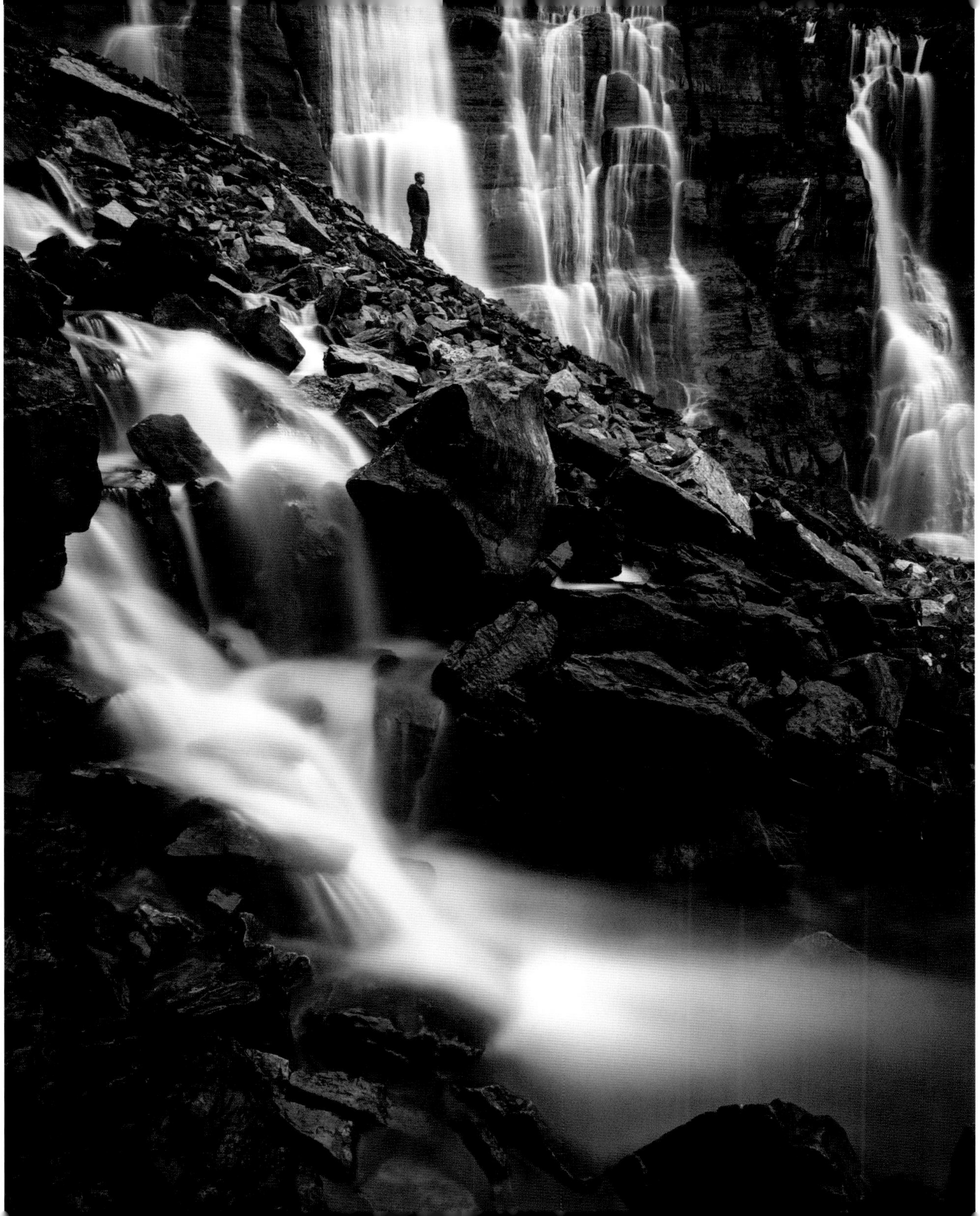

TITLE

Soar

After an afternoon of dramatic hiking in the mountains of Iceland, I stumbled upon this scene from high above, looking down on an incredible black sand beach.

Location: Vestmannaeyjar, Iceland

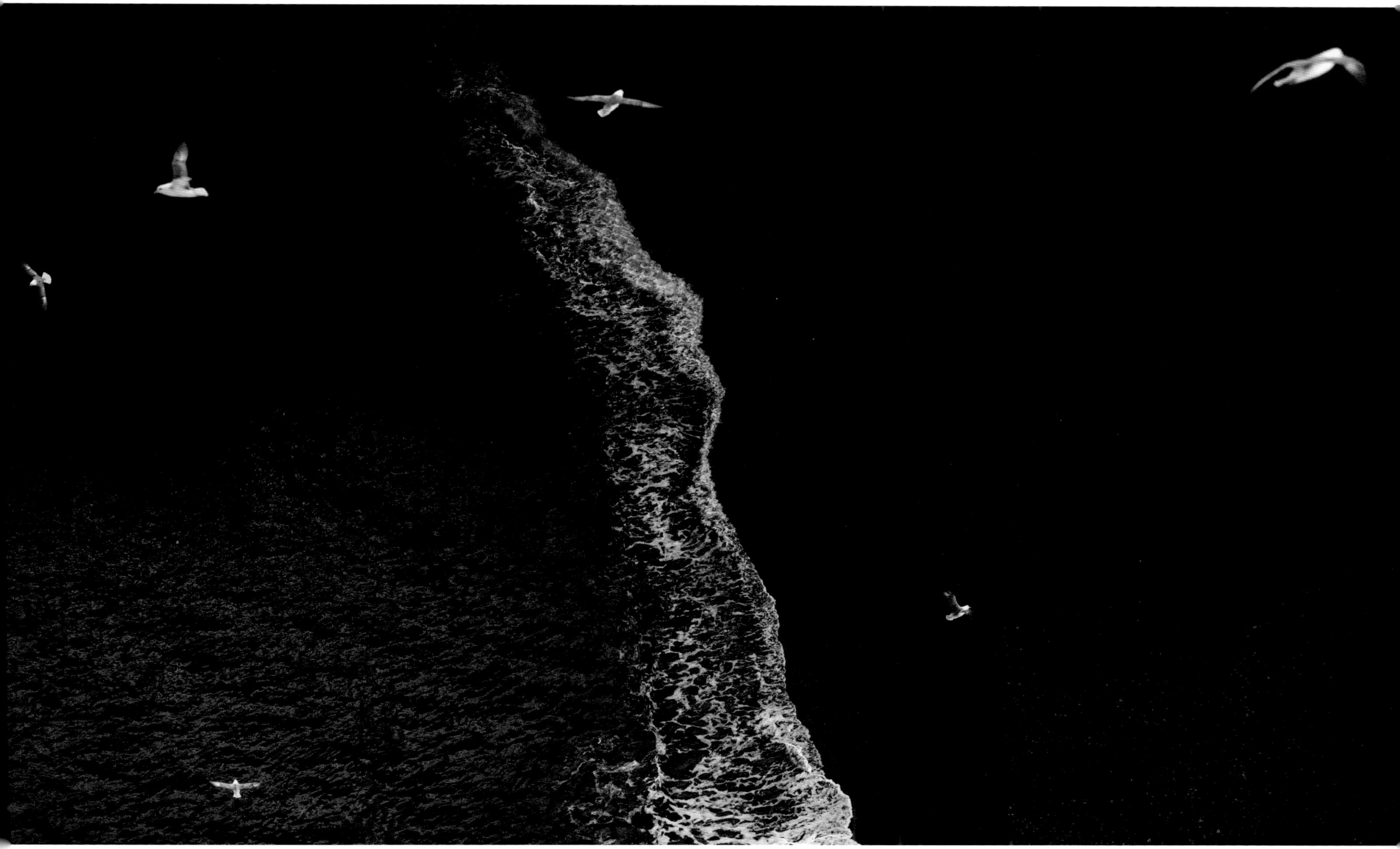

TITLE

Still

When you spend a lot of time exploring a place, you get to know its nuances – its many secrets. Here, at Canoe Cove on Prince Edward Island, I know of a rock that only reveals itself when the tide hits a certain point. A perfect place to take it all in.

Location: Canoe Cove, Prince Edward Island, Canada

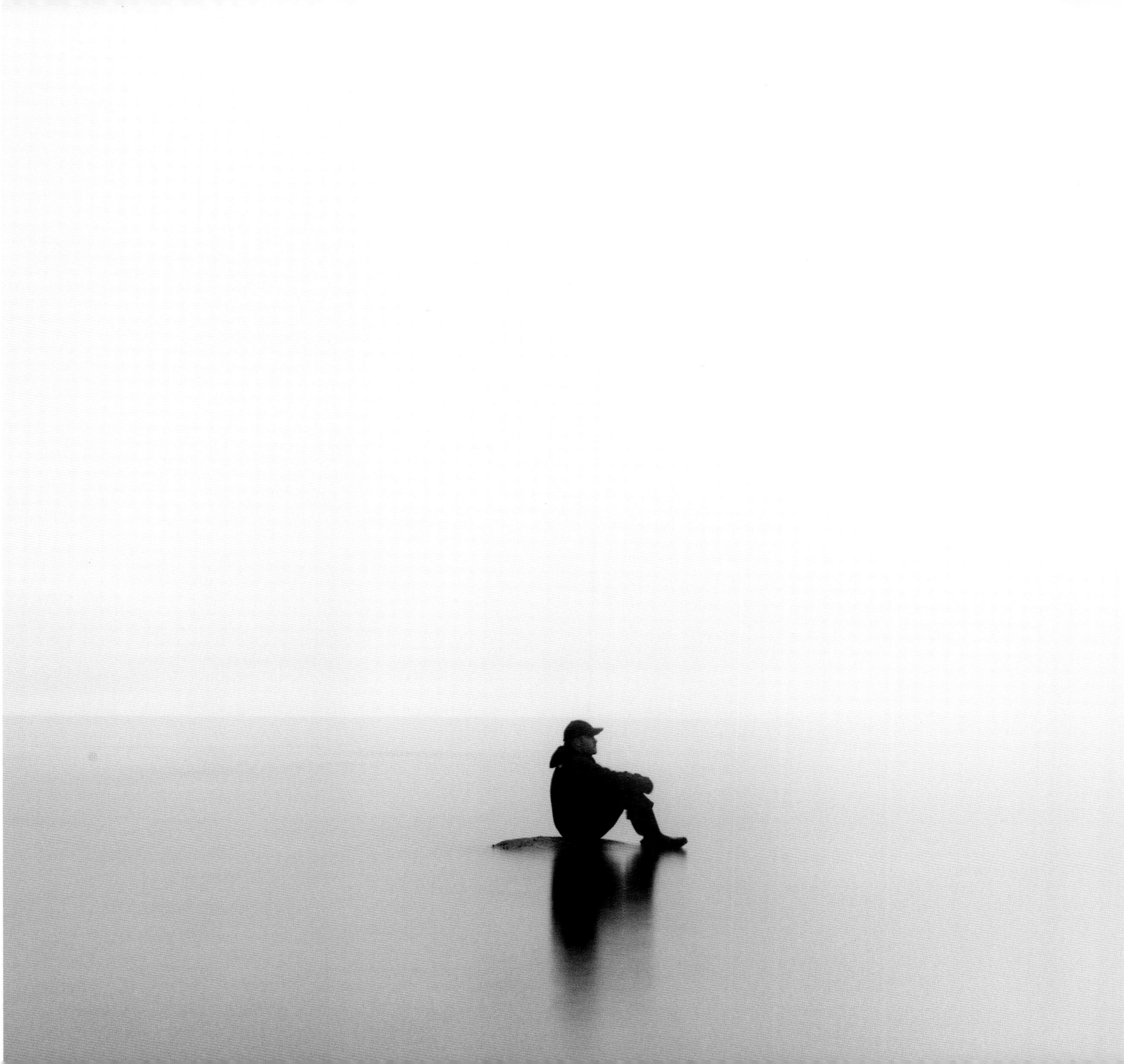

TITLE

We Come in Peace

Photography isn't about dramatic locations; photography is about recognizing the potential in your surroundings and seeking the truth within. This image was from a simple countryside stroll in rural Nova Scotia, and it's one of my favourites.

Location: Afton, Nova Scotia, Canada

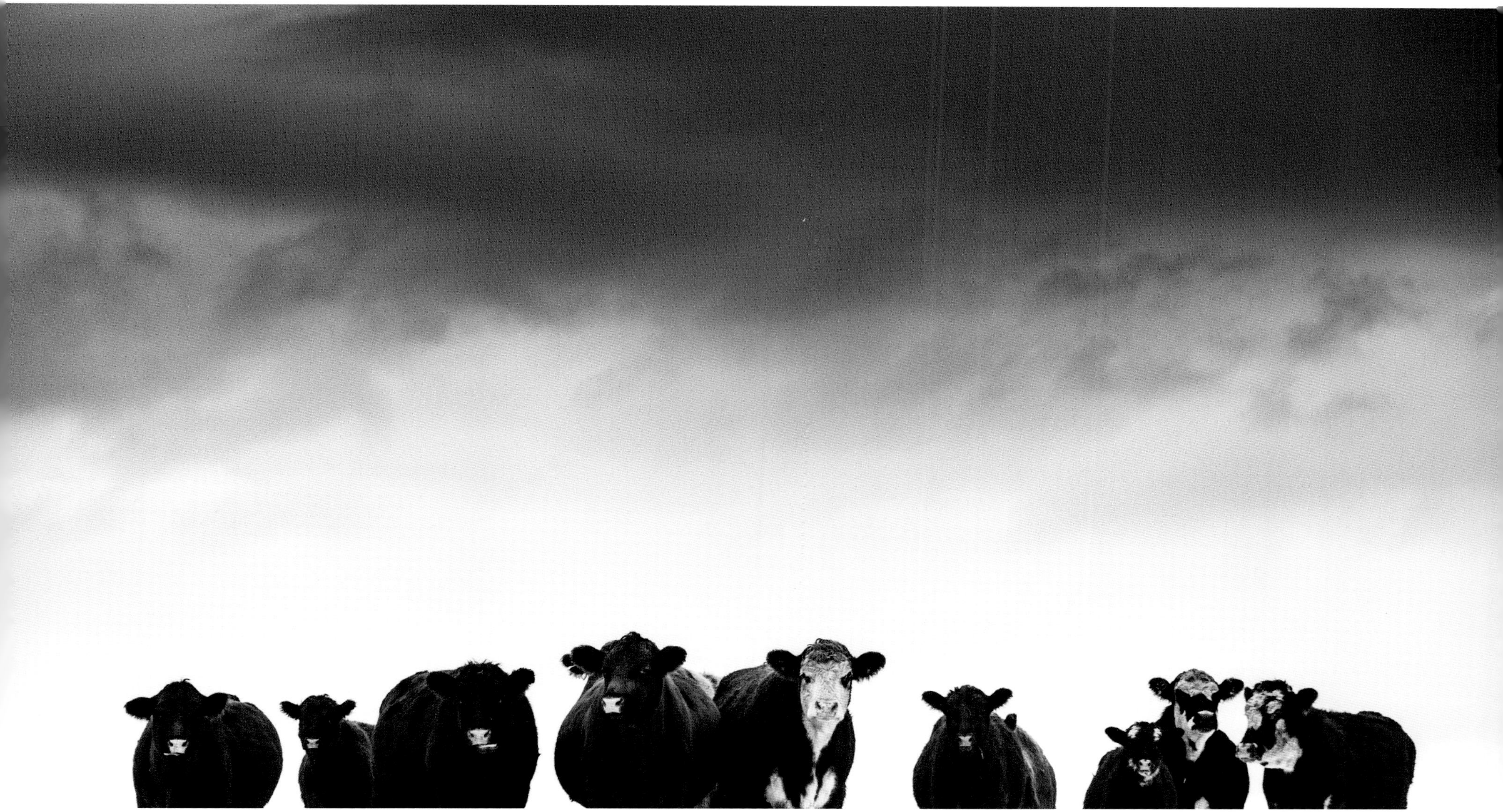

TITLE

Sparkle and Shine

Photographers often like to photograph with other photographers. I'm no exception. A result of this, though, is often that the other photographer becomes the story I focus on as much as my environment; it can sometimes lead to "gold" in the field. Here, my friend Stephen DesRoches takes in his dramatic surroundings on Disko Island in Greenland while I'm just fascinated with the light dancing around him.

Location: Qeqertarsuaq, Greenland

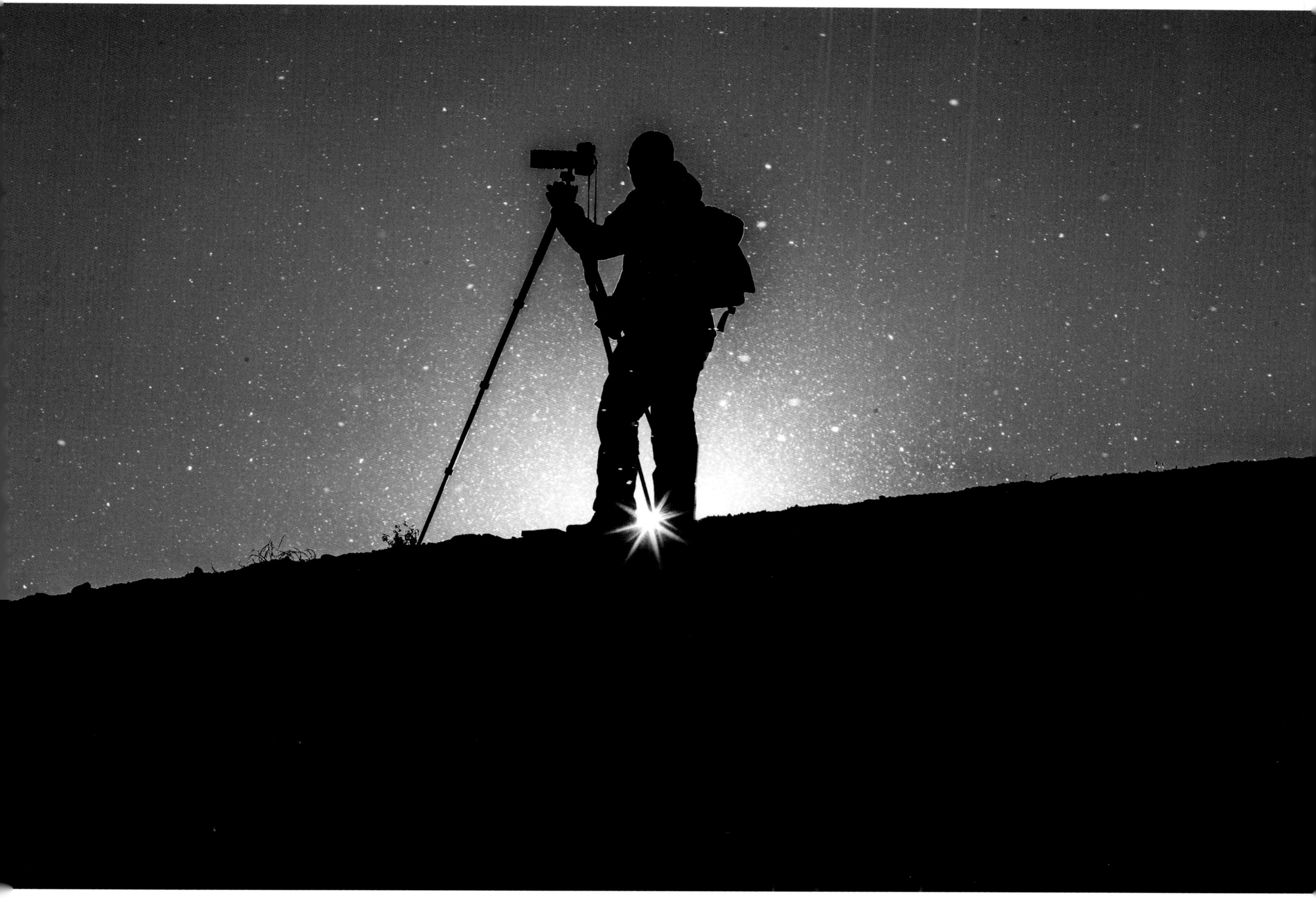

TITLE

Lie and Wait

Harsh light can become dramatically moody when underexposed in black and white photography. This was photographed in the harsh sun and heat of an African afternoon; my patient subject was content to sit in the sun and wait for unsuspecting prey…luckily, not us.

Location: Chobe National Park, Botswana

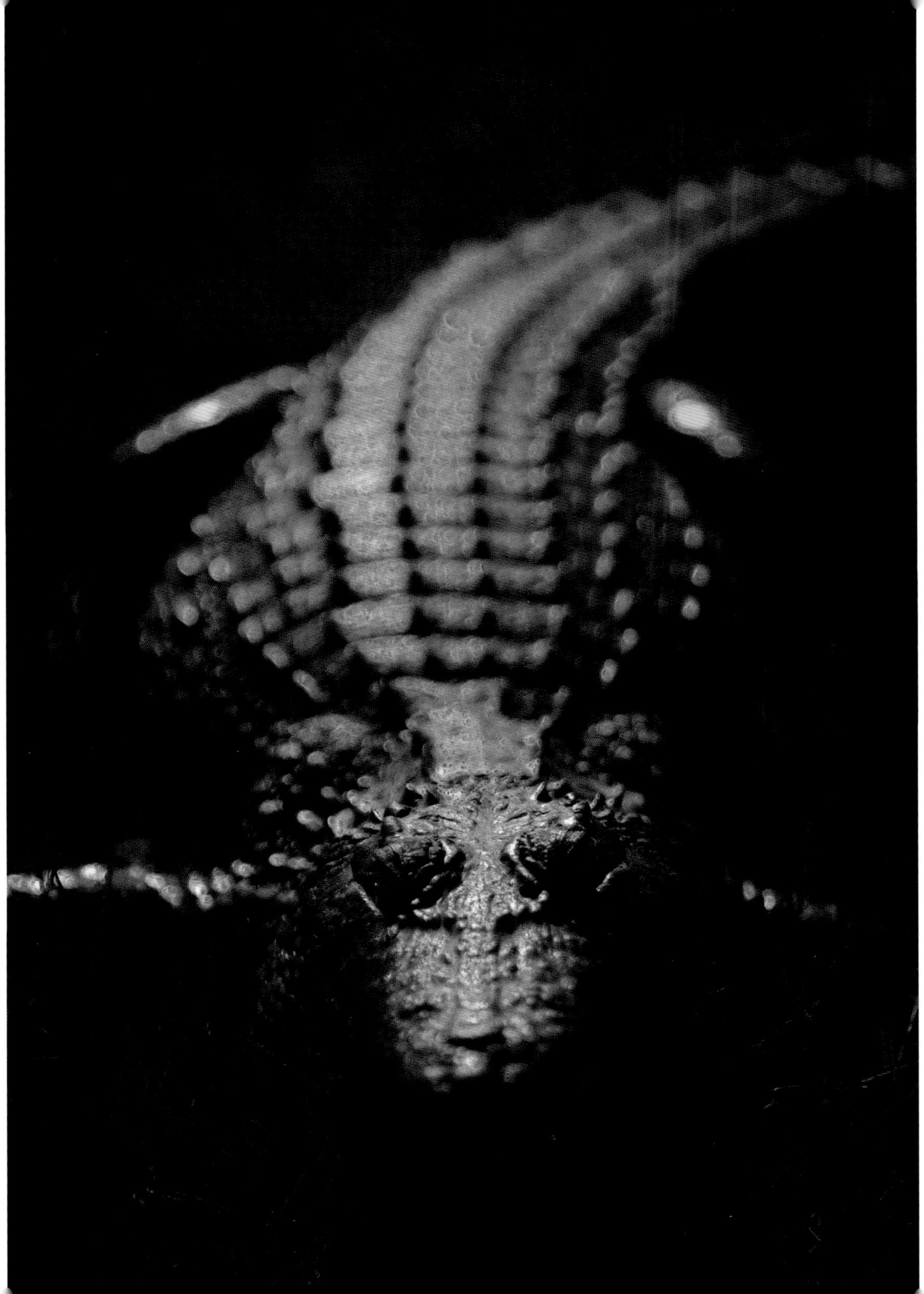

TITLE

Breakwater

Just down the shore from my mother's place in Bayfield, Nova Scotia, is a unique world of black and white drama. I love finding these gems, and the stories they tell.

Location: Bayfield, Nova Scotia

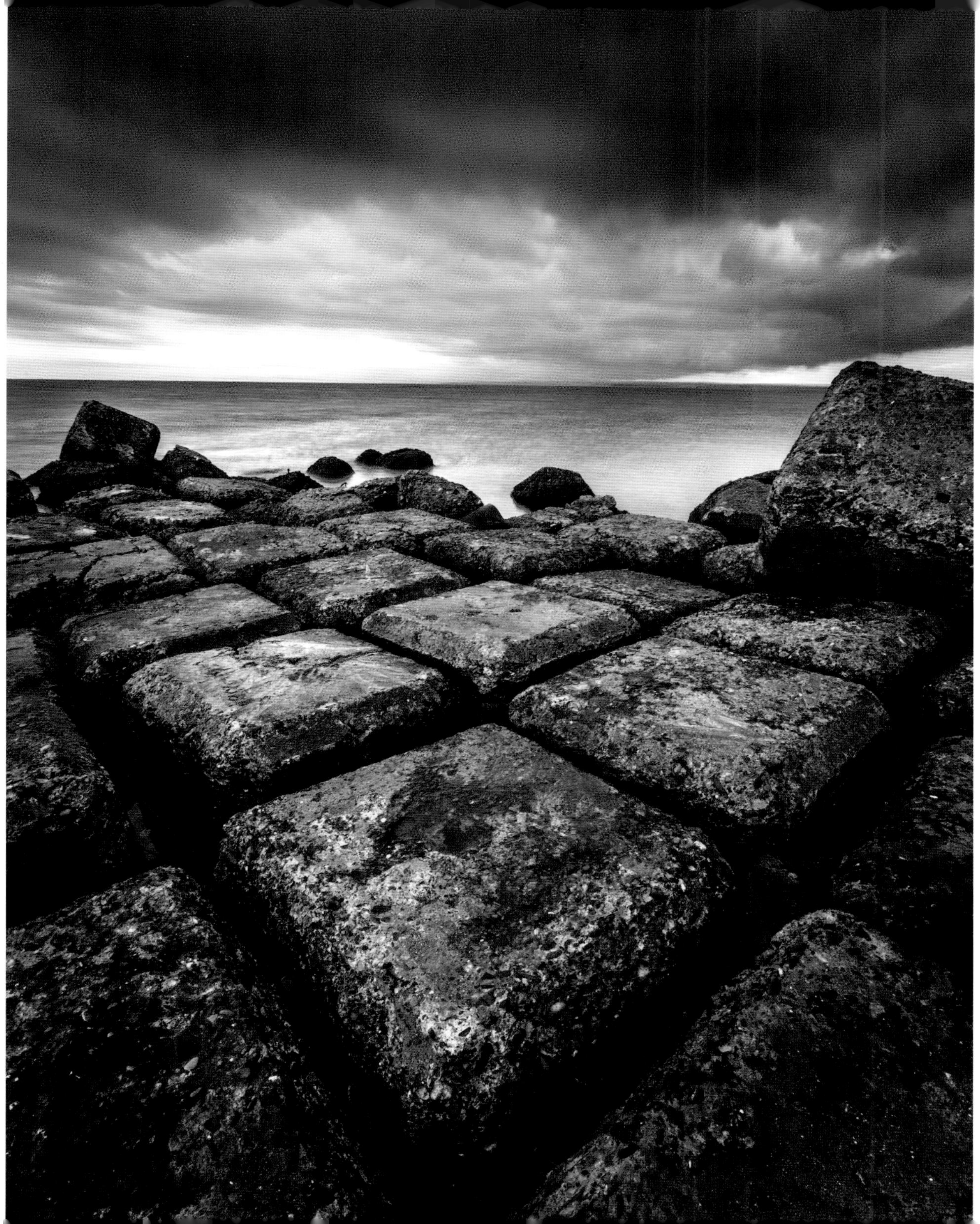

TITLE

The Pass

The Himalaya of Bhutan is one of the most beautiful and dramatic places on earth. With some of the world's highest peaks, the Himalaya is no place for the frail, and you're reminded of that around every bend.

Location: Chomolhari Trek, Bhutan

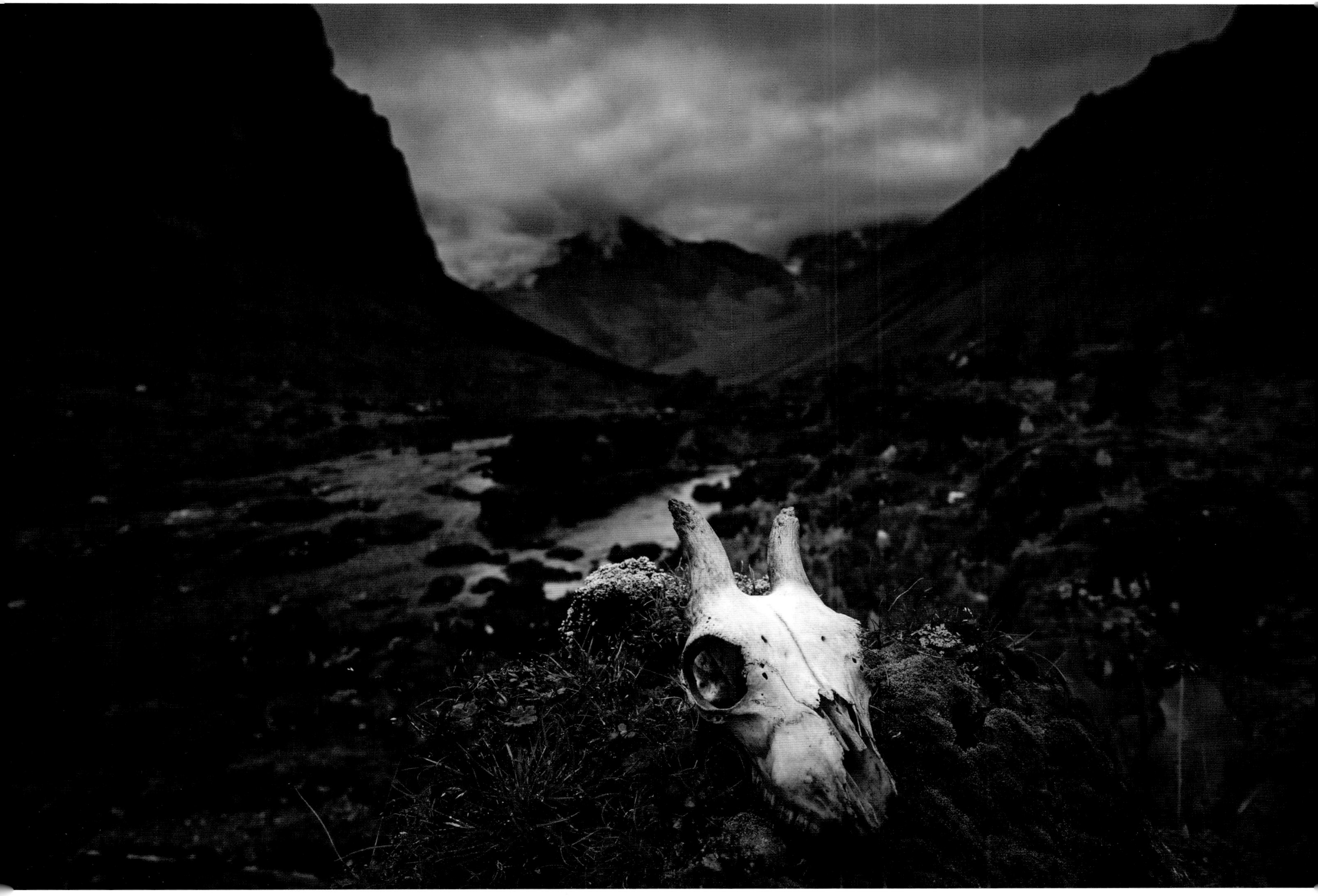

TITLE

Up and Away

Often, in nature photography, you're trying to get away from humanity, avoiding roads and power lines and people and anything that's not purely our natural environment. To close your eyes to the occasional visual beauty carved by humanity, however, would be folly.

Location: Gjógv Valley, Faroe Islands

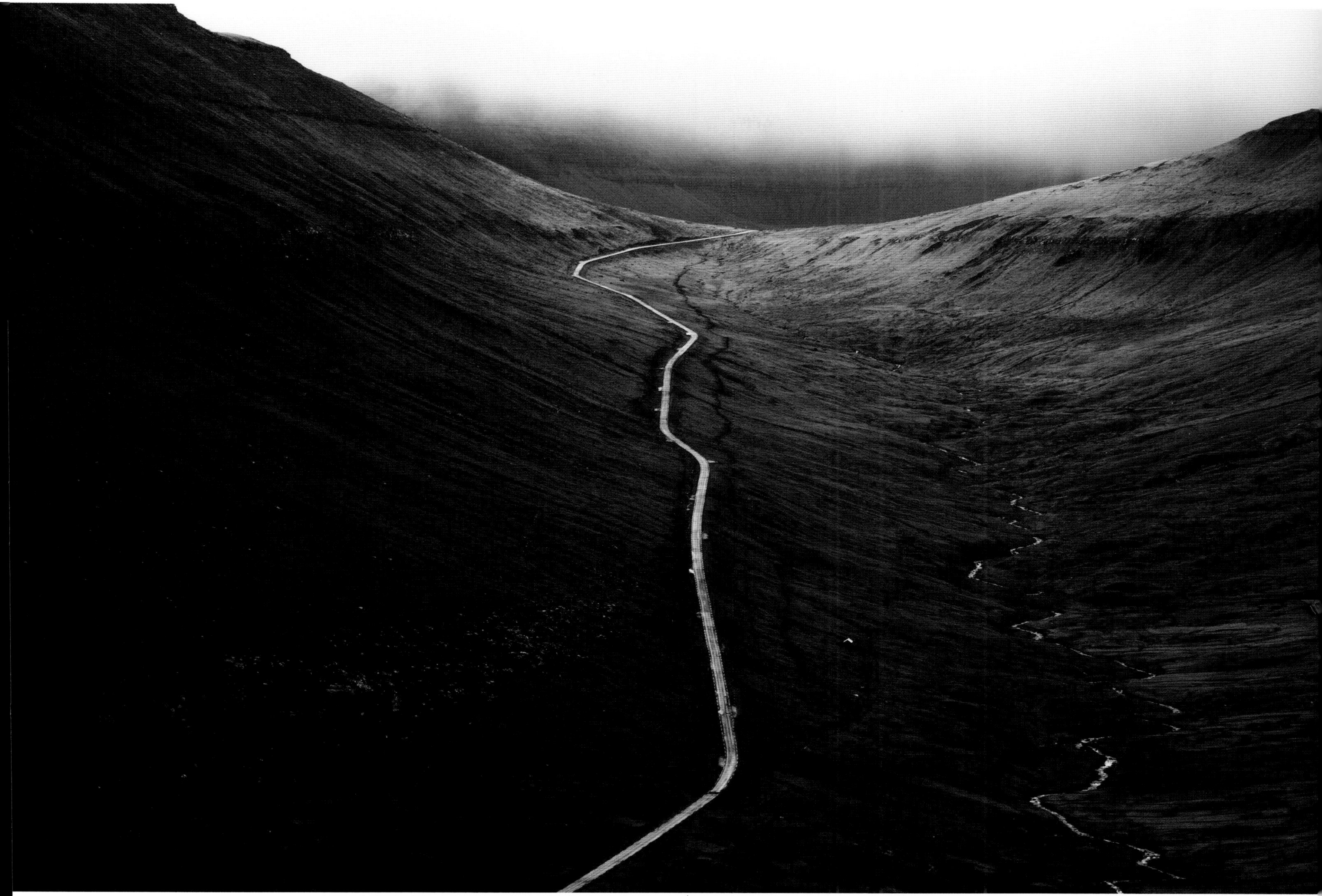

TITLE

The Visitor

Living in rural Prince Edward Island, I am fortunate to stumble upon a lot of beautiful "wild," including in my own backyard. This beautiful visitor appeared one day in my back field, stopping for a moment to consider my presence before trotting lazily on its way.

Location: Long Creek, Prince Edward Island, Canada

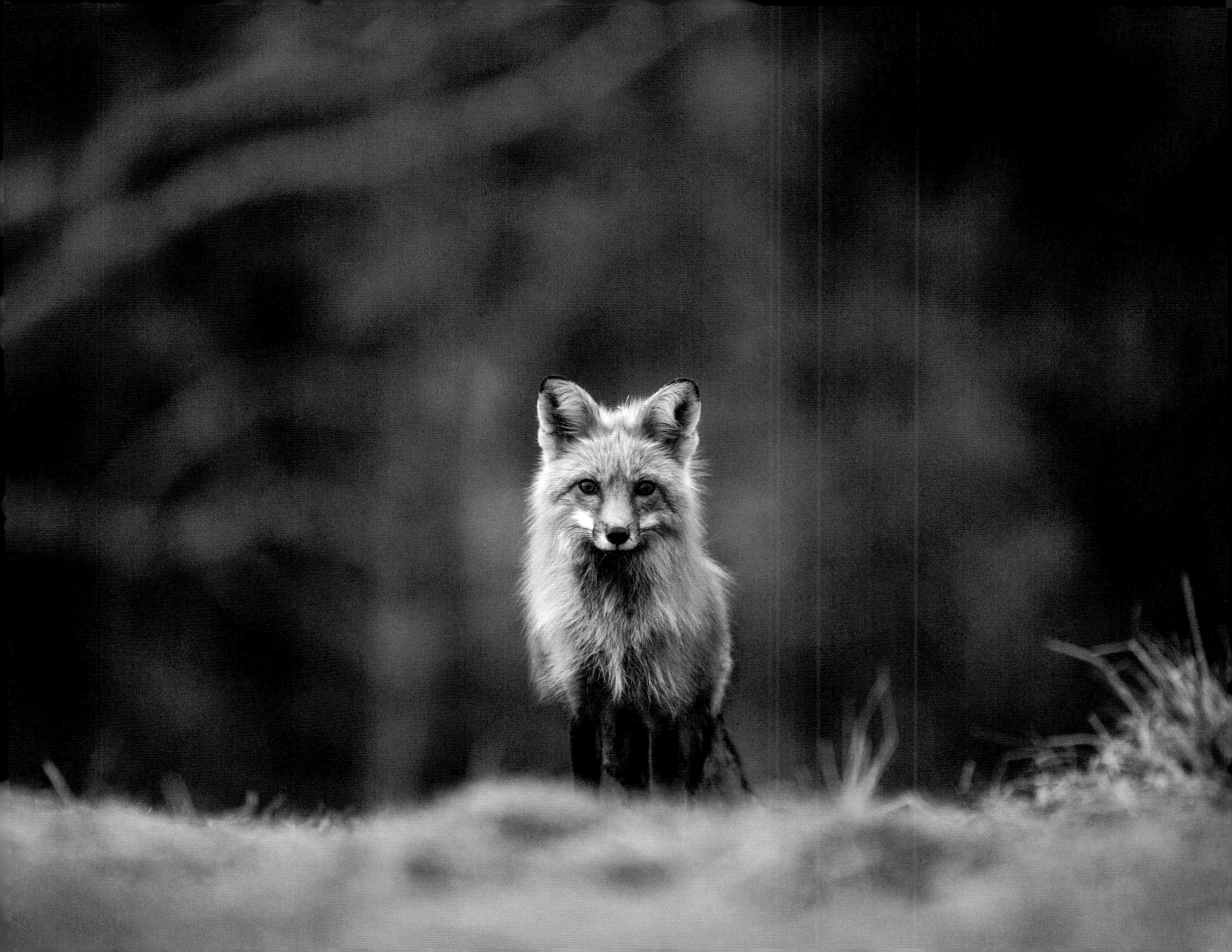

TITLE

Tumbling Down

The ancient, rugged, heavily textured landscape in Auyuittuq National Park on Baffin Island, in the Canadian Arctic. A land of waterfalls and unforgiving terrain.

Location: Auyuittuq National Park, Nunavut, Canada

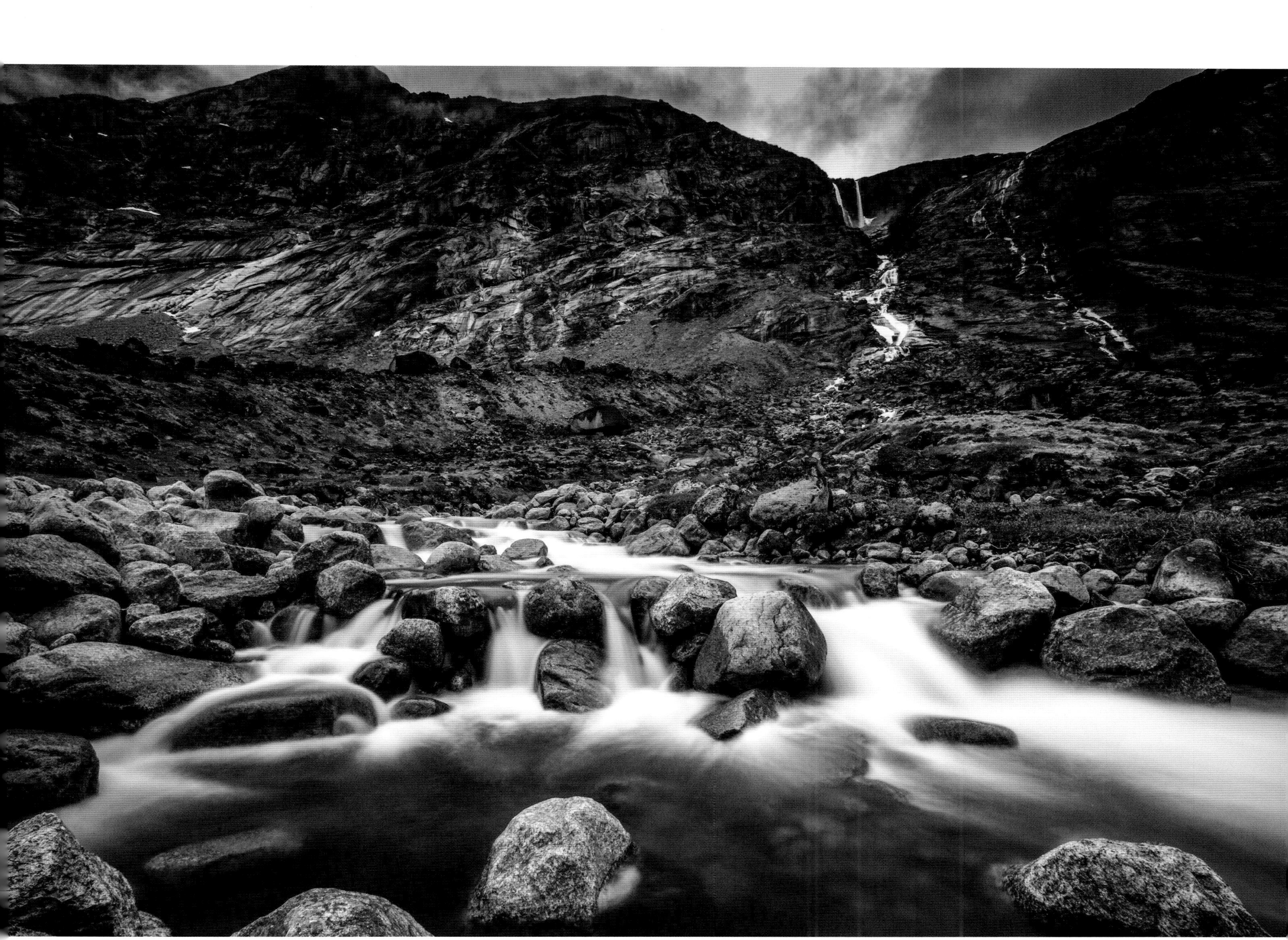

TITLE

New-found Shores

One of my best friends, Curtis Jones – a Newfoundlander like no other – taking in the dramatic shores of the land and sea he loves so much. Home. A child of the salt and the sea.

Location: St. Bride's, Newfoundland, Canada

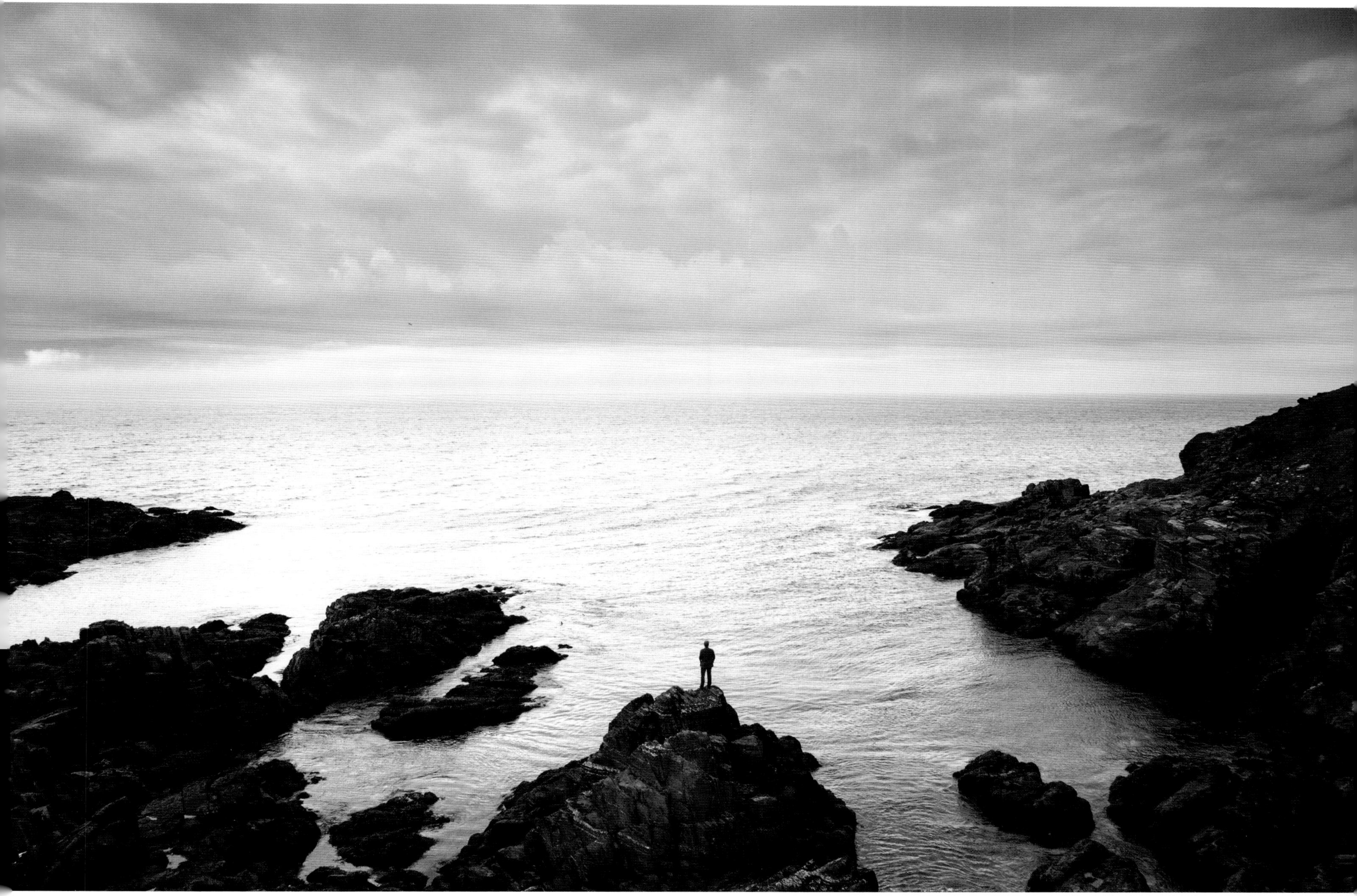

TITLE

Family Gathering

There's certainly more famous and "epic" wildlife in Botswana – many photographers seek out the Big Five, which includes the African elephant, lion, Cape buffalo, leopard and rhinoceros – but for pure observational "fun," I'll take a family of baboons any day.

Location: Chobe National Park, Botswana

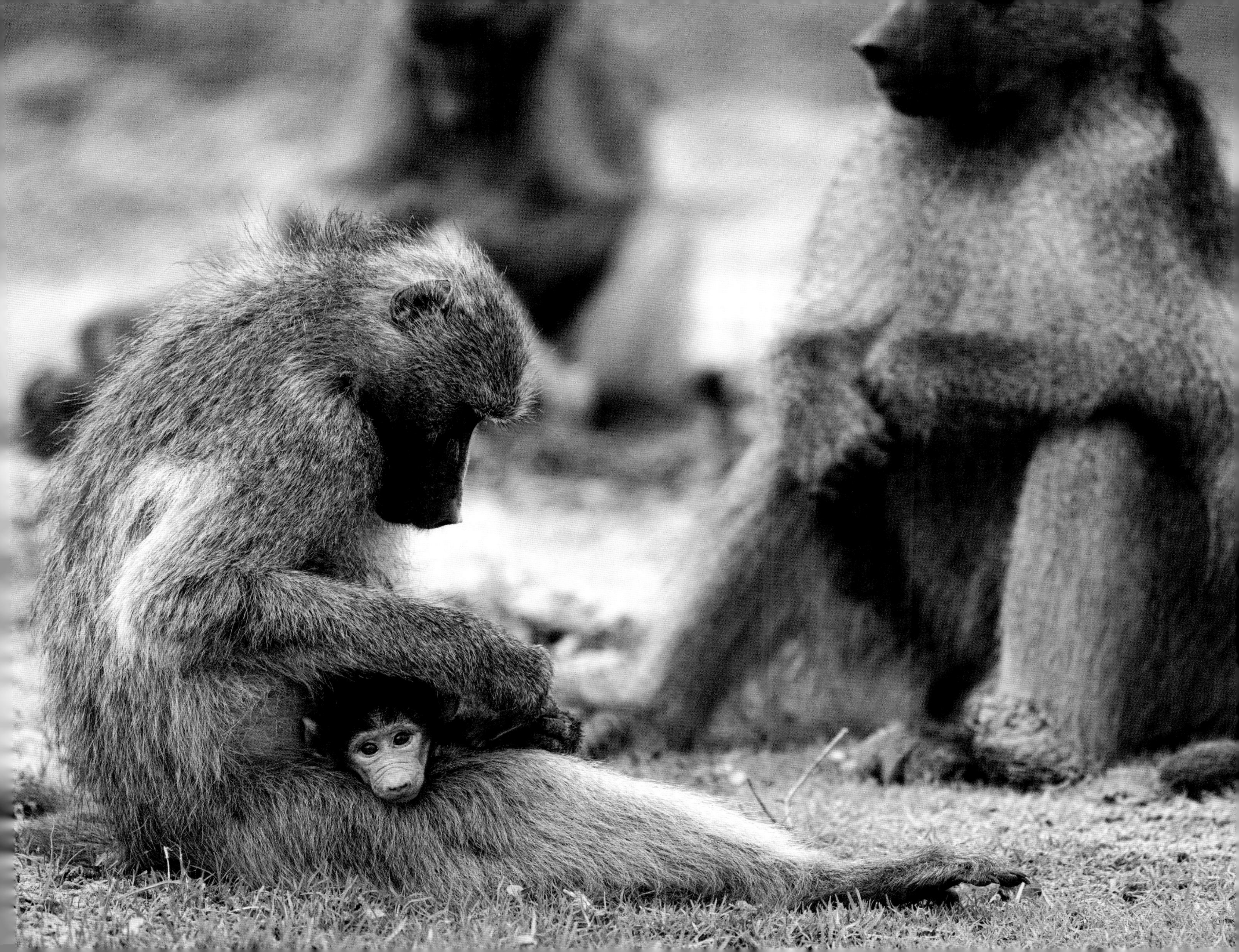

TITLE

The Gift

Anyone who wanders the seaside coast knows that the true gift is not what you might find along the shores while beachcombing, but simply the experience of being out in the salt air and breathing in the ocean.

Location: Canoe Cove, Prince Edward Island, Canada

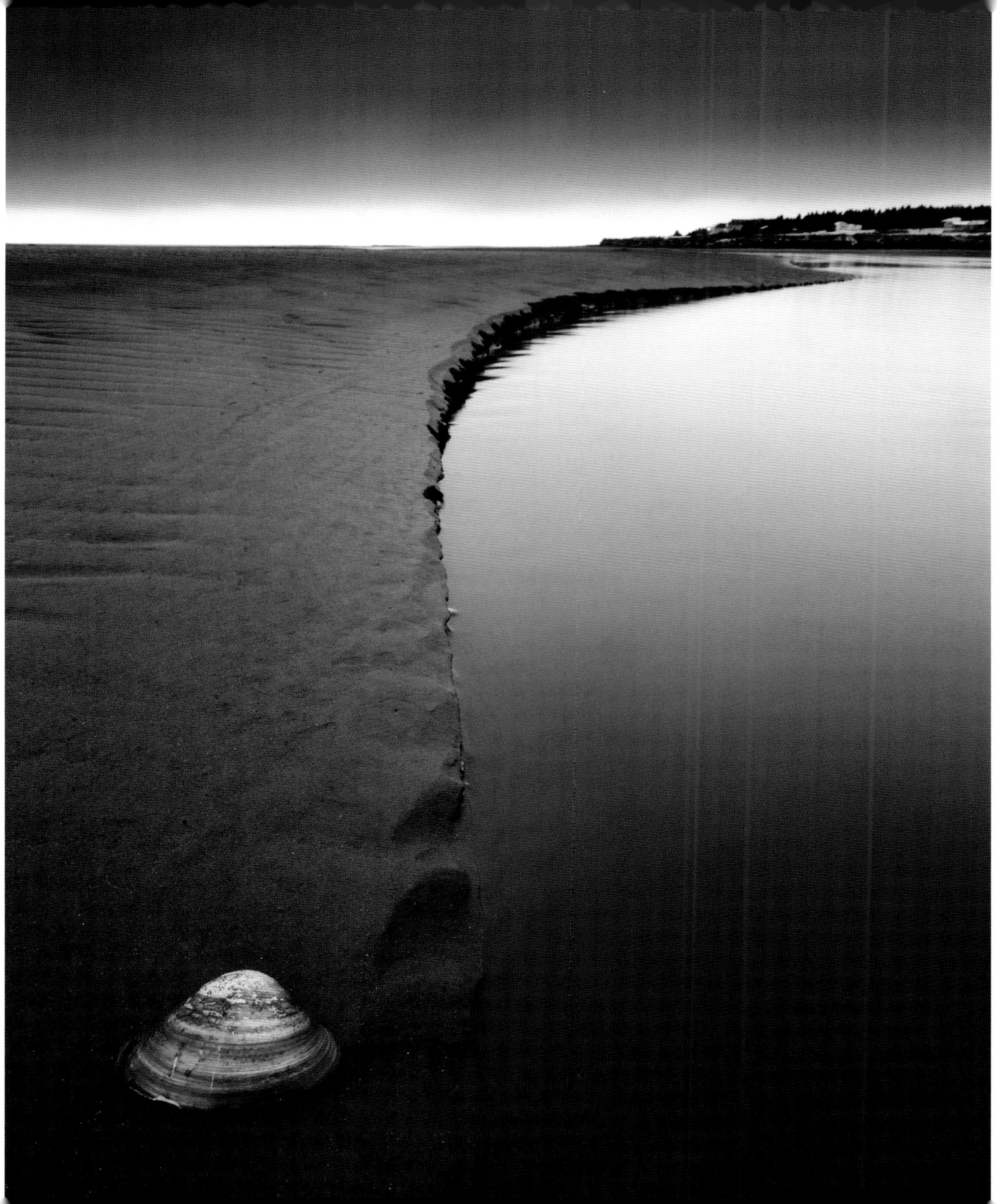

TITLE

The Standoff

Greenland sled dogs have a moment of confrontation in this Ilulissat street scene. Sled dogs have been an important part of the Greenlandic way of life for over 1,000 years.

Location: Ilulissat, Greenland

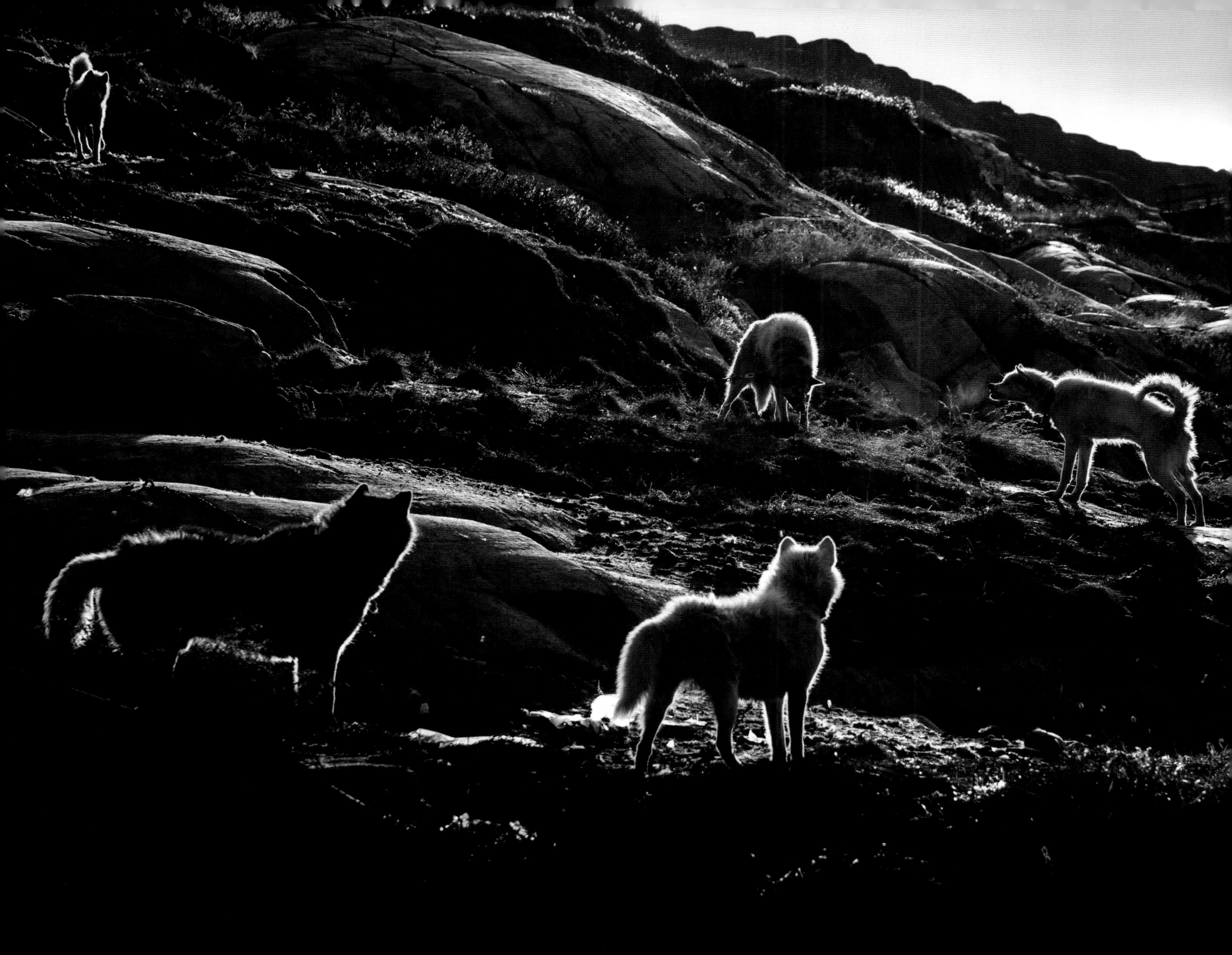

TITLE

Titans

Over my 20 years of photography, I have found myself on many commercial projects. Here, a "little" scene I stumbled upon at a diamond mine on a winter day in the Canadian sub-Arctic. A day of rest for these titans of industry.

Location: The Barrenlands, Northwest Territories, Canada

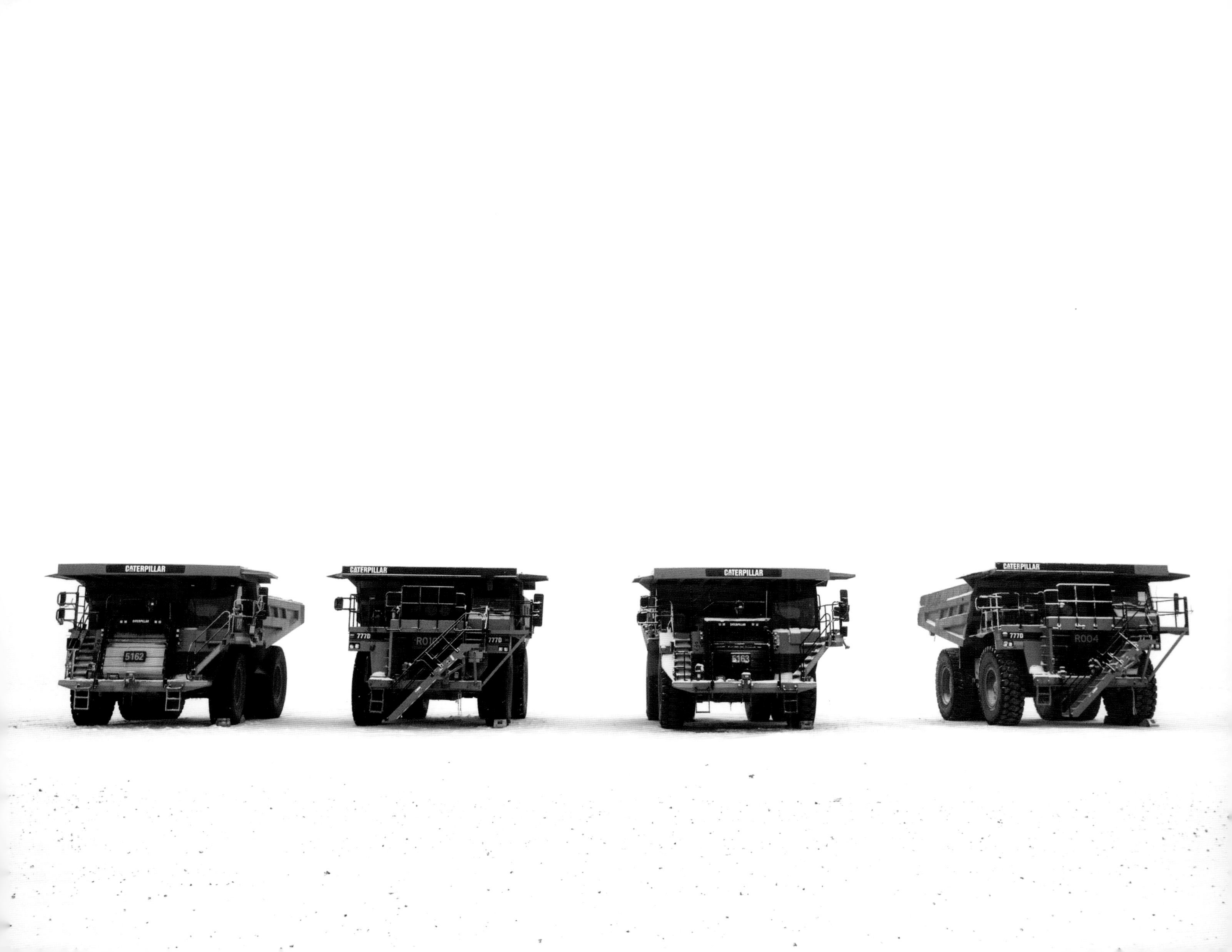
CATERPILLAR
5162
CATERPILLAR
777D
777D
CATERPILLAR
CATERPILLAR
777D
R004

TITLE

Backsplash

The black sand beaches of Qeqertarsuaq in Greenland always form a striking contrast to the bits of pieces of nearby icebergs that get broken down and wash up on its shores.

Location: Qeqertarsuaq, Greenland

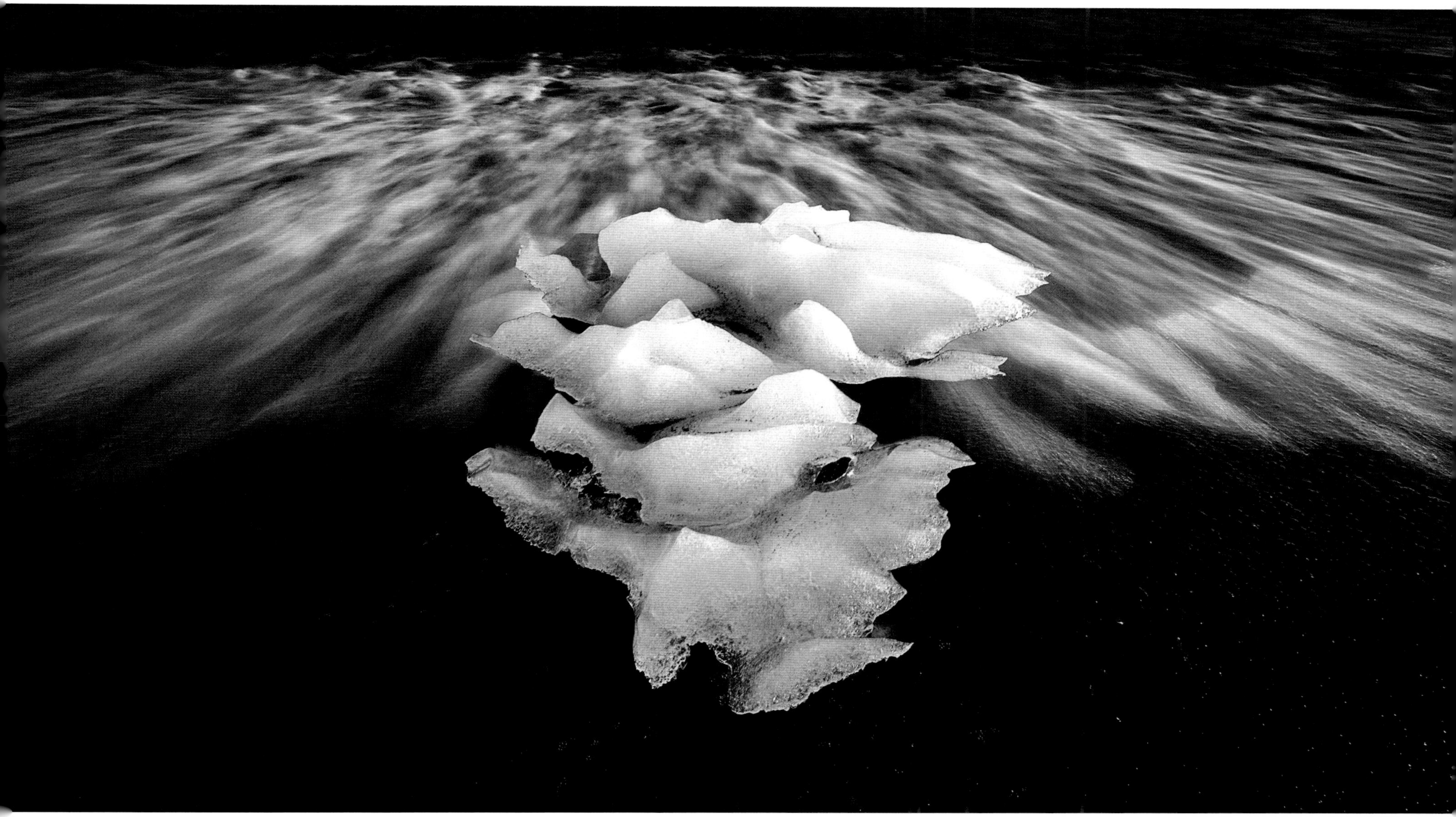

TITLE

Finding Form

At the heart of black and white is the interplay between light and shadow, lightness and darkness, structure, story and form. Here is a scene in rural Prince Edward Island where I, as photographer, was looking to "play" and to challenge myself to find out what I could see.

Location: Queens County, Prince Edward Island, Canada

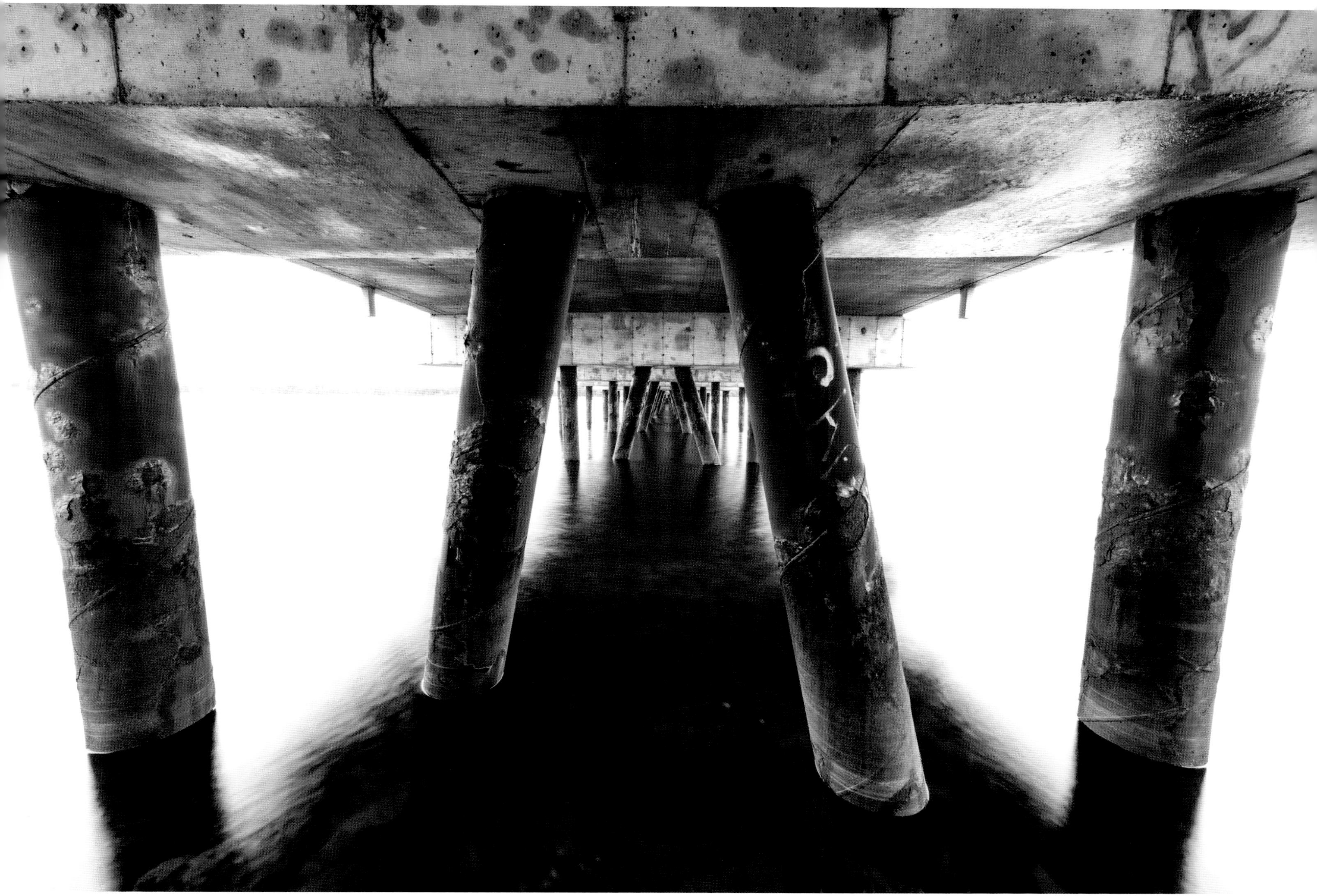

TITLE

Home upon Home

Architectural and cityscape photography is not something I do often (as a photographer who resides in the countryside), but I always enjoy the challenge of analyzing humanscapes for visually interesting scenes.

Location: Southern Florida, United States

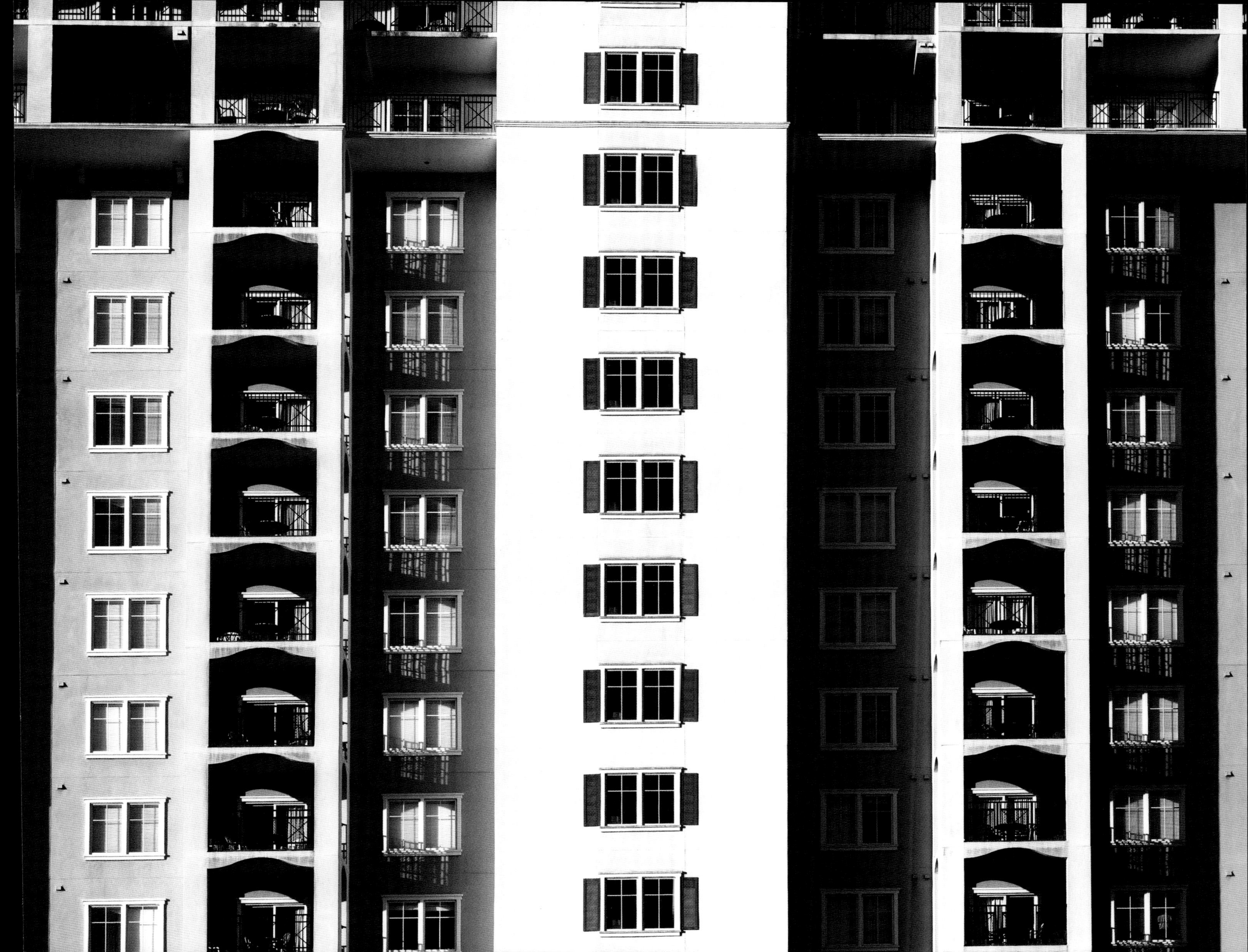

TITLE

Float

The first time I had the opportunity to sail from southern Argentina to Antarctica (I would later return many times), our initial stop was South Georgia, which would become one of my favourite places in the world due to the incredible geography and wildlife found there. This was the first iceberg we spotted that year as we approached this formidably beautiful island.

Location: South Georgia, Antarctica

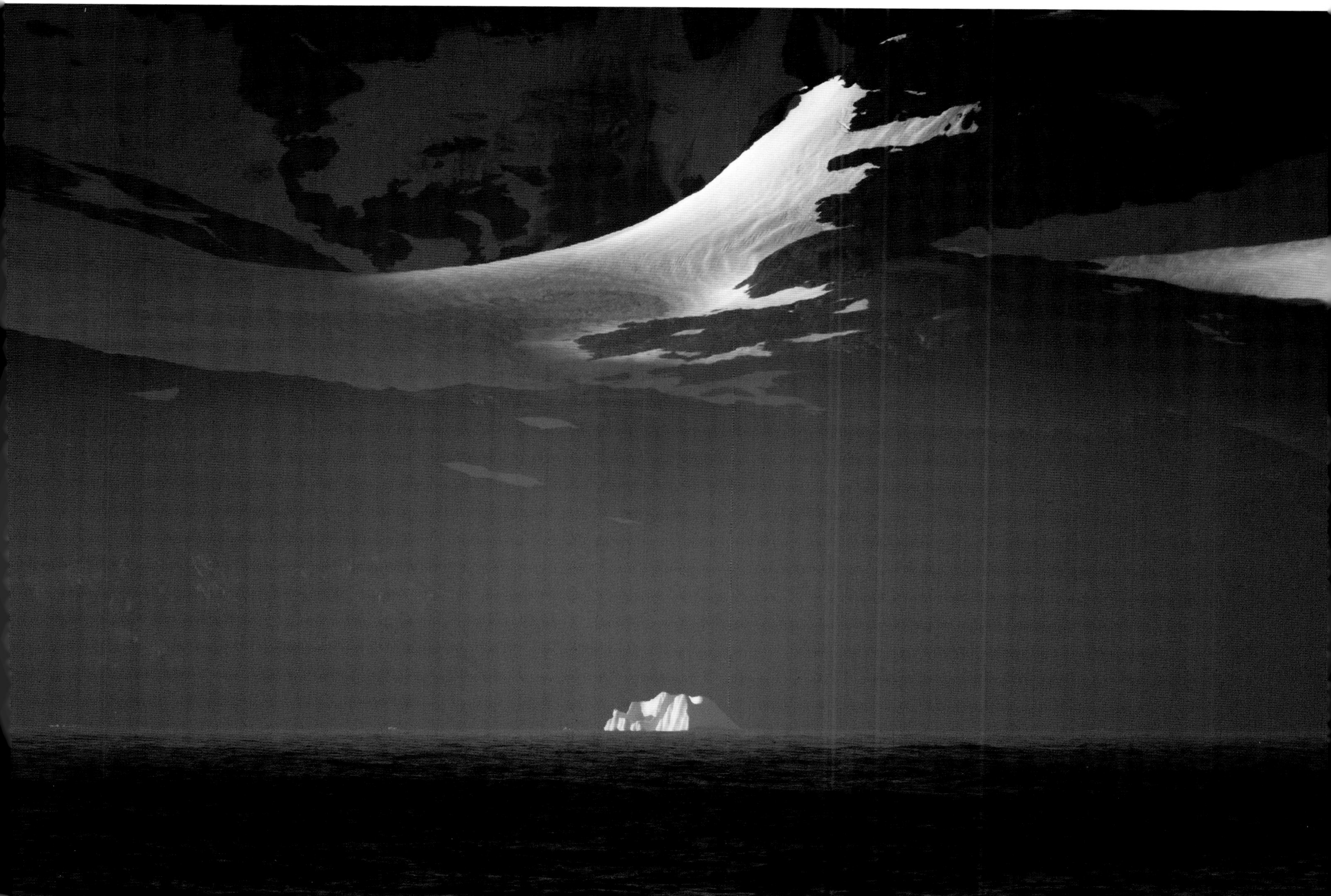

TITLE

The Mirror

After you've photographed your first 1,000 penguins and gotten over the sheer unique "cuteness" of them (they really are), you remember to look for the unusual, photographically, in attempts to make not only cute images but strong ones. This quiet moment of a gentoo penguin sipping on some trapped meltwater provided not only a unique moment but a sizeable amount of cute factor too.

Location: Antarctic Peninsula, Antarctica

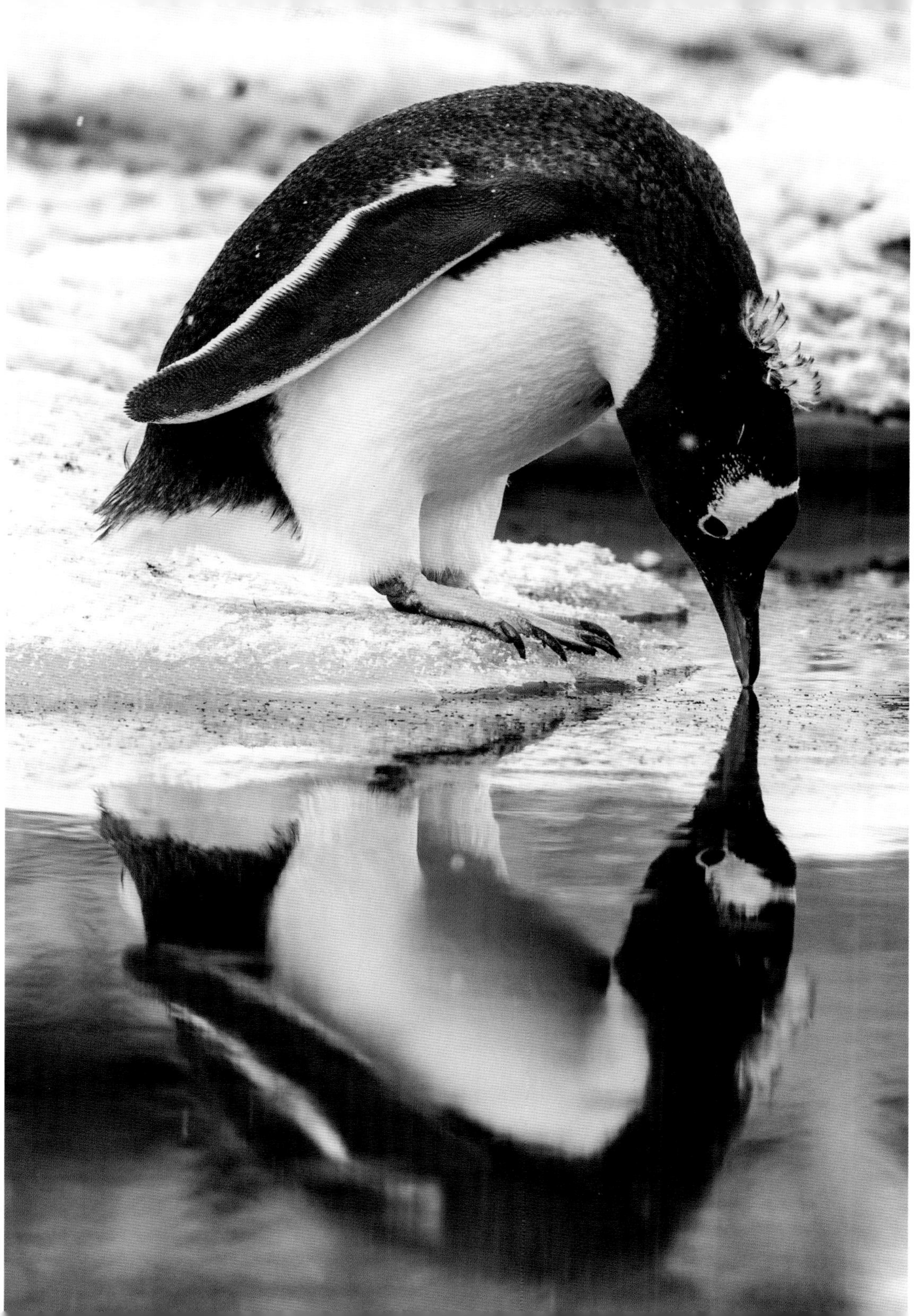

TITLE

Ancient Gazes

In the African wilds, a reliable source of fresh water becomes a magnet for diverse wildlife. On this day we sat waiting in a wildlife blind, a multitude of elephants continuously emerged from the wilderness, stopping to hydrate before continuing on.

Location: Okavango, Botswana

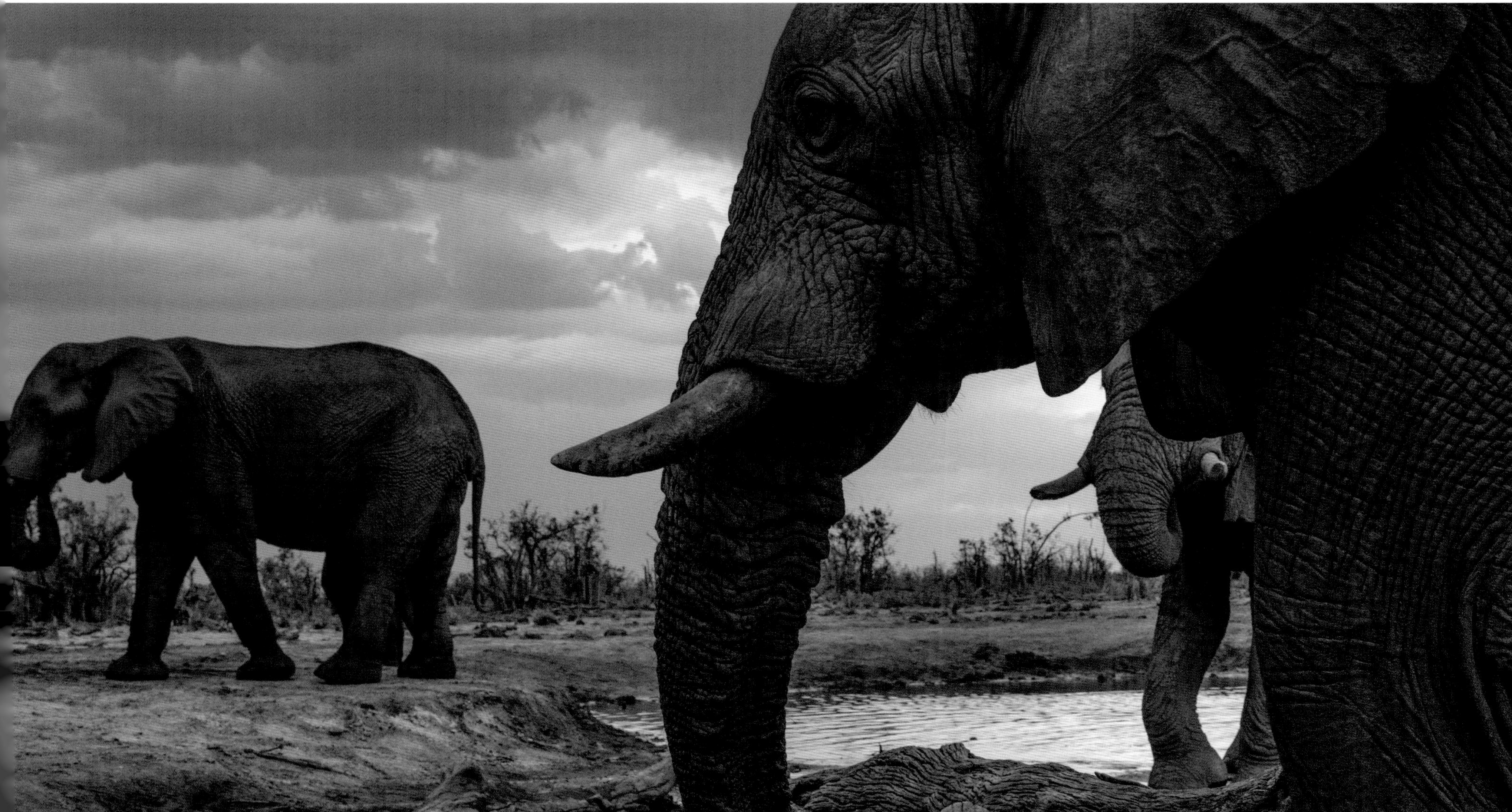

TITLE

The Wanderer

Just a moment of light, lines and exploration in the hills of the always-dramatic Faroe Islands – a place where the weather is as much a part of the landscape as the physical ground you walk on.

Location: Faroe Islands

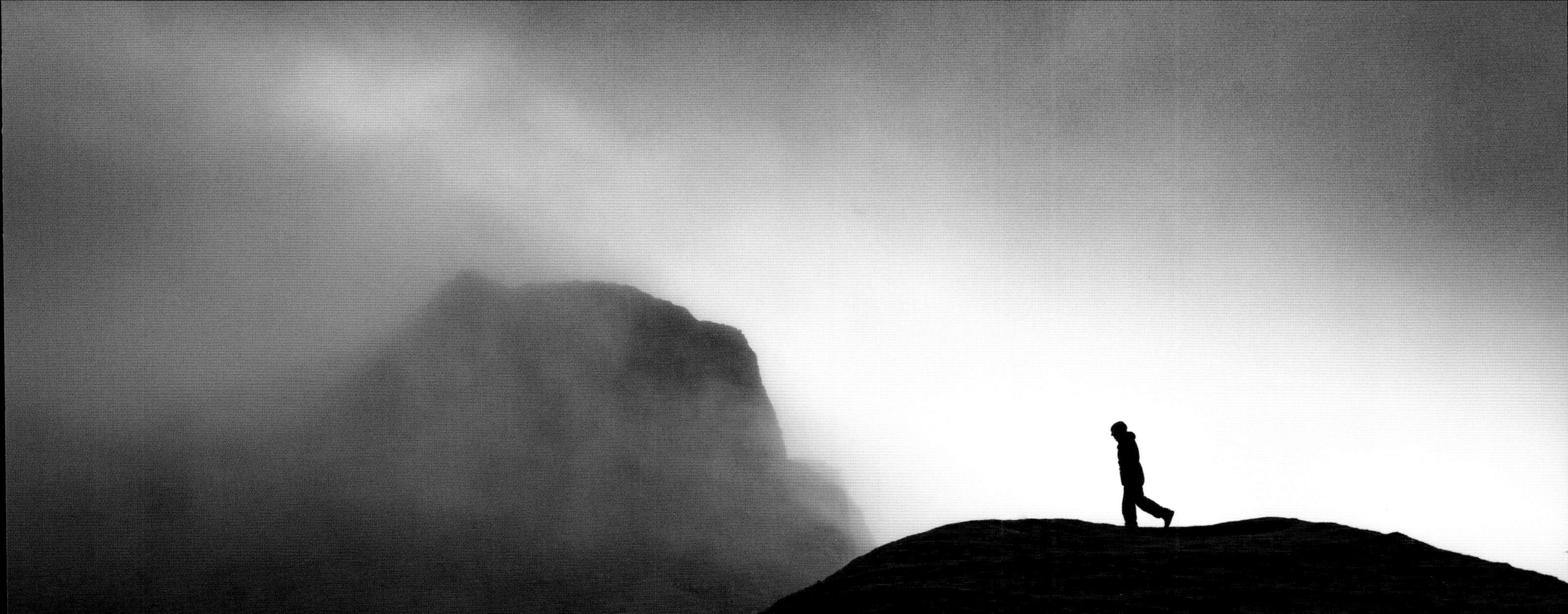

TITLE

Red Shores

Nature photography is the art of noticing the quiet moments of beauty that surround you. When I stroll the shores of Prince Edward Island I find myself looking down as often as up – and even though the Island is known for its incredible colour, I often find myself seeing it with a monochromatic gaze.

Location: Canoe Cove, Prince Edward Island, Canada

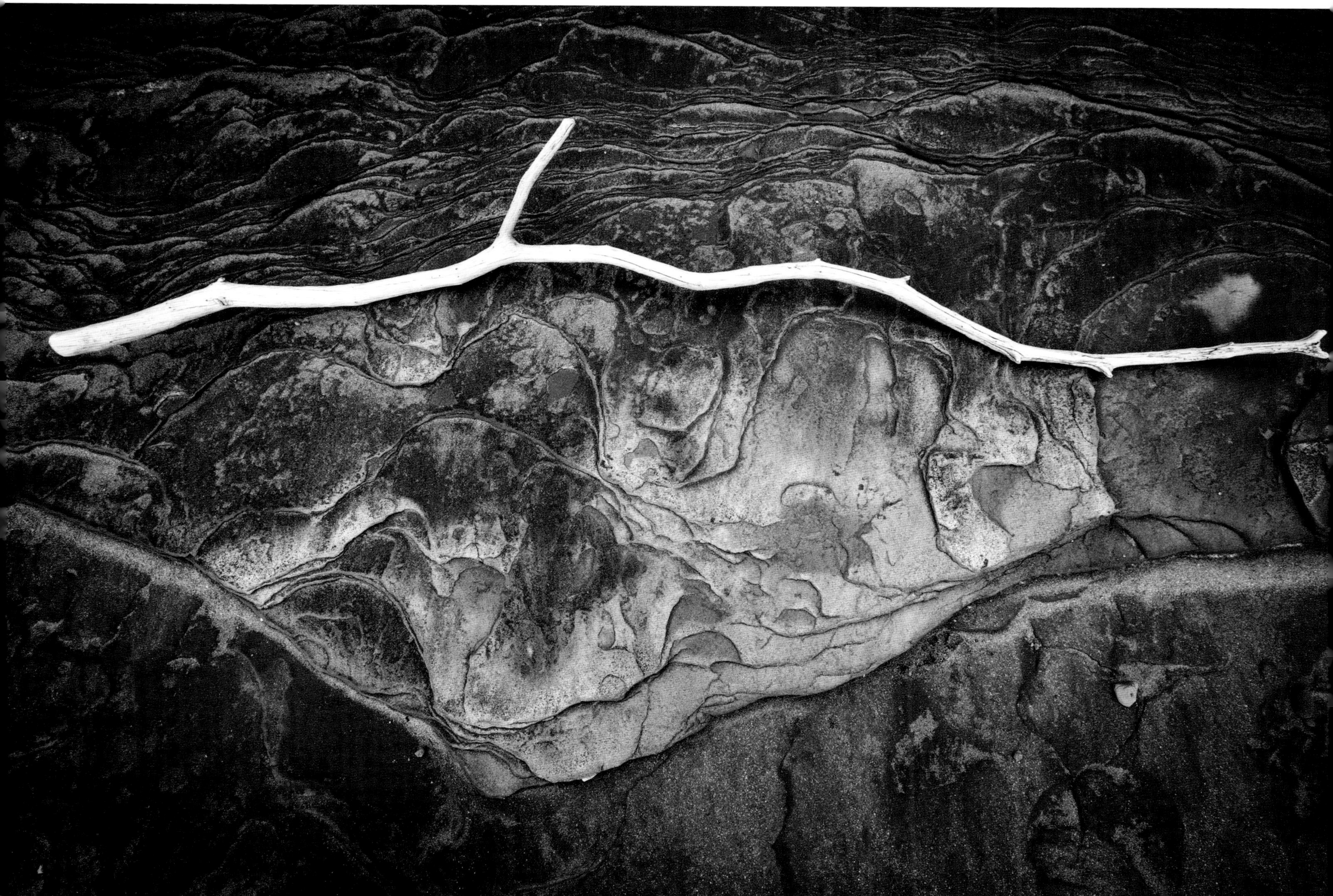

TITLE

Gone but Not Forgotten

An eerie moment of dust-blown beauty, honouring what once lived. Deadvlei, Namibia. In a place normally known for its bright, colourful sand dunes, this dramatic evening featured a dust storm that was hell on equipment but made for perfect photographic conditions.

Location: Deadvlei, Namibia

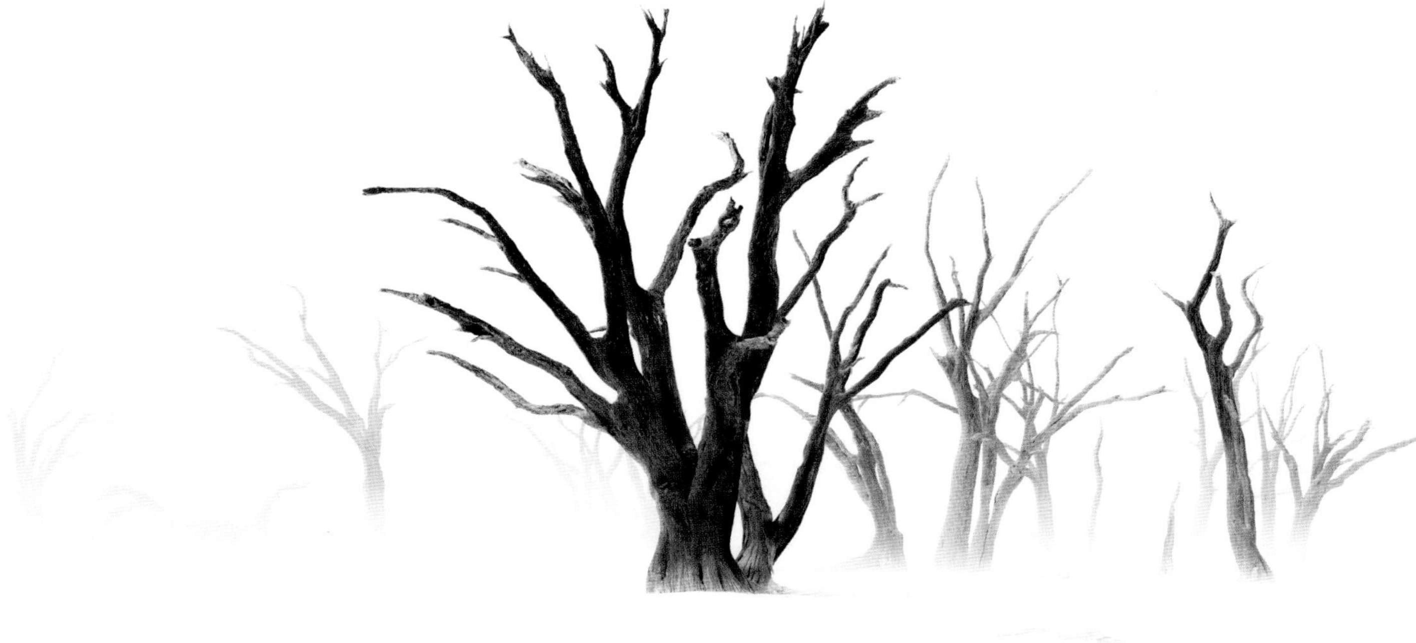

TITLE

An Afternoon Stroll

Foxes have been featured in my images almost as long as I've been a photographer. My home province of Prince Edward Island is abundant with them, but so was my previous home of a decade: Yellowknife, in Canada's North.

Location: Yellowknife, Northwest Territories, Canada

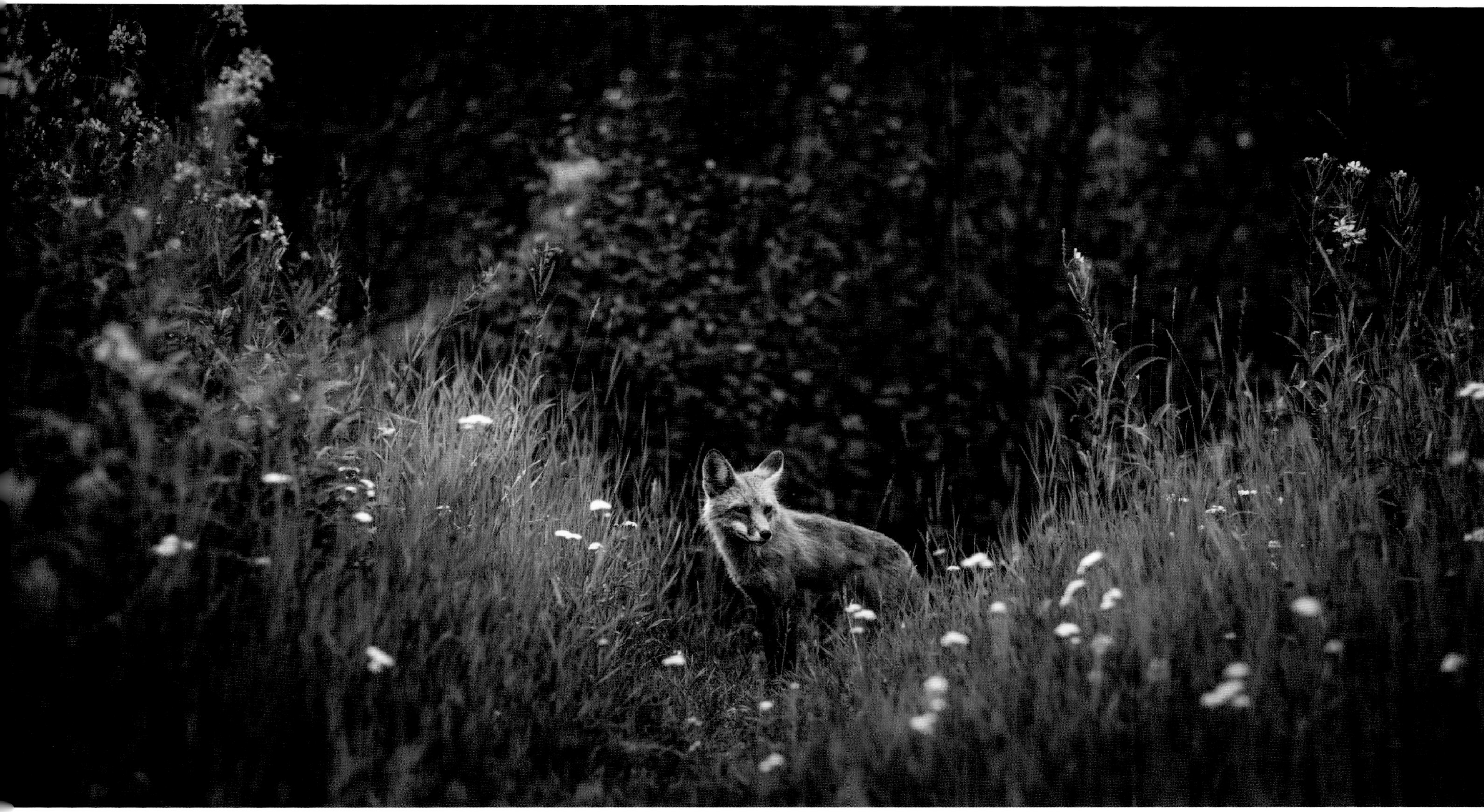

TITLE

The North Atlantic

The power of nature always leaves me in awe – how quickly weather can change from sunny to a state of fury, and how calm can give way to chaos in a matter of moments. As a photographer, I've found many of my favourite images have come from being "on the edge" of fury; this state often gives way to compelling and memorable conditions, if only you're willing to risk a little.

Location: North Atlantic Ocean, Faroe Islands

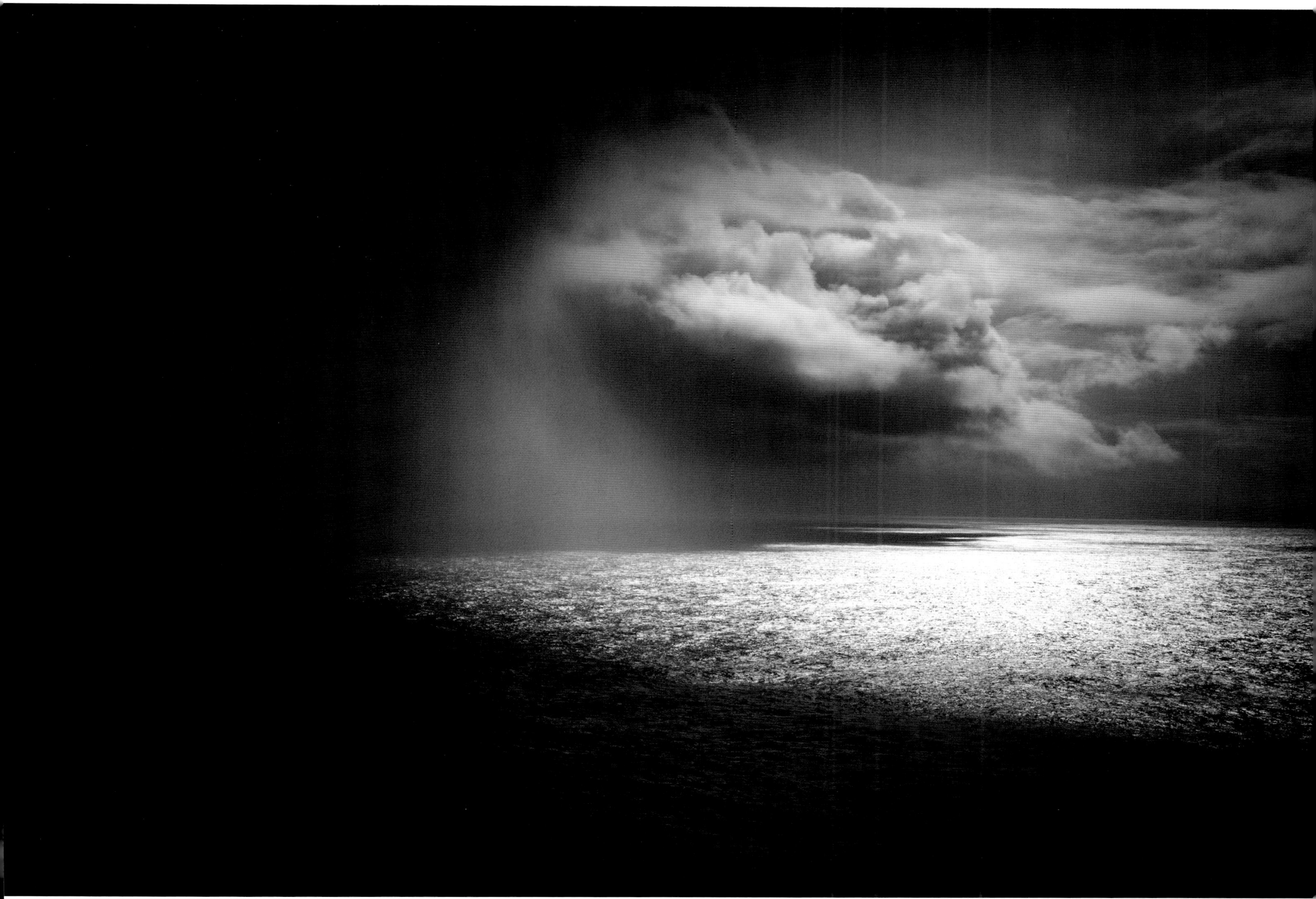

TITLE

Focus

Much of nature is messy and chaotic and overwhelming with its abundance of lines and textures and visual stimuli. One of my favourite personal challenges in these environments is to "connect the dots," so to speak, and cut through the visual chaos to find simplicity in the tangle.

Location: Banff National Park, Alberta, Canada

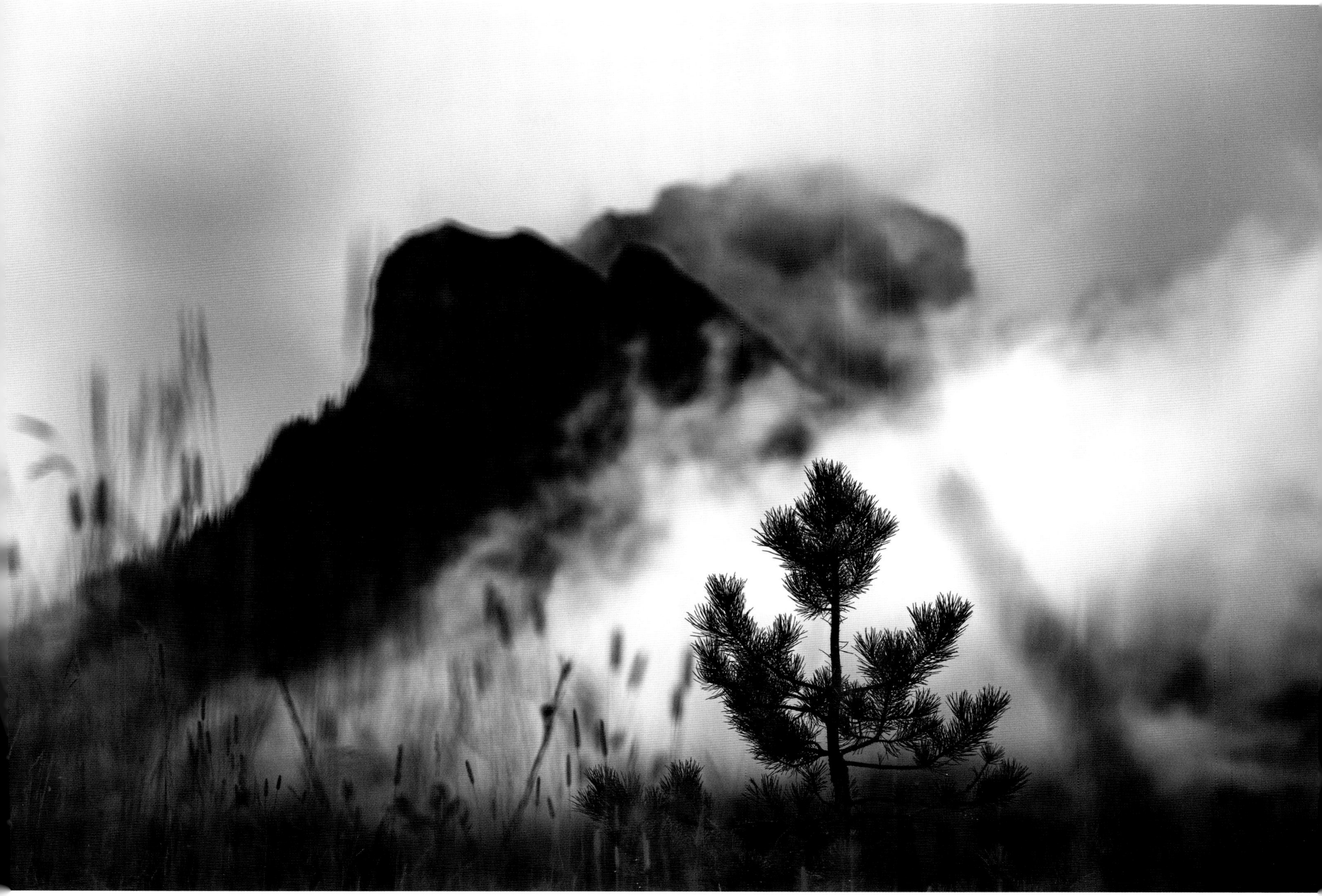

TITLE

In Frame

I once heard a photographer lecture on how he "found his composition first, and then let the story come to the composition." That lesson stuck with me, and it has changed how I photograph; I now find something visually appealing, and then "will" a subject to fall into frame – as in this simple moment in the tiny seaside village of Gjógv.

Location: Gjógv, Faroe Islands

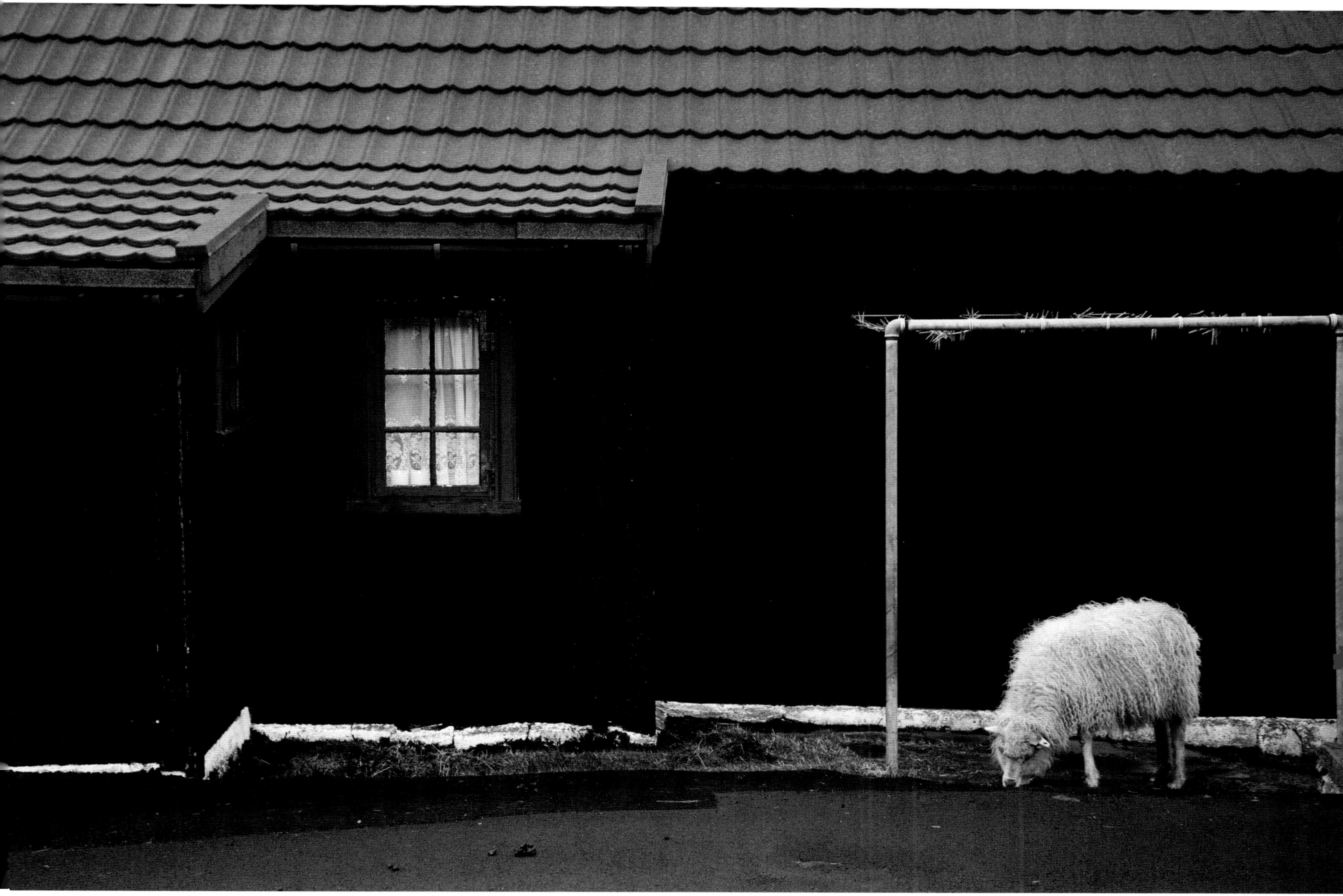

TITLE

Stand Out

There's always one in every crowd, isn't there? Whenever I photograph mass groupings of animals (penguins, oryx, zebras, bison or – in this case – Cape buffalo), I'm always on the lookout for the individual who is exhibiting a behaviour that is unique or against the grain.

Location: Okavango, Botswana

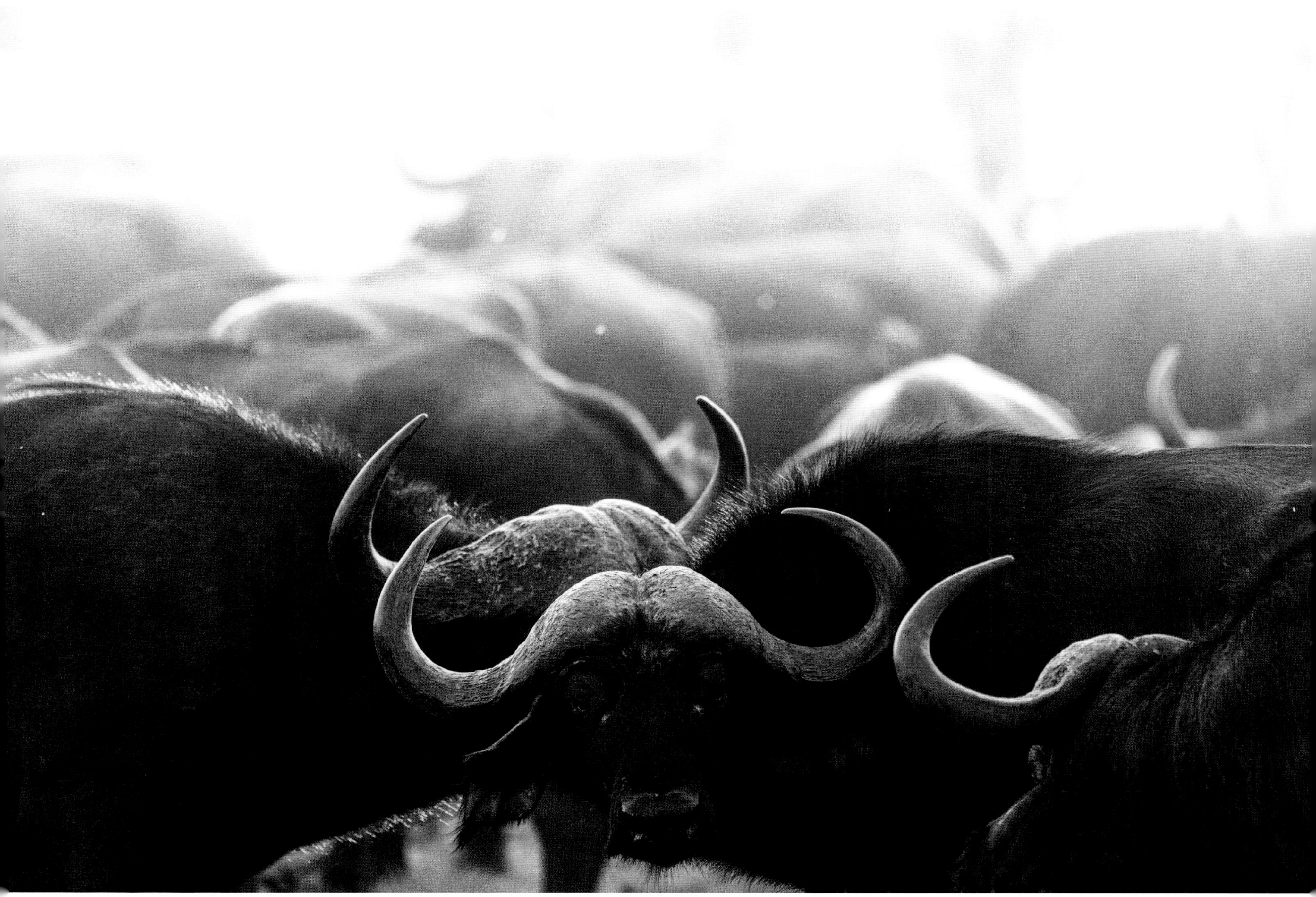

TITLE

Summer Bliss

As a photographer who has made literally millions of images over the course of his career, I can say with absolute certainty the most precious of my photographs are those of my children.

Location: Kouchibouguac National Park, New Brunswick, Canada

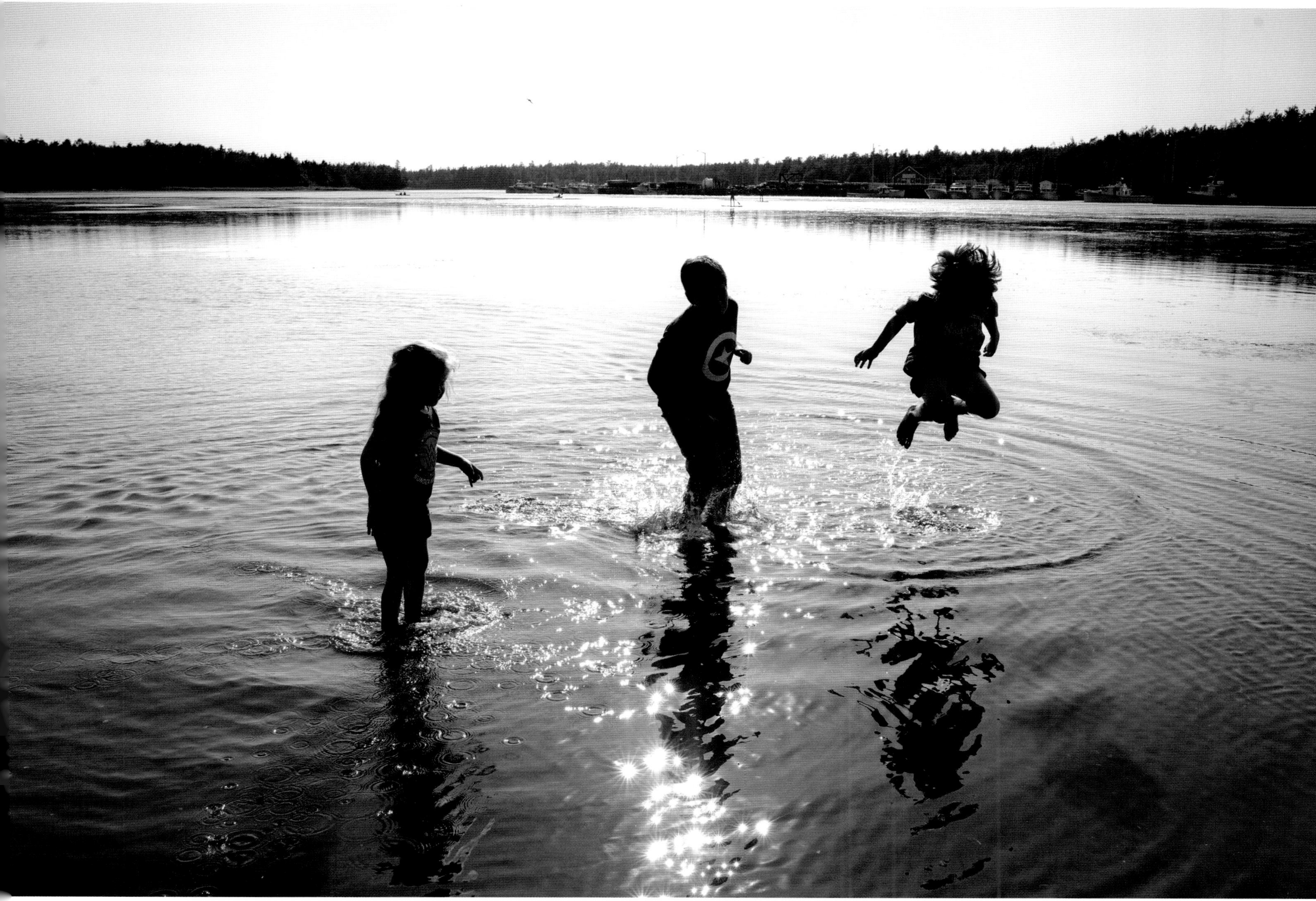

TITLE

The Boats of Ilulissat

This is a chaotic scene, looking down upon the messy network of boats in the main harbour of Ilulissat, Greenland, but one that I feel still holds a certain visual balance and symmetry.

Location: Ilulissat, Greenland

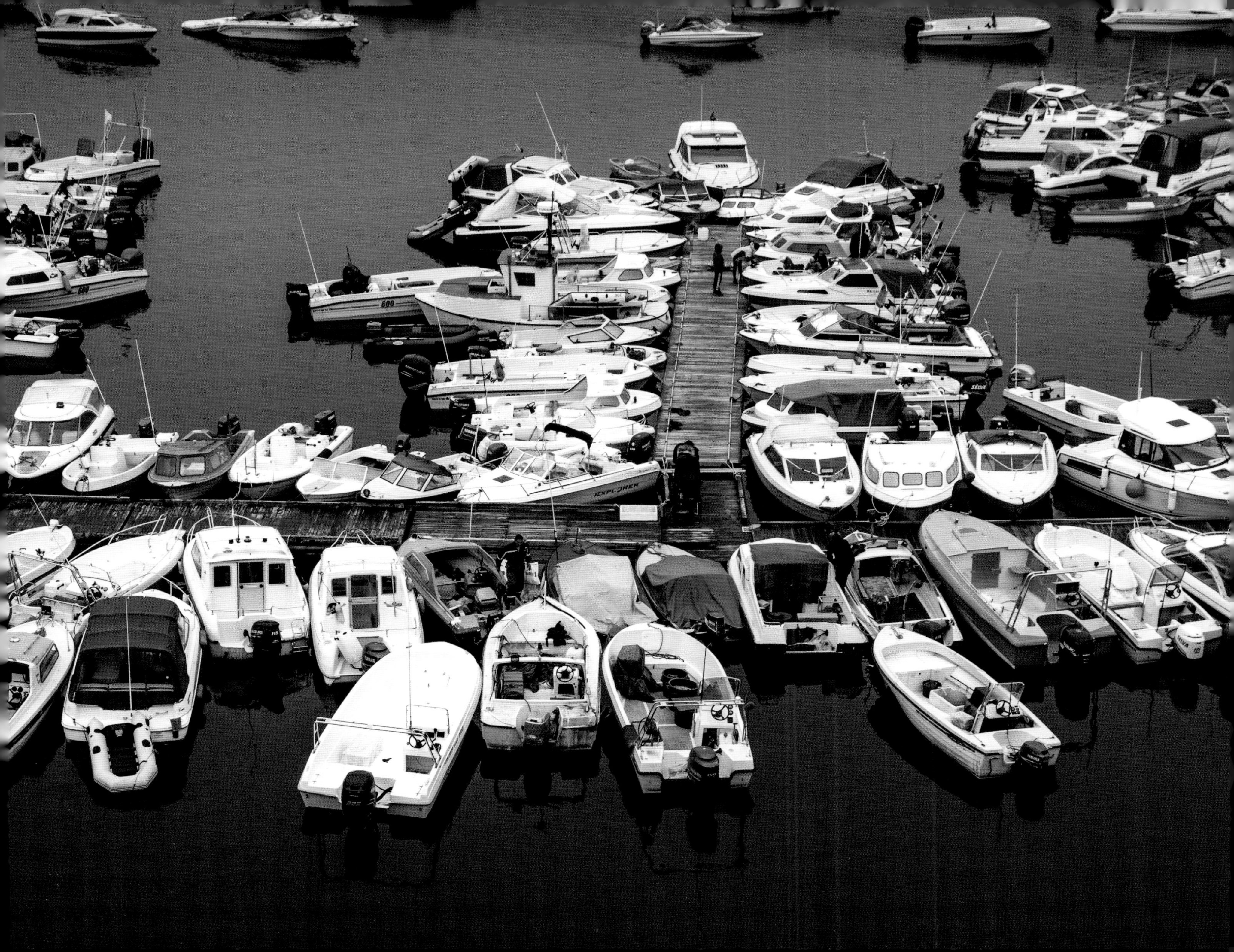
EXPLORER
600

TITLE

Beasts of Beauty

A hot, harsh day along the Chobe River provided a great contrast between the overexposed shoreline foliage and the impressive mass of these African elephants. It is not uncommon to see hundreds of these beautiful creatures at once along the river's shores.

Location: Chobe National Park, Botswana

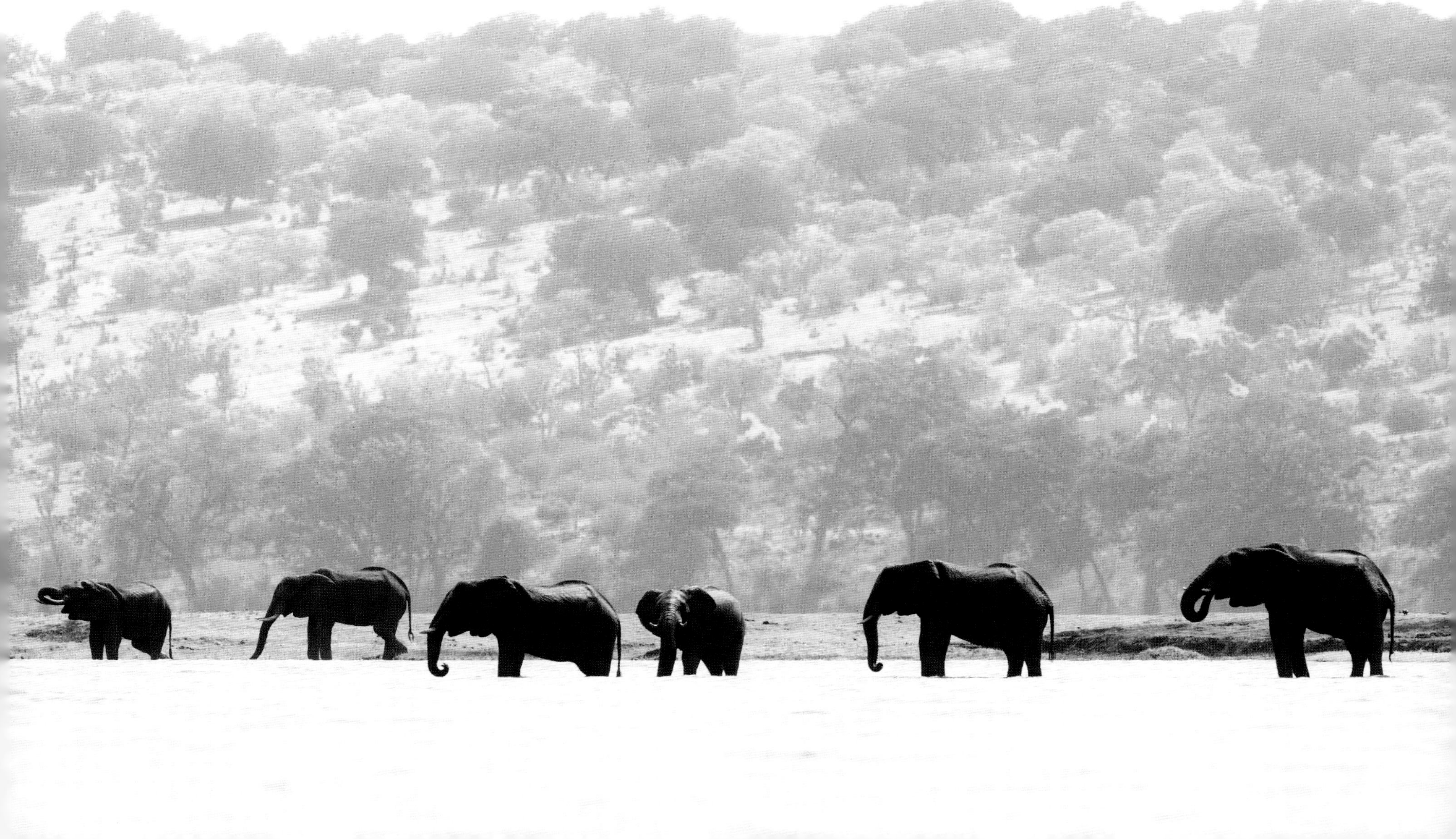

TITLE

Black Swan

More from the black sand beaches of Qeqertarsuaq, Greenland. I liked this scene because you can see the origin story of this “growler” (a small chunk of an iceberg) in the background. Icebergs come in to shore and slowly get smashed apart by weather and tidal forces, and the beaches there get littered with their beauty.

Location: Qeqertarsuaq, Greenland

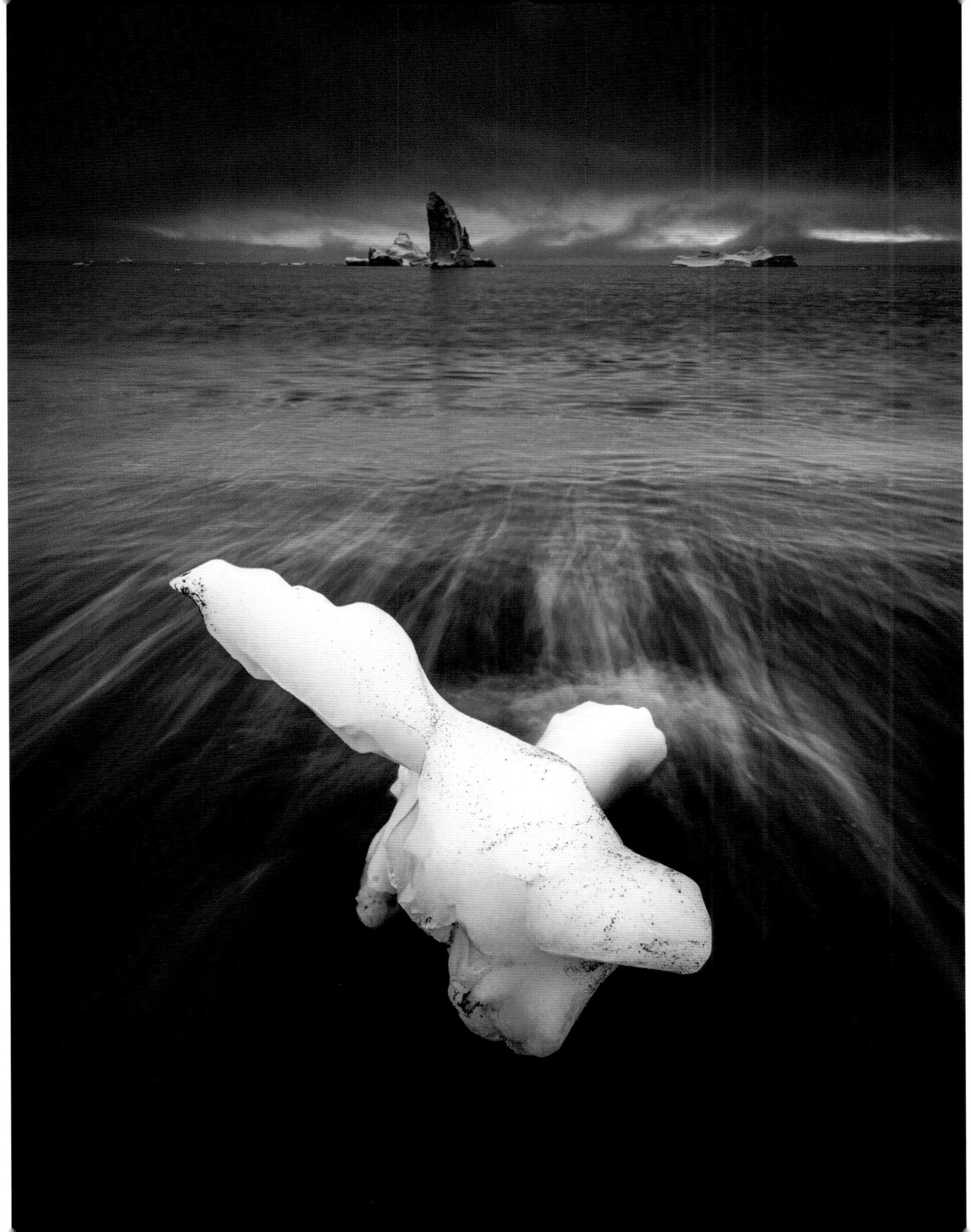

TITLE

Cut Throat

I love looking at a scene and asking myself, "How can I 'one-up' what I'm seeing?" Photography is an artistic expression, and I love – in the absence of a compelling narrative – trying to figure one out, even if it means injecting myself into the scene.

Location: Kolmanskop, Namibia

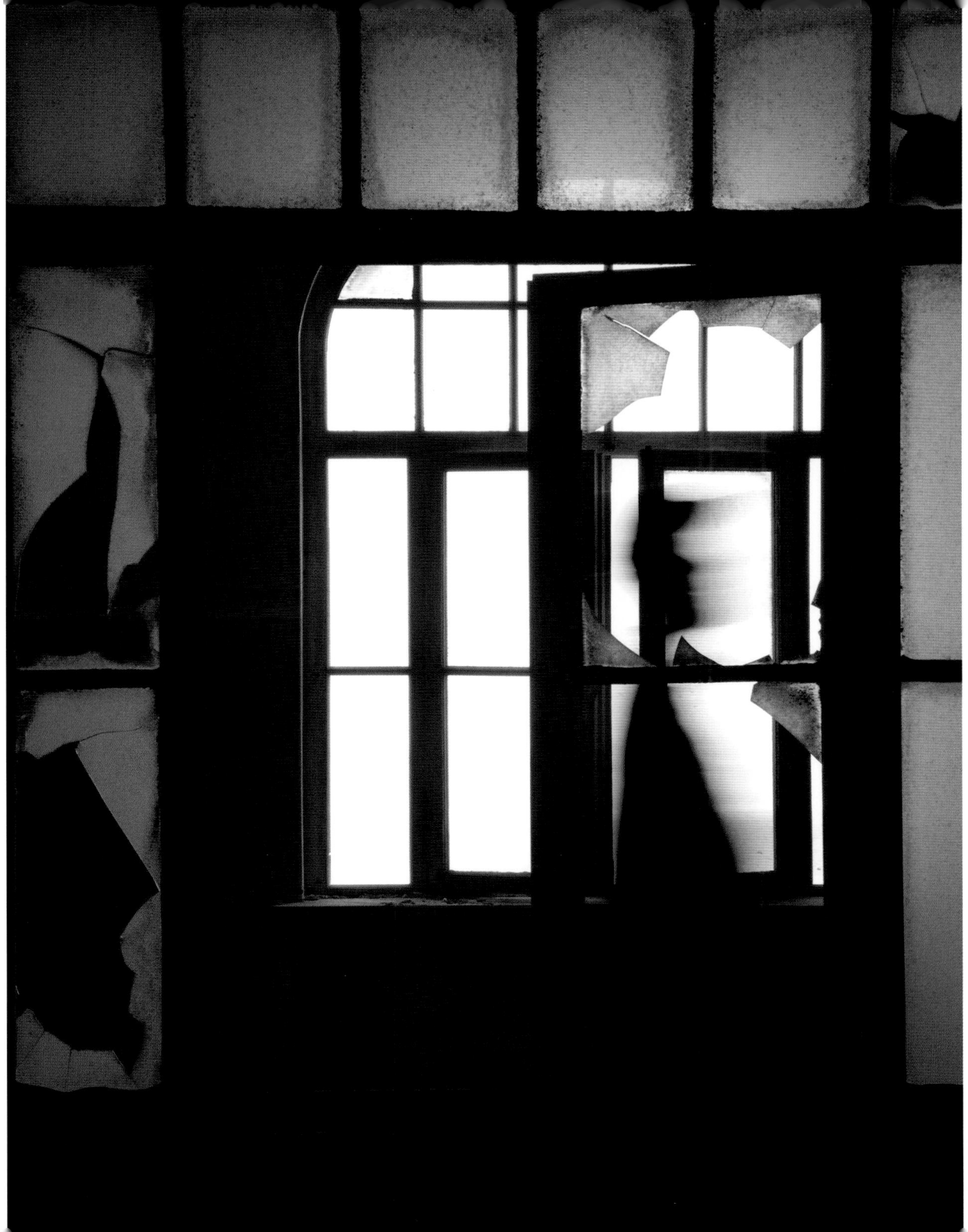

TITLE

The Shimmer

It's a bold choice as a photographer to shift into monochromatic mode when witnessing some of the most beautiful displays of colour the universe has to offer, standing under the aurora borealis, but there's a beautiful narrative in the contrasting tones they provide. Sometimes it's a story worth telling.

Location: Ilulissat, Greenland

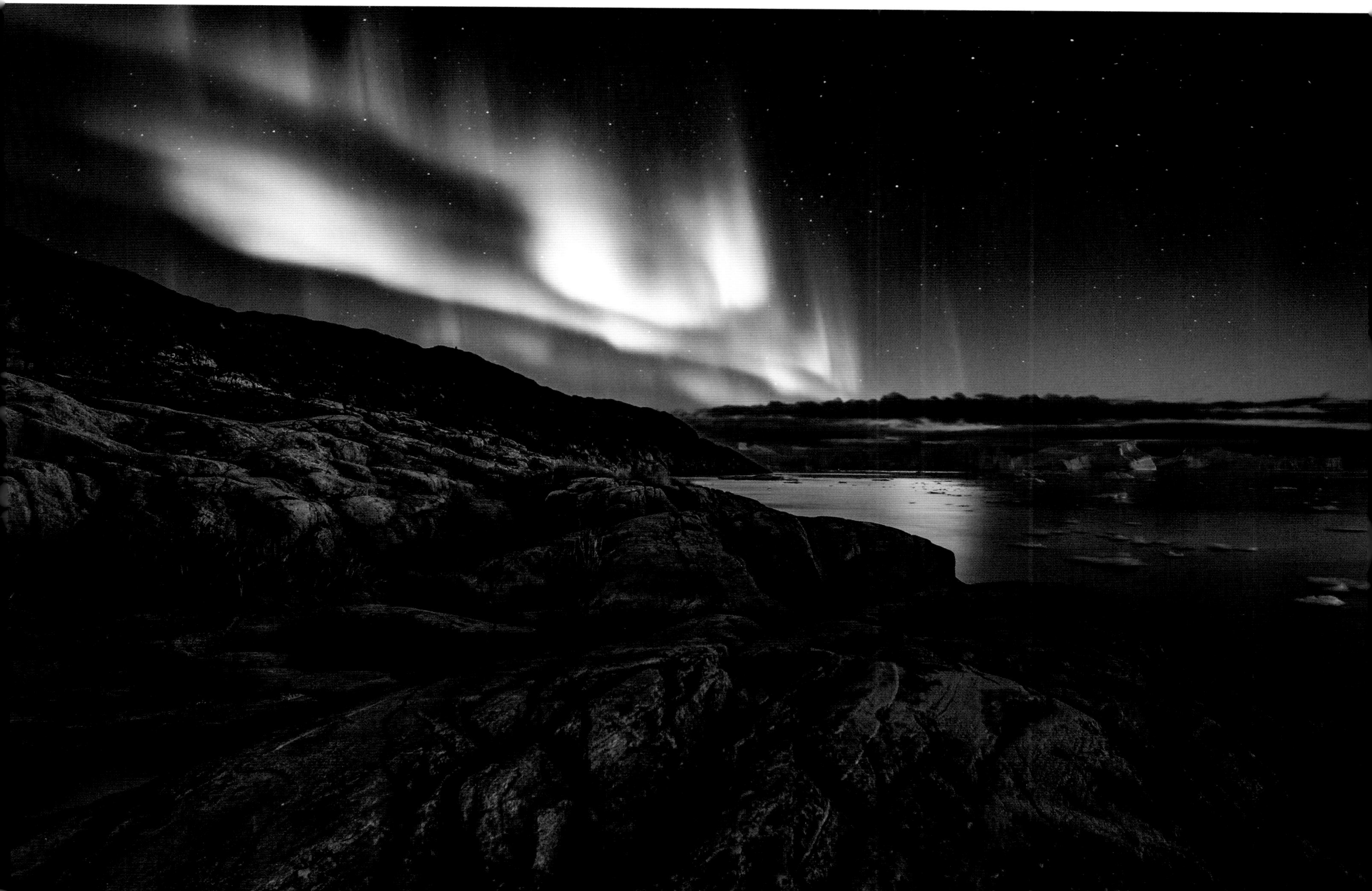

TITLE

Days Gone By

There's perhaps no subject as "built" for black and white photography as the beautiful zebra, for obvious reasons.

Location: Etosha, Namibia

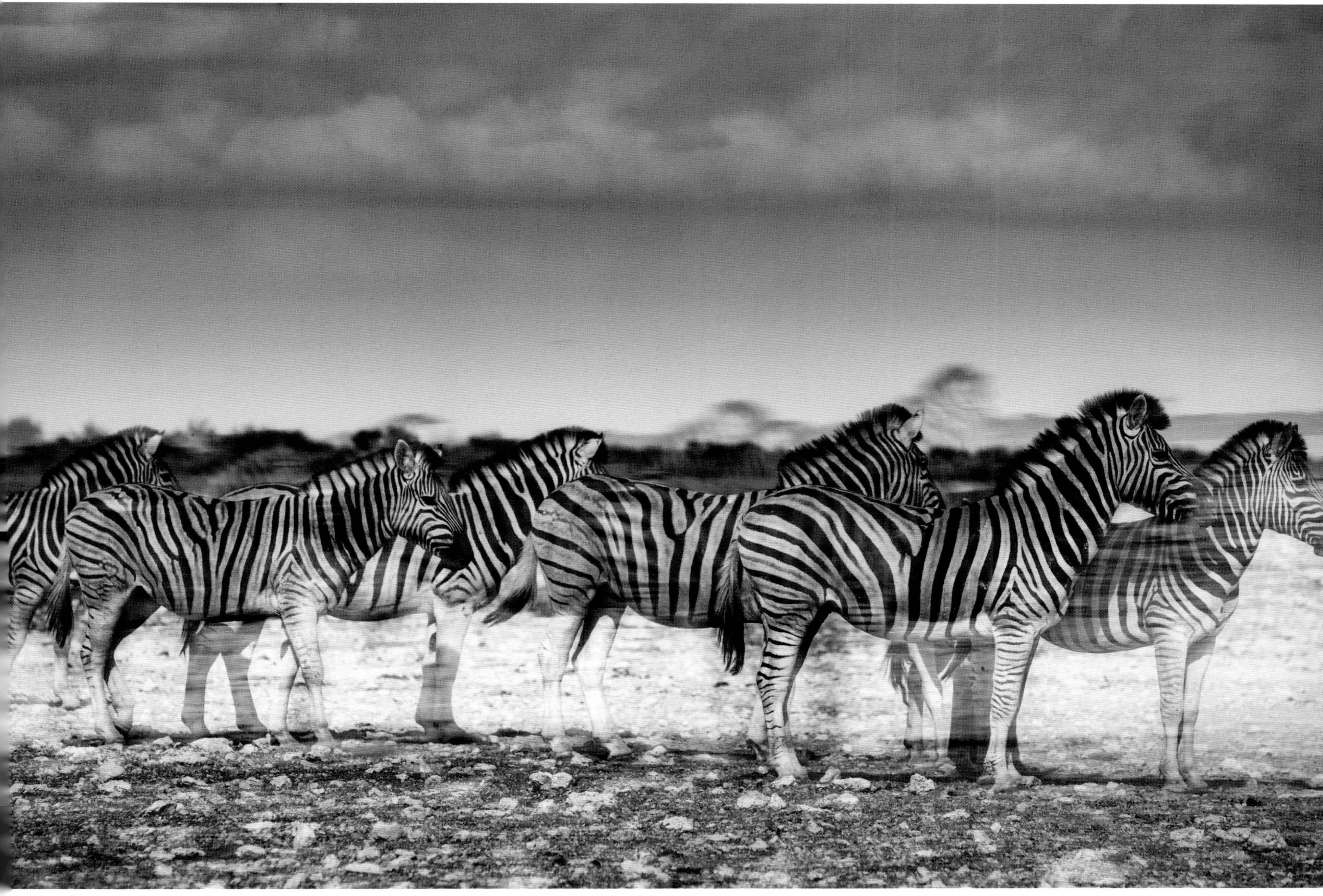

TITLE

Island Layers

Some photographers are drawn to the rich colours of morning or evening magic light, and while I certainly love "magic light," I would say I am more drawn to the mysterious beauty of fog, mist and low-hanging clouds for my own work.

Location: Vancouver Island, British Columbia, Canada

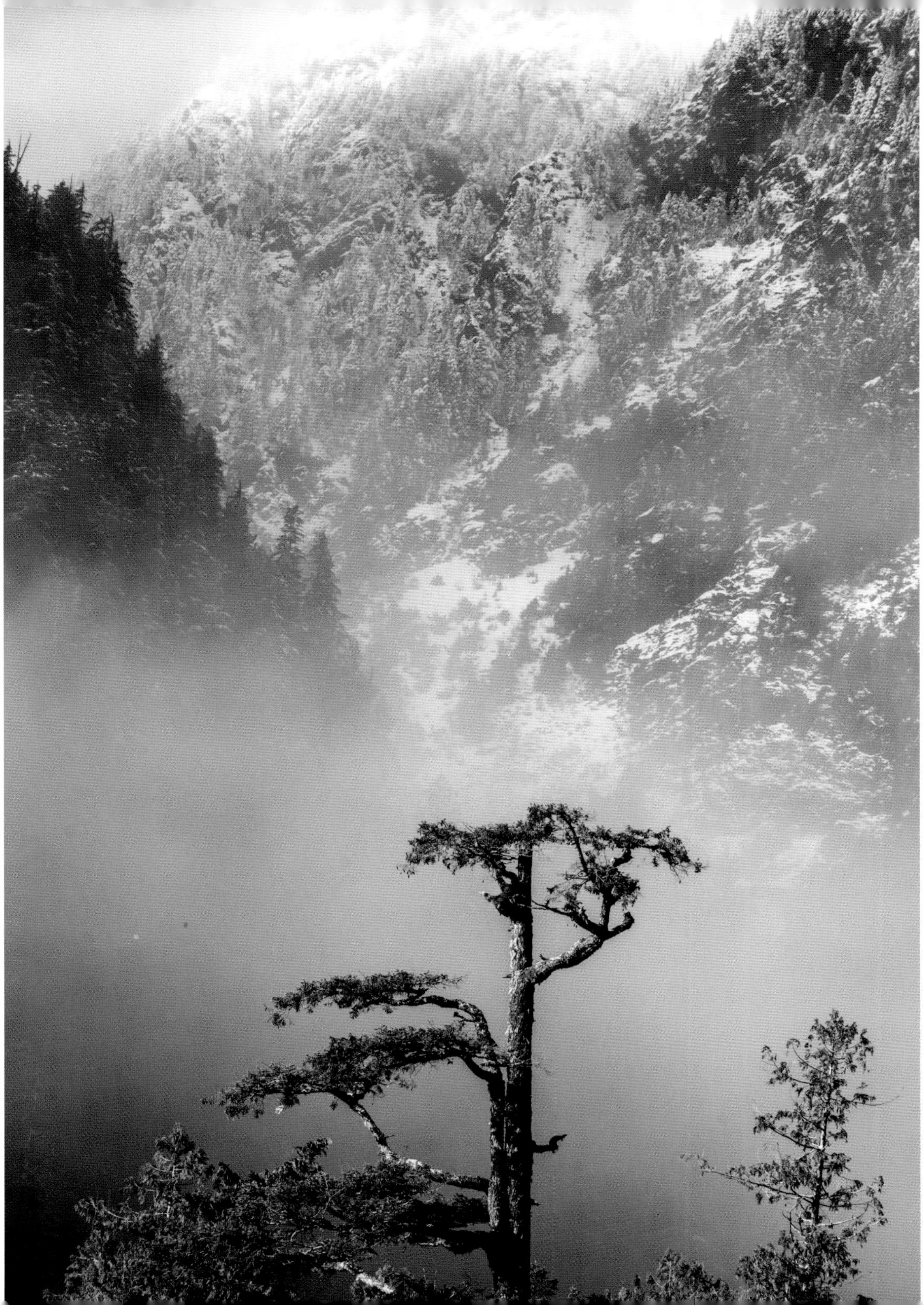

TITLE

Wild Winds

Exploring the Faroe Islands leads to the most unexpected delights – generally caused by ferocious weather, which the islands are known for. Here, incredible winds blow a waterfall often sideways; later that morning the waterfall would, at times, blow straight up.

Location: Saksun, Faroe Islands

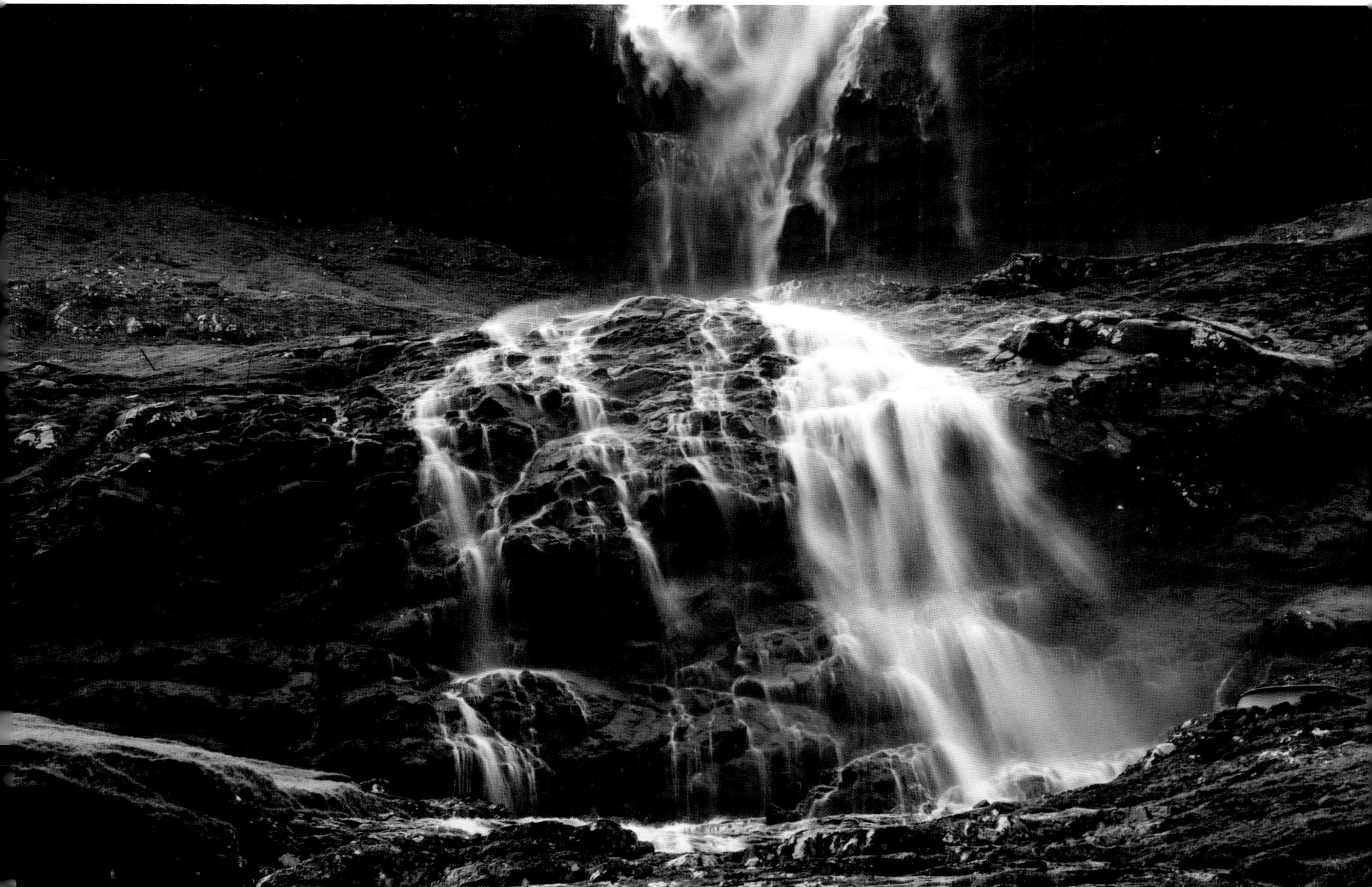

TITLE

Polar Contrast

Contrast is one of the first components of black and white photography that photographers learn and lock onto, and I'm no exception: I'm always on the lookout for clean, visually compelling scenes that showcase the relationship between light, dark and everything in between. Antarctica, with its bright glaciers and snow, often provides an incredible canvas for high-contrast images.

Location: Antarctic Peninsula, Antarctica

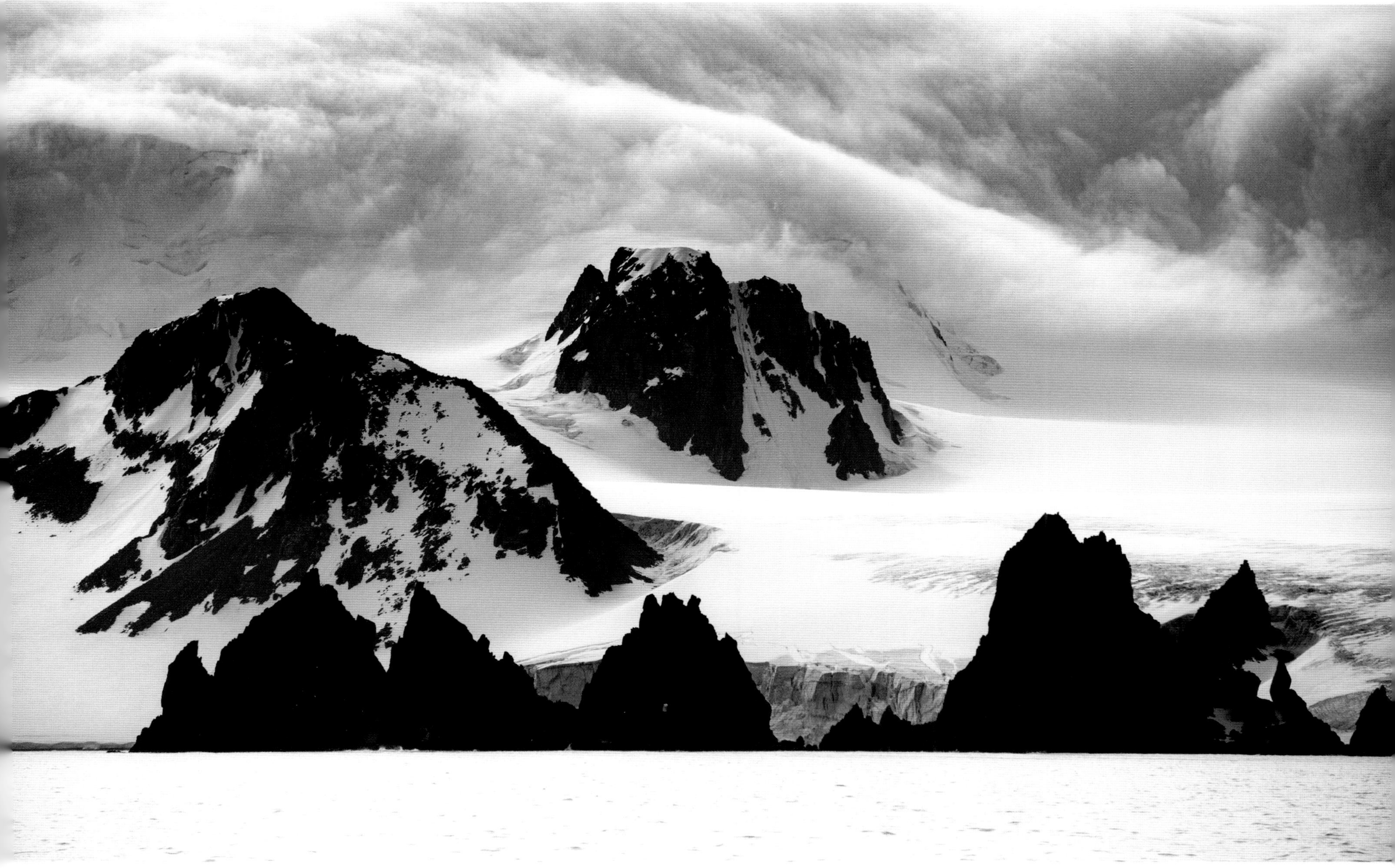

TITLE

The Highland Heart

I've photographed the grounds of the Ardvreck Castle ruins, in the Scottish Highlands, many times over the years. As with any location that you spend time getting to know, the more time you give to a place, the more it rewards you. This was the one and only time I saw a small flock of sheep grazing their way past the sixteenth-century ruins.

Location: Loch Assynt, Scotland, United Kingdom

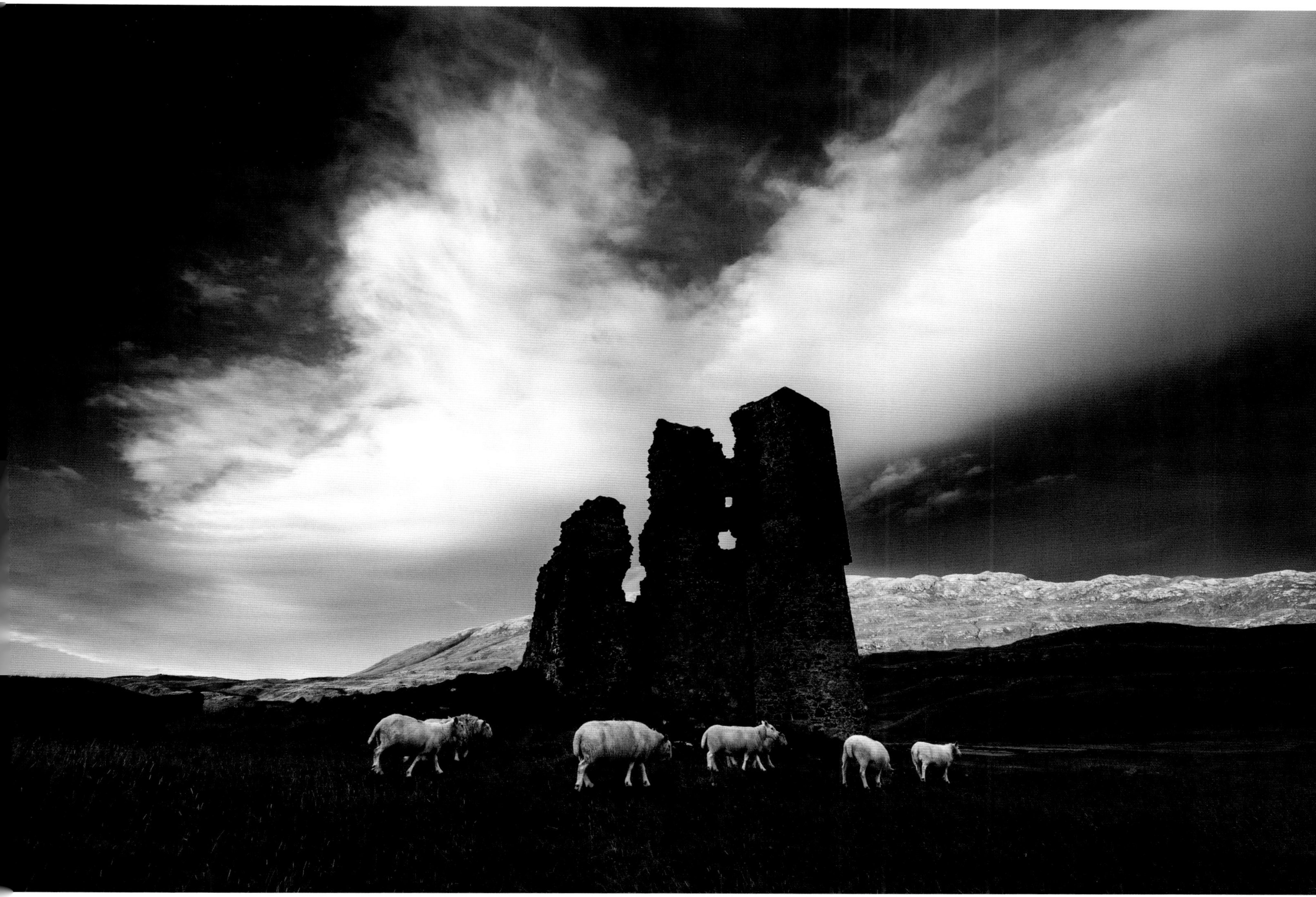

TITLE

Who Goes There?

While I would not want to be any closer to these two (hippos are amongst the most dangerous of African animals), what's not to love, photographically, about a pair of cantankerous hippopotami?

Location: Chobe National Park, Botswana

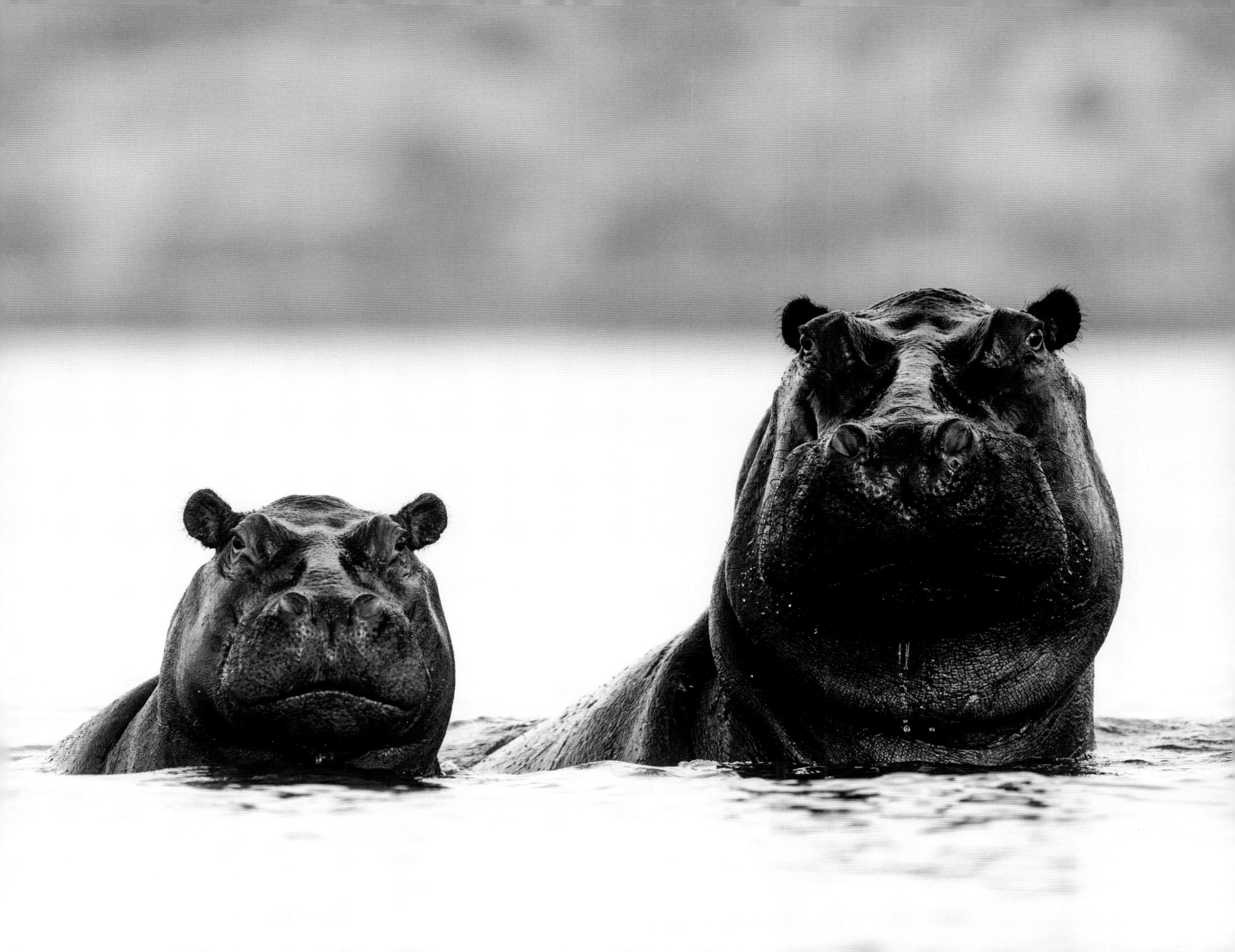

TITLE

Local Gossip

The Cliffs of Moher in Ireland are one of the most stunningly beautiful areas of the legendary country, but I struggled, photographically, to create anything "unique" that I felt hadn't been already shot. My creative solace was found in the parking lot as I walked back to my family's parked rental van, and I stumbled upon these two up on its roof.

Location: Cliffs of Moher, Ireland, United Kingdom

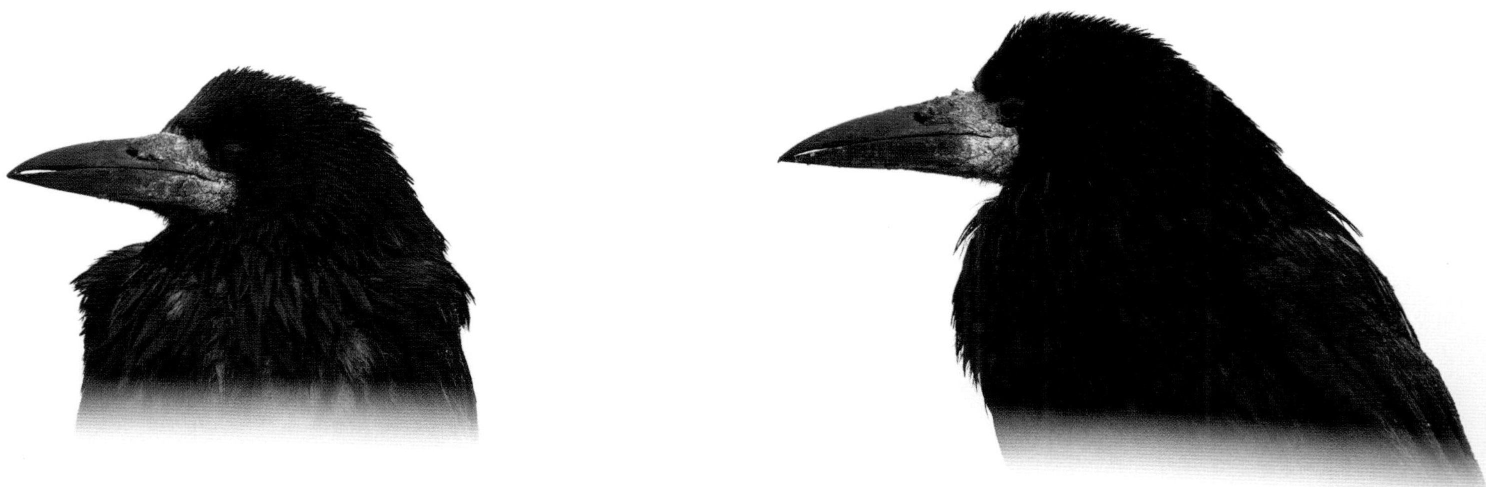

TITLE

The Stand

Do you ever want to feel like we're a lot smaller than we give ourselves credit for (and I don't mean simply in size)? Spend an hour or two observing nature. Make it part of your routine. From the tiniest birds that grace our tree branches to the largest of animals, there's beauty happening out there to witness and learn from – if only we got out of our heads more.

Location: Okavango, Botswana

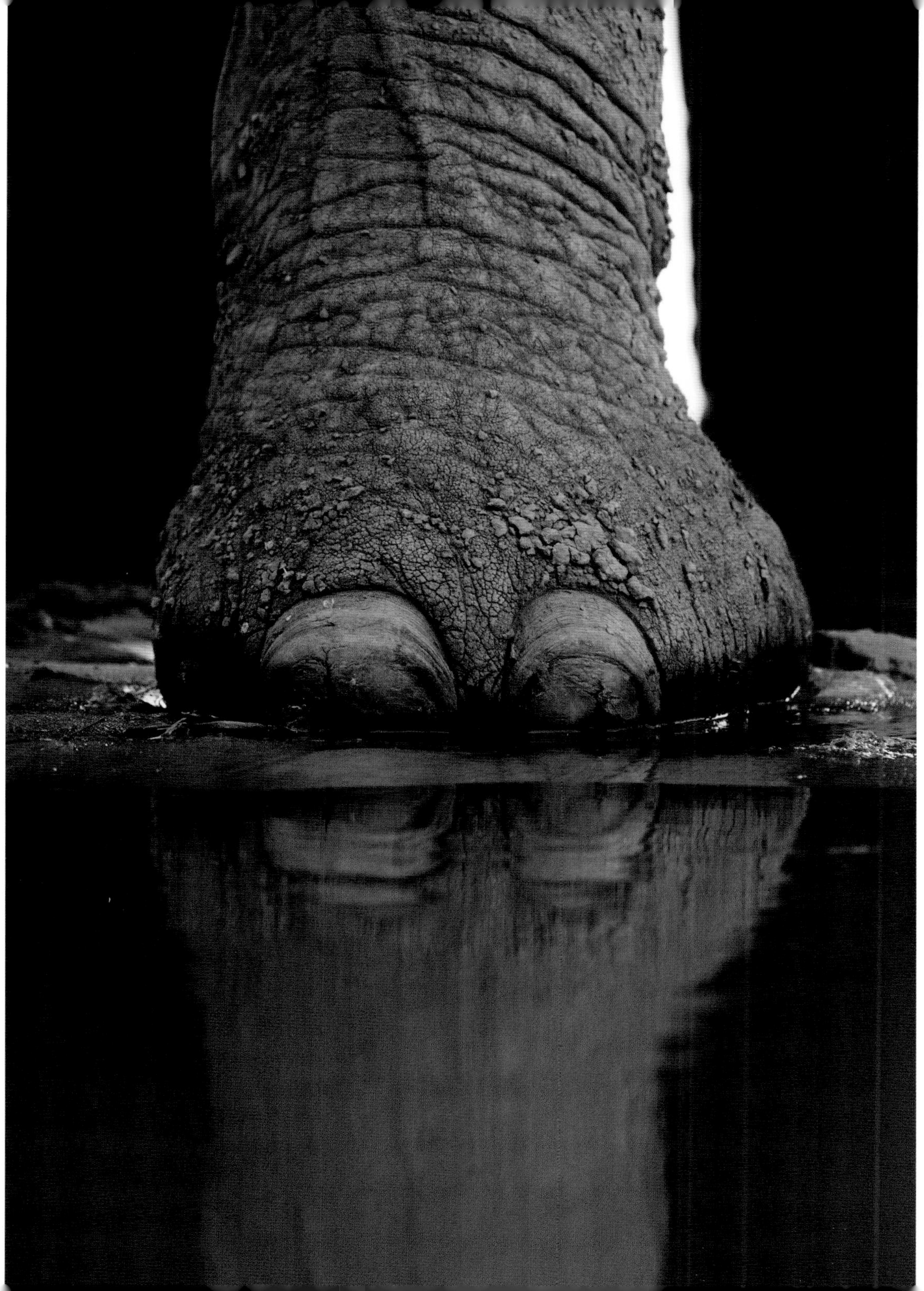

TITLE

The Other Side

A moody oceanside scene in the Azores, an autonomous region of Portugal and a stunning archipelago of dramatic beauty. A family stroll.

Location: The Azores, Portugal

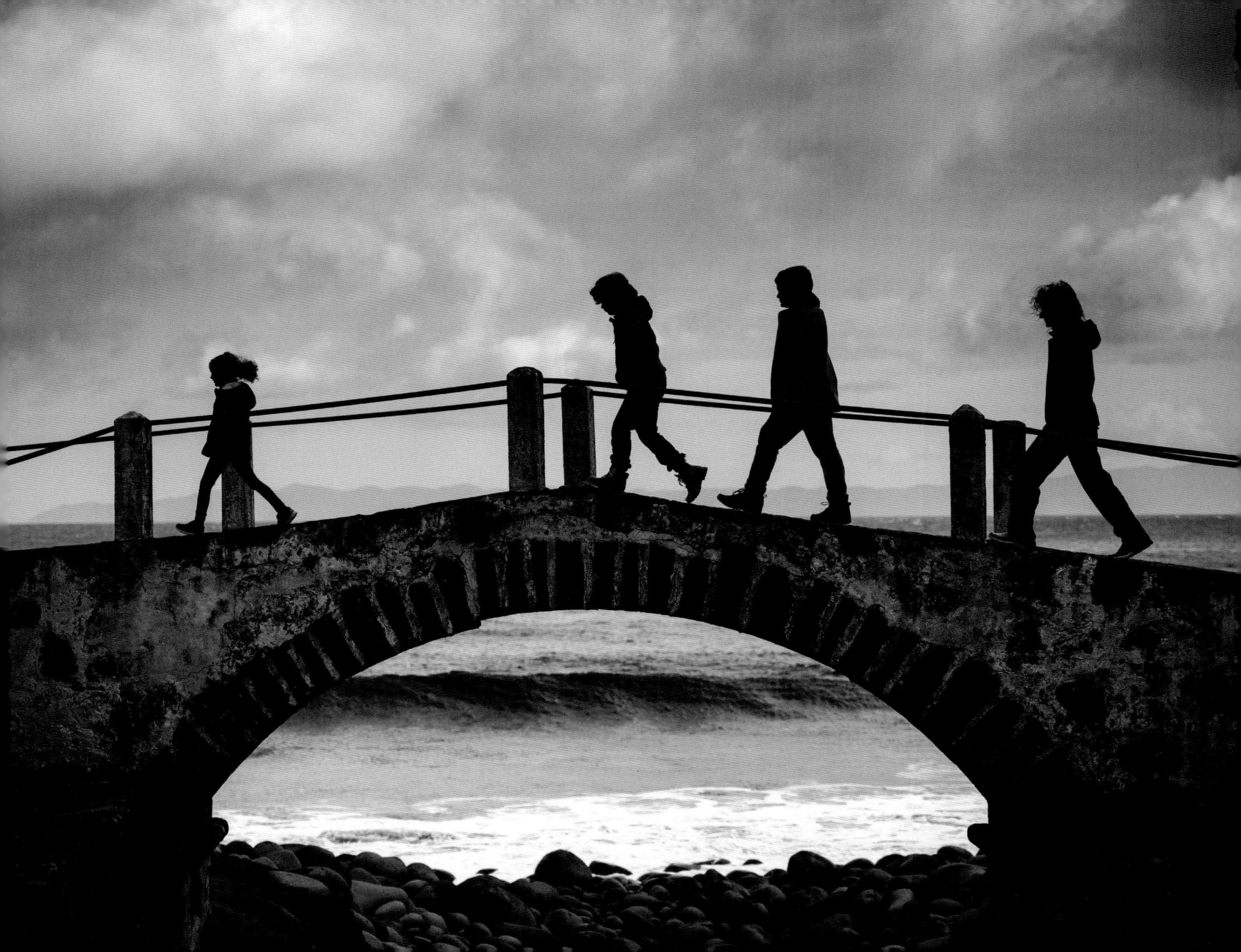

TITLE

Into the Churn

One of the things that fascinates me most in photography is how acutely in tune with "time" you become. I always thought prior to my entry into photography that a "moment is just a moment." Since picking up a camera, however, I've become aware that 1/1000 of a second has a different mood than 1/3 of second, which has a different poetry than 4 seconds. All allow light and motion to dance a slightly different dance, each with its own characteristics and beauty. Here, 2 seconds is my muse.

Location: The Azores, Portugal

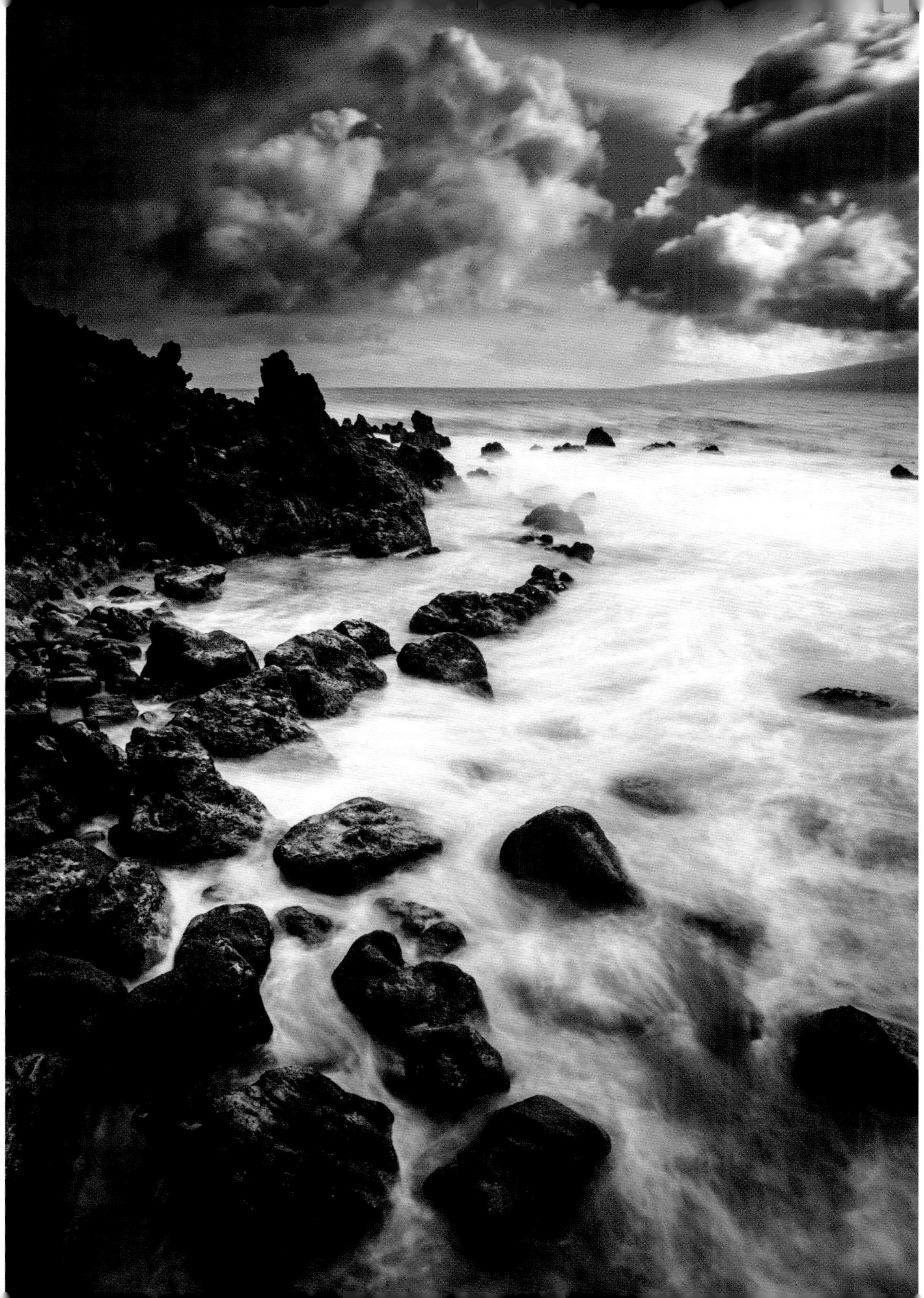

TITLE

Whale Tale

Observing the observers. A small team heads out in a Zodiac on the brisk waters of the Antarctic Peninsula, on the "hunt" for minke whales as part of a scientific research program.

Location: Antarctic Peninsula, Antarctica

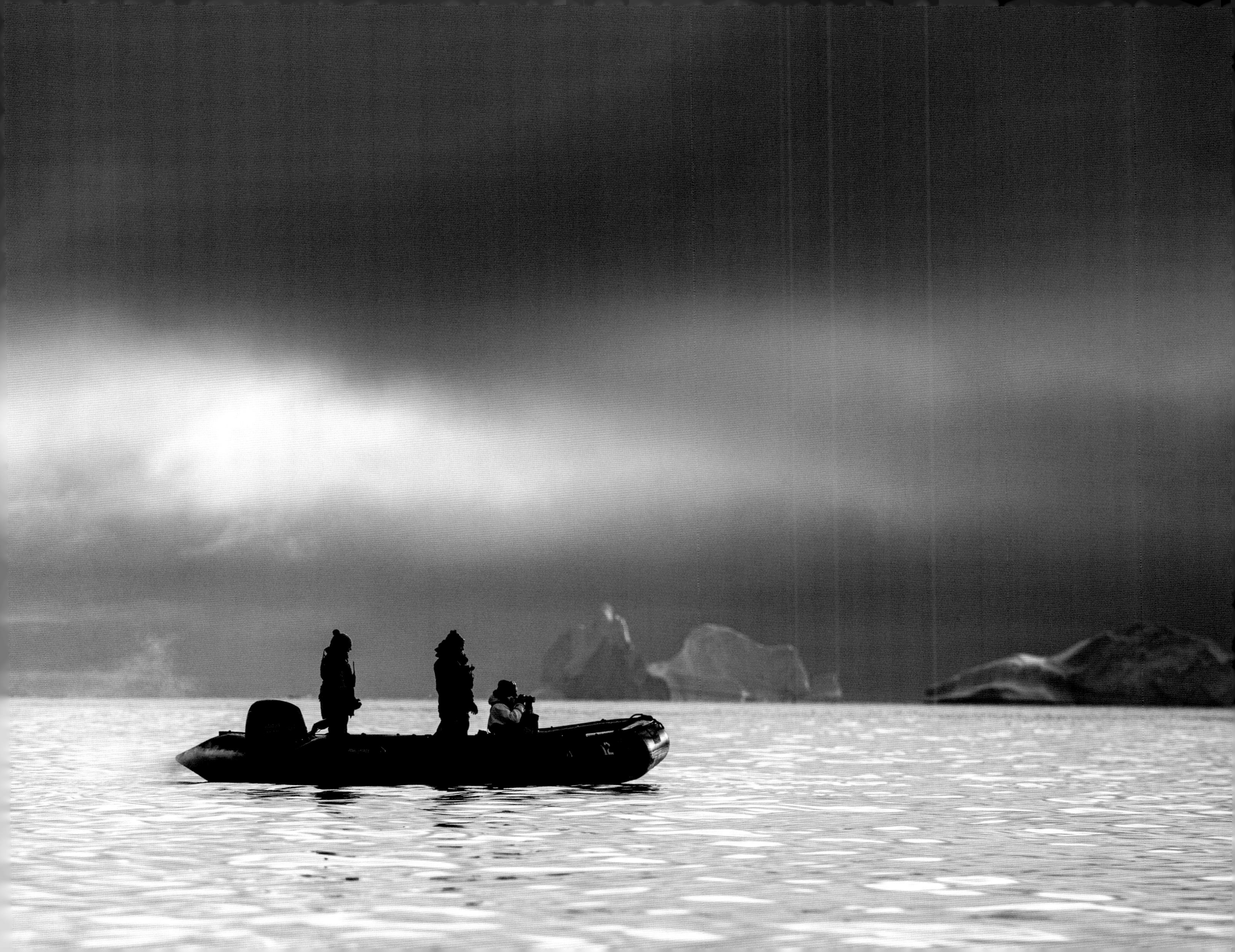

TITLE

Pretty Places

A rare sunny day in the Gjógv valley on the Faroese island of Eysturoy, an idyllic place dotted by small houses and sheep farms.

Location: Gjógv Valley, Faroe Islands

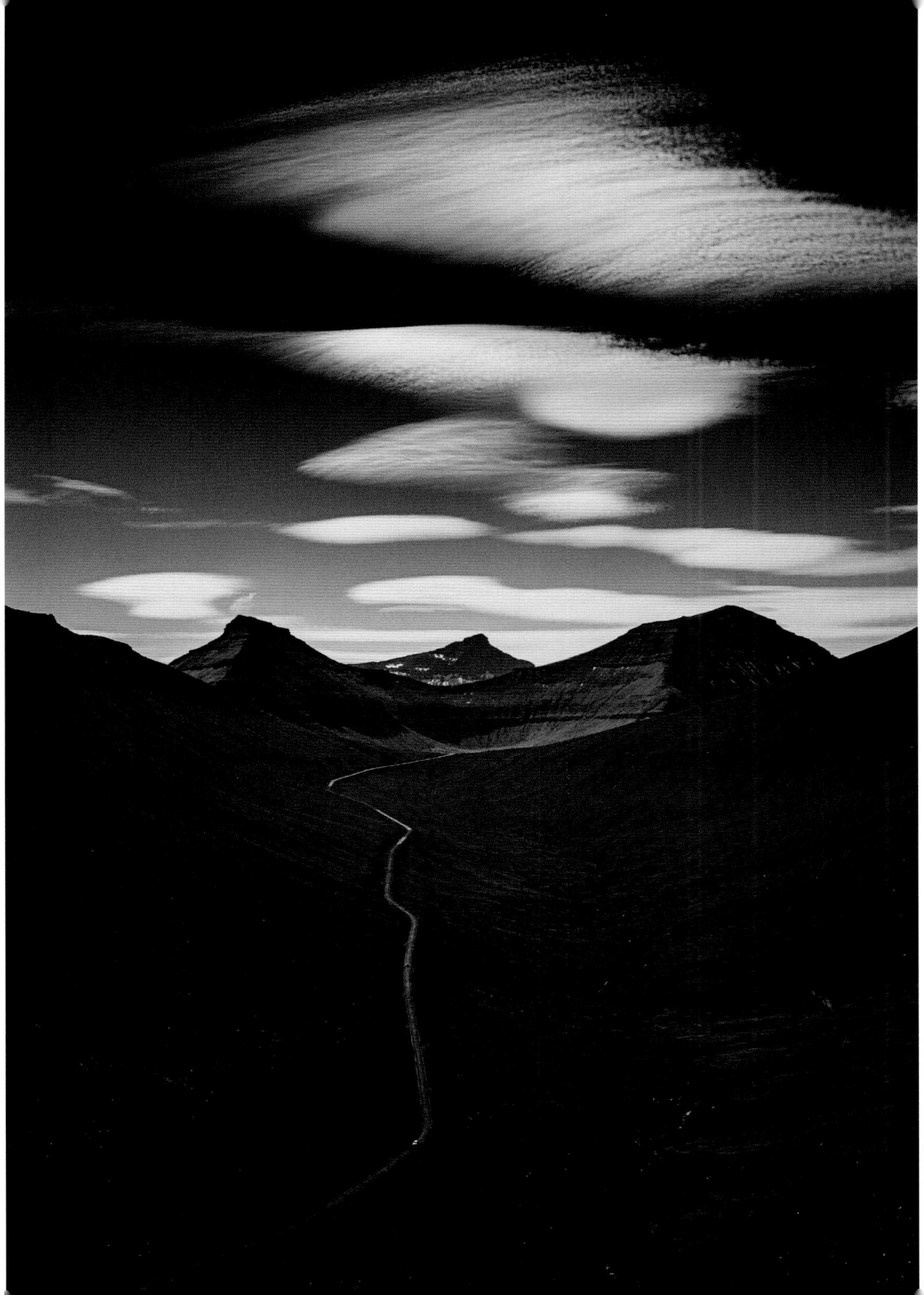

TITLE

Wild Horses Couldn't Drag Me Away

I was pleased with this image, I'm not going to lie...because this image was born out of anticipation and patience. I had seen these horses deeper within another sand dune near sunset but saw that this "valley" still had a small sliver of light. I guessed their trajectory and positioned myself just in time to be at the right angle and vantage point to capture some beautiful backlight on the small herd. They posed for only a few seconds before wandering out of the light and into the dusk.

Location: Khongoryn Els, Mongolia

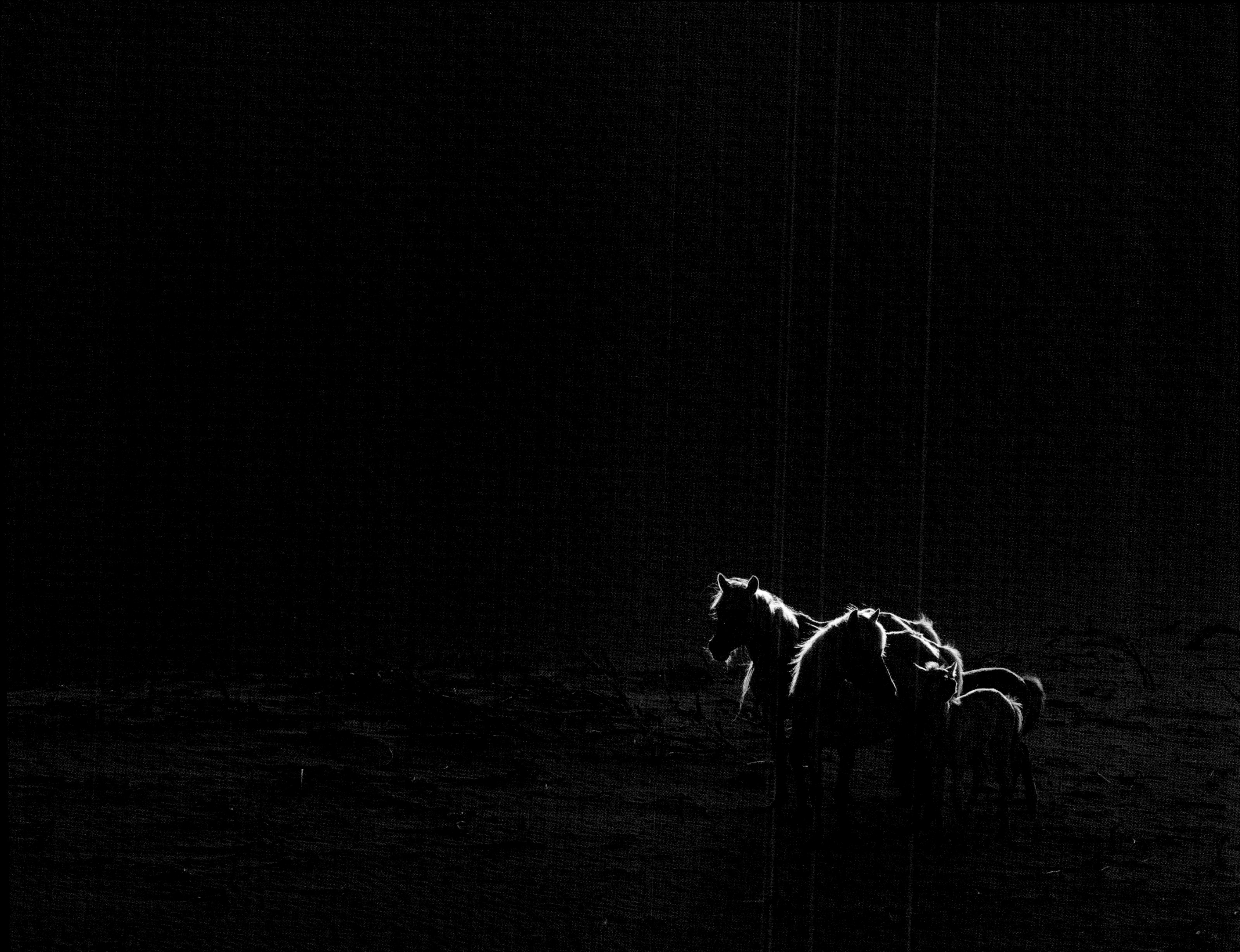

TITLE

The Ice Trail

Kluane National Park is one of those places I go to in my dreams. It's one of the national parks I've spent the most time in during my career, and when I need to relax or meditate, I often find myself soaring above its dramatic peaks or imagining myself breathing in its incredibly fresh air.

Location: Kaskawulsh Glacier, Yukon, Canada

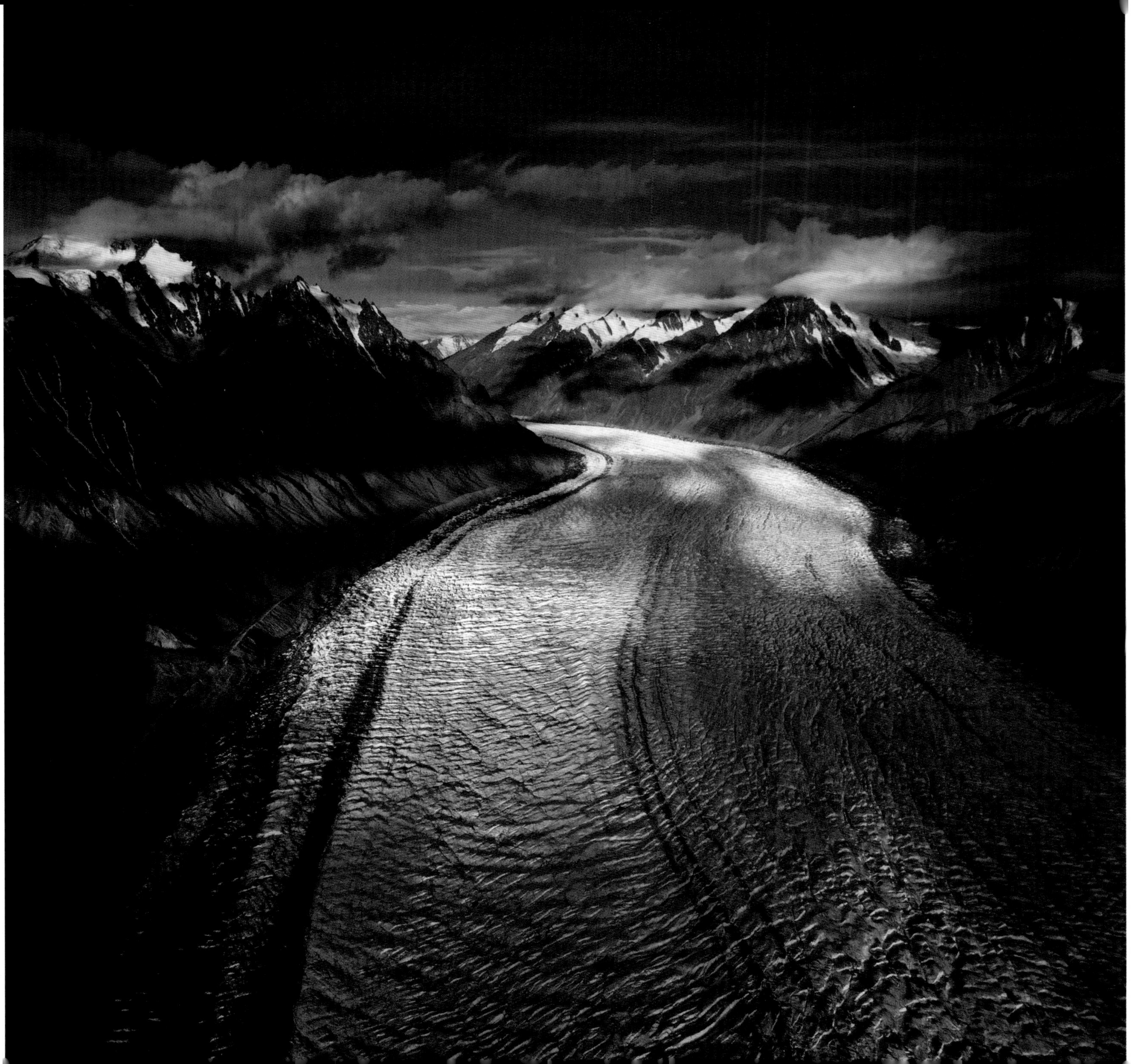

TITLE

Force of Nature

As formidable as Cape buffalo are, they can still find themselves victims to other predators, like the Nile crocodile, which are numerous in the Chobe River. Cape buffalo pick their routes across water crossings carefully, stick together, and swim at remarkable speeds to minimize their risk during these crossings.

Location: Chobe National Park, Botswana

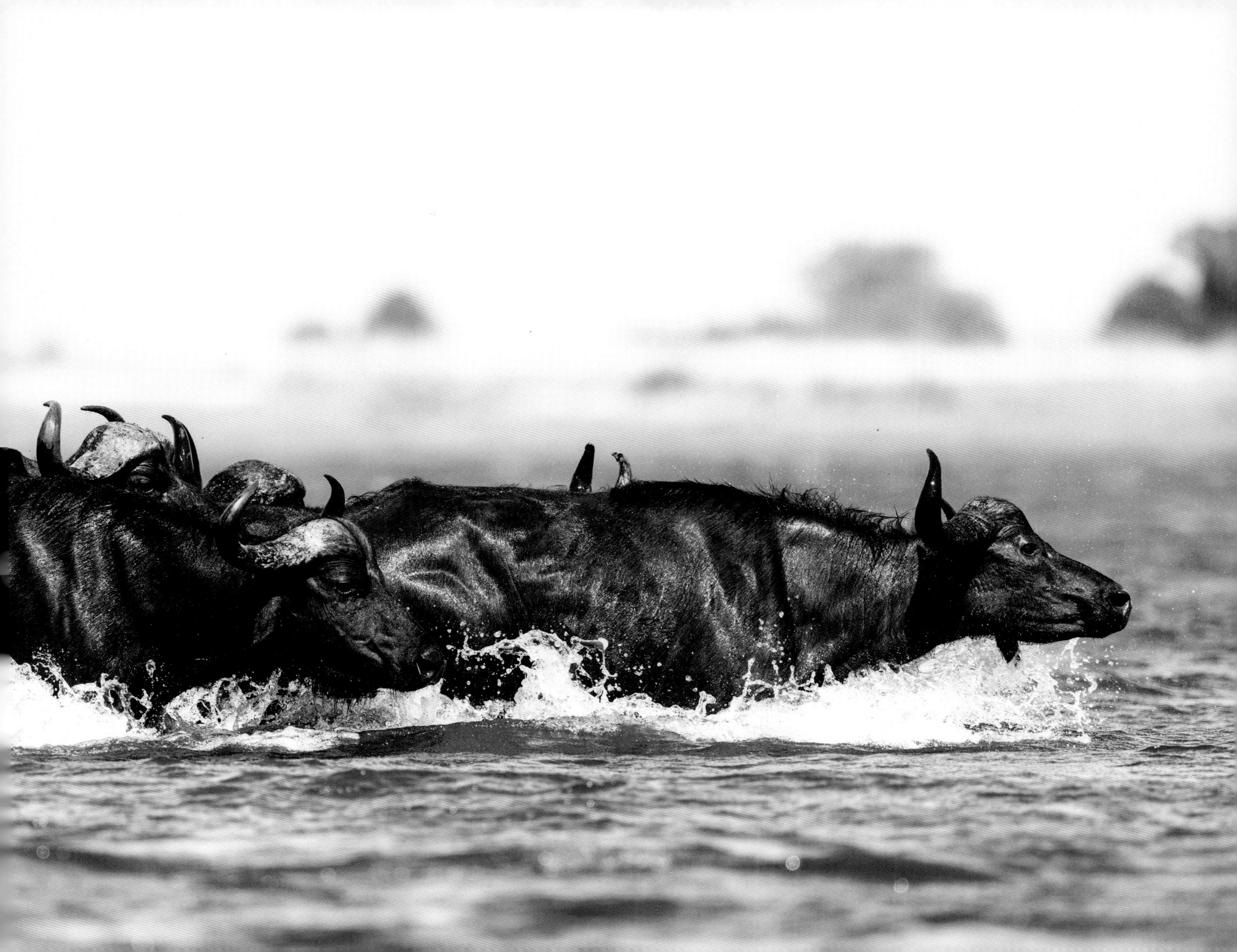

TITLE

Vágar

The Faroe Islands have the highest sea cliffs in Europe, and some of the highest in the world. To walk along their edges is an exercise in deep breathing and shaky legs, no matter how seasoned you are to heights. Here, in the Lake Sørvágsvatn area of the island of Vágar, are some of the most impressive (or terrifying, depending on your point of view).

Location: Sørvágsvatn, Faroe Islands

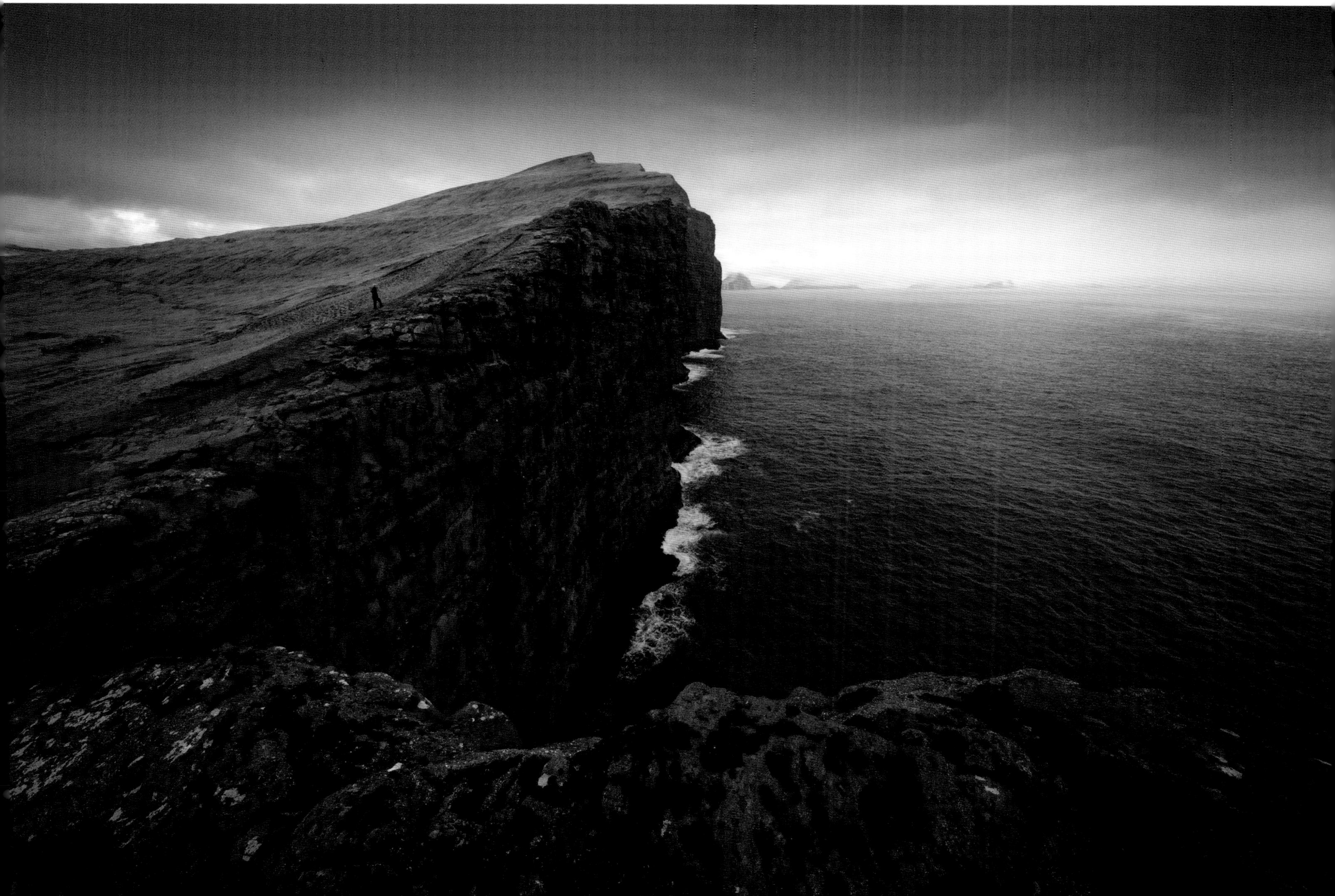

TITLE

To Be Seen

There's nothing quite like seeing your first elephant in the wild, where elephants are meant to be. All wildlife gets my respect, of course, but there's something about peering into the eyes of such an intelligent creature that stirs something in your soul; how anyone could hurt these majestic creatures is beyond my comprehension.

Location: Chobe National Park, Botswana

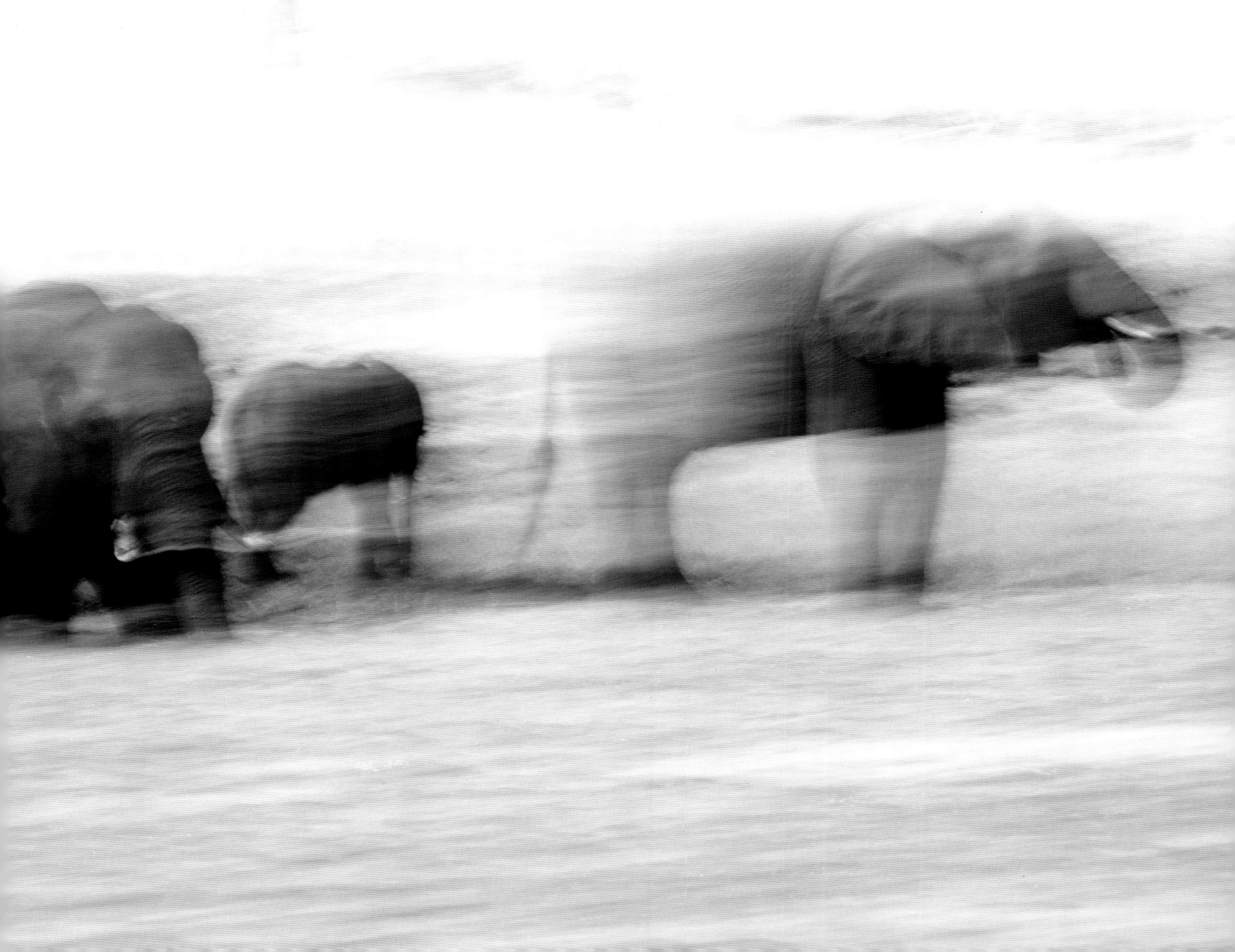

TITLE

Let Sleeping Dogs Lie

If you ever had the opportunity to go to Bhutan, you know it has one of the highest dogs-to-people ratios in the world; whether you're in the cities or the countryside (or even high in the mountains!) you're bound to come across dogs. Loud by night (historic protectionism), and often lazy by day, they're a huge part of the Bhutanese experience.

Location: Paro, Bhutan

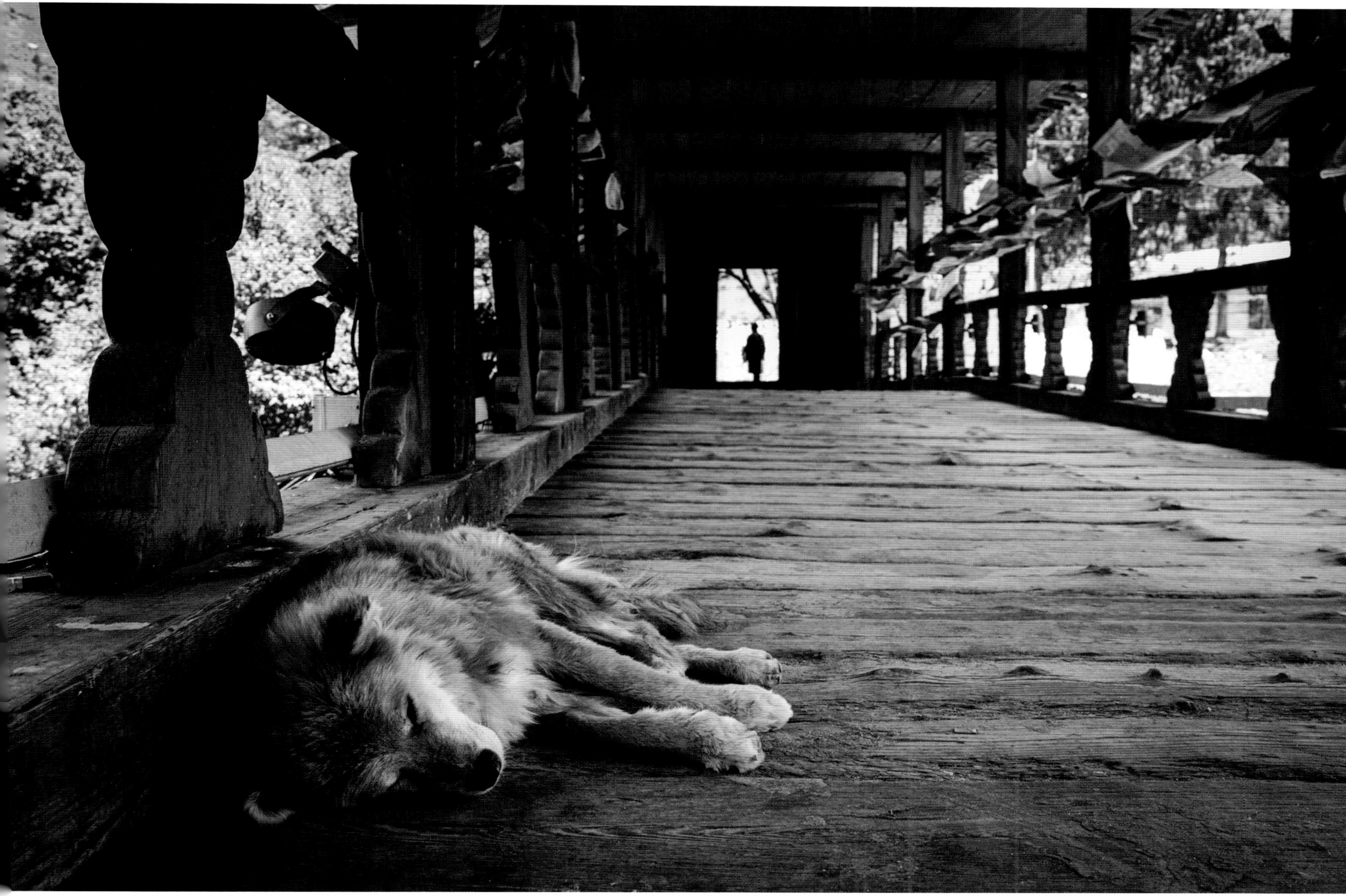

TITLE

Nature's Gaze

While I most often love photographing wildlife from an environmental perspective – meaning an animal simply living or interacting with its natural environment – I have a growing series of "portraits" of the wildlife I encounter, and try to put to use my years of experience photographing portraits of people to try to represent another side to the creatures of the wild.

Location: Brackley, Prince Edward Island, Canada

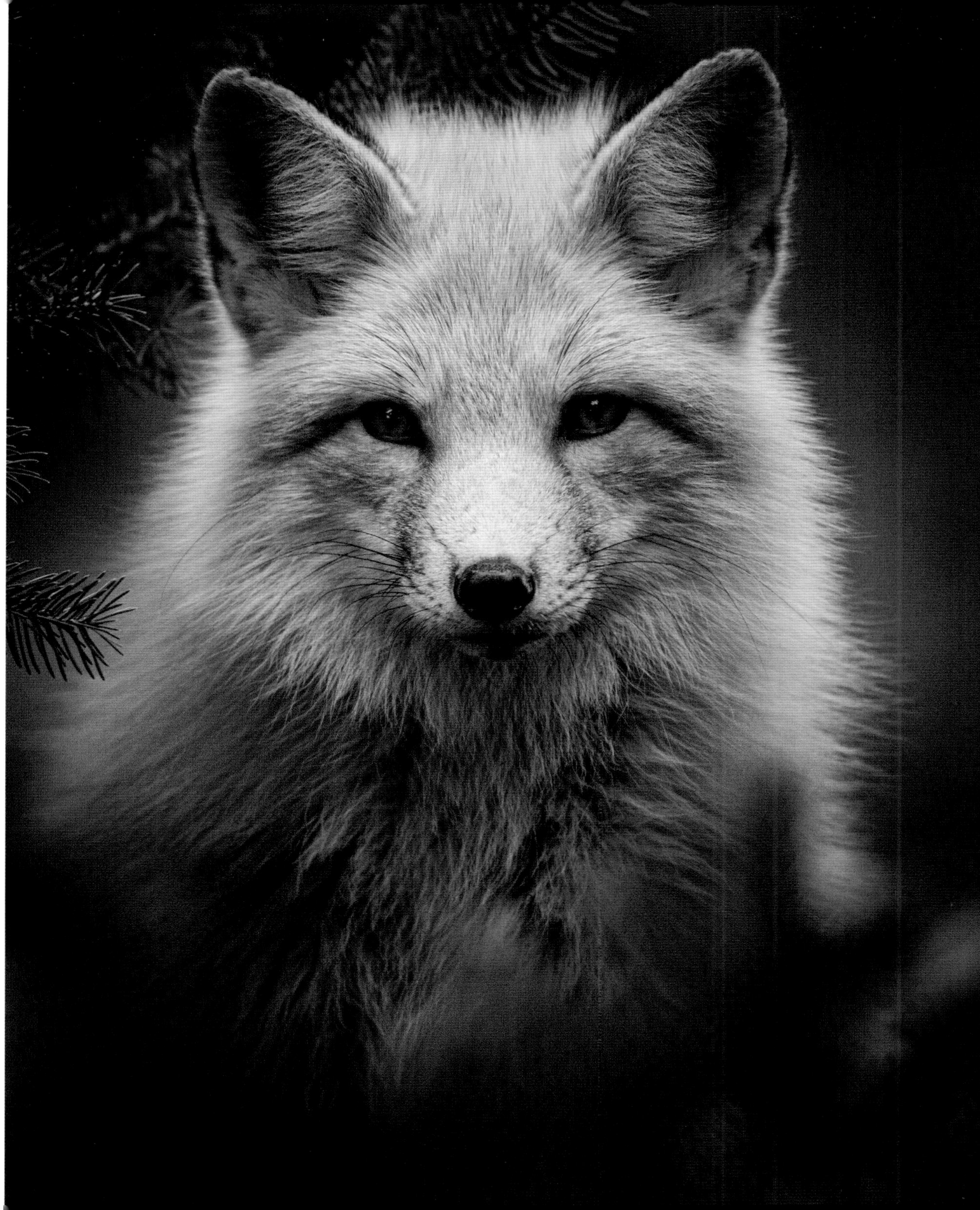

TITLE

An Autumn Day

No deep meanings here – just a depiction of a glorious autumn day in the Faroese countryside. Light, life and beautiful tones.

Location: Sandavágur, Faroe Islands

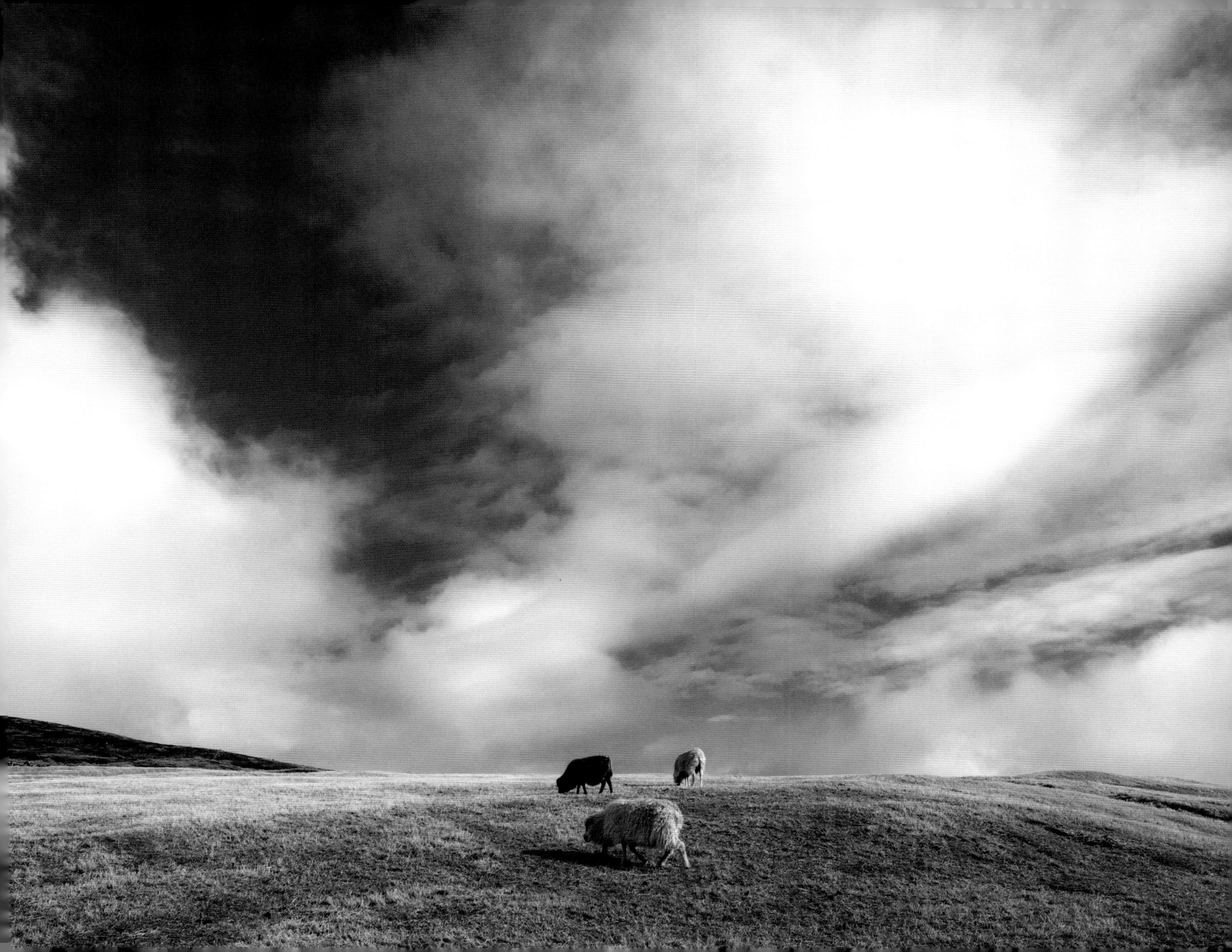

TITLE

Explore

This scene, witnessed one day while out on a hike somewhere along the Antarctic Peninsula, is indicative of the type of "cleanliness" of composition that I'm always on the lookout for: clean, with a sense of not only symmetry but story as well.

Location: Antarctic Peninsula, Antarctica

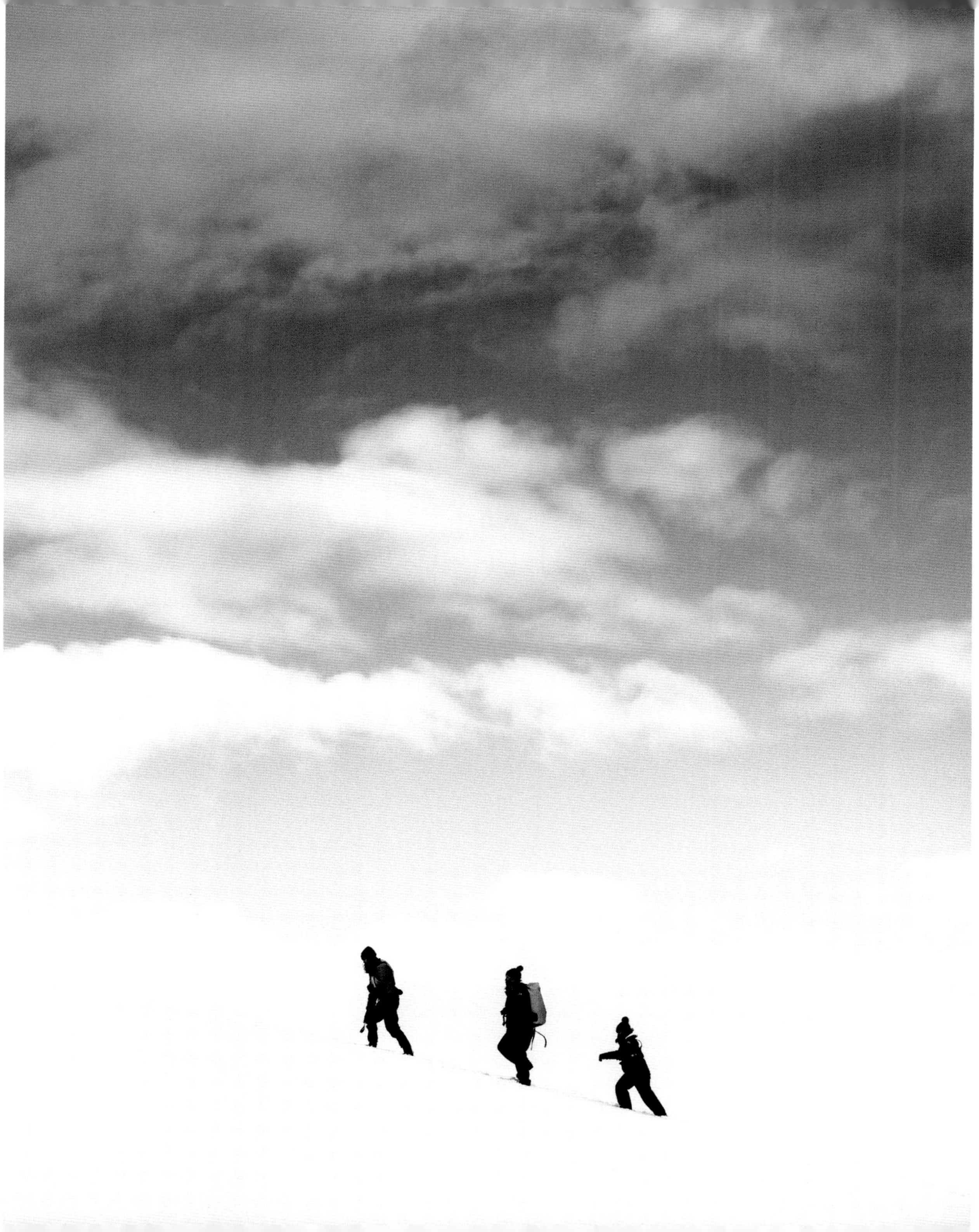

TITLE

The Protector

We almost drove past this little beauty, which was nestled safely in the arms of its mother within the confines of two trees. I'd spotted just a slight movement as we drove by 50 metres away, and our group was able to stop in time to observe a sweet and tender series of moments.

Location: Okavango, Botswana

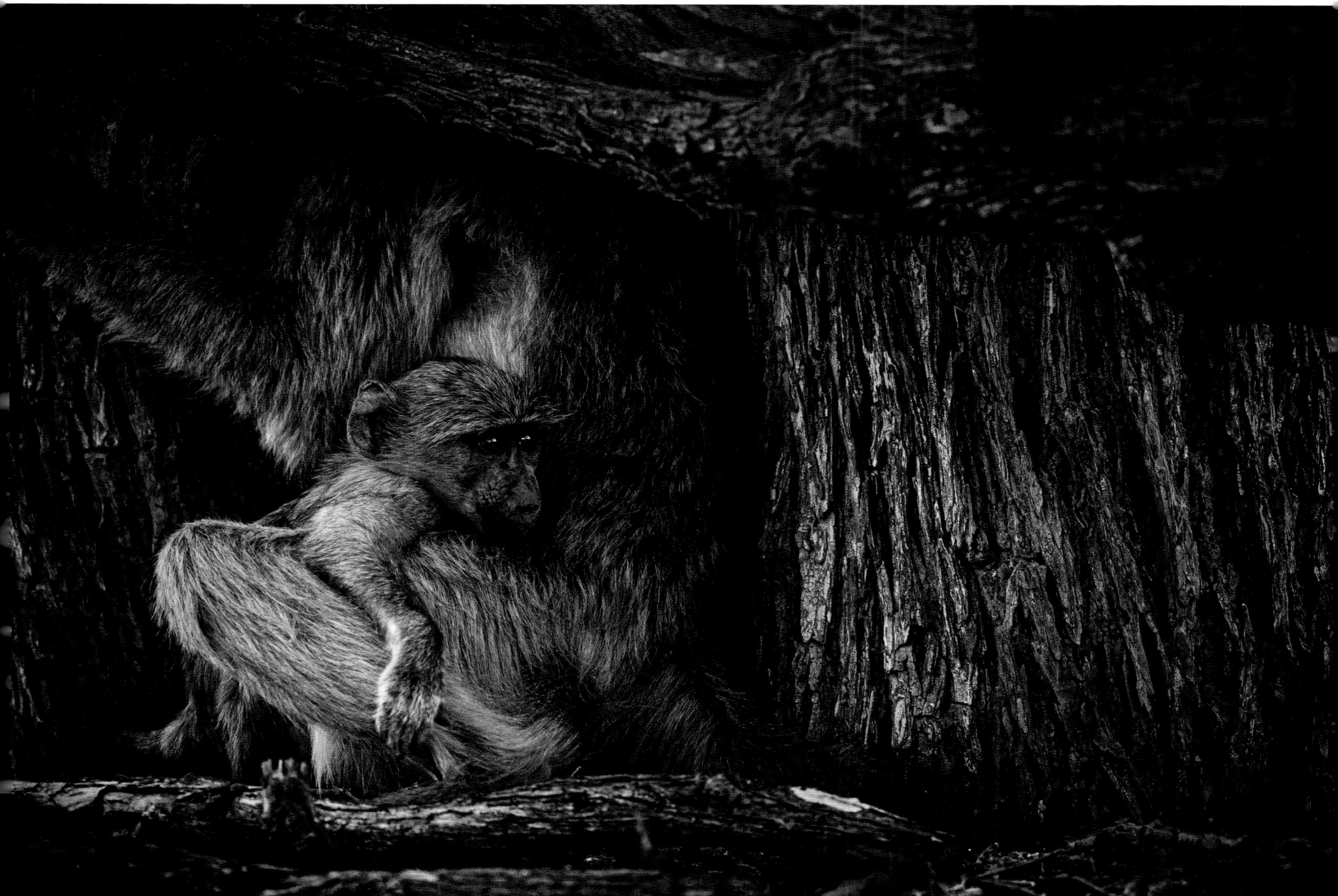

TITLE

The Climb

Sometimes moments occur in nature that leave you shaking your head – the happenstances and the coincidences. In this image, I was observing and photographing a continuous succession of massive waves crashing into a sea tower. In this frame – and I didn't realize it until I loaded it on my computer afterward – the waves took on almost exactly the same shape as the rocky tower.

Location: Valahnúkamöl, Iceland

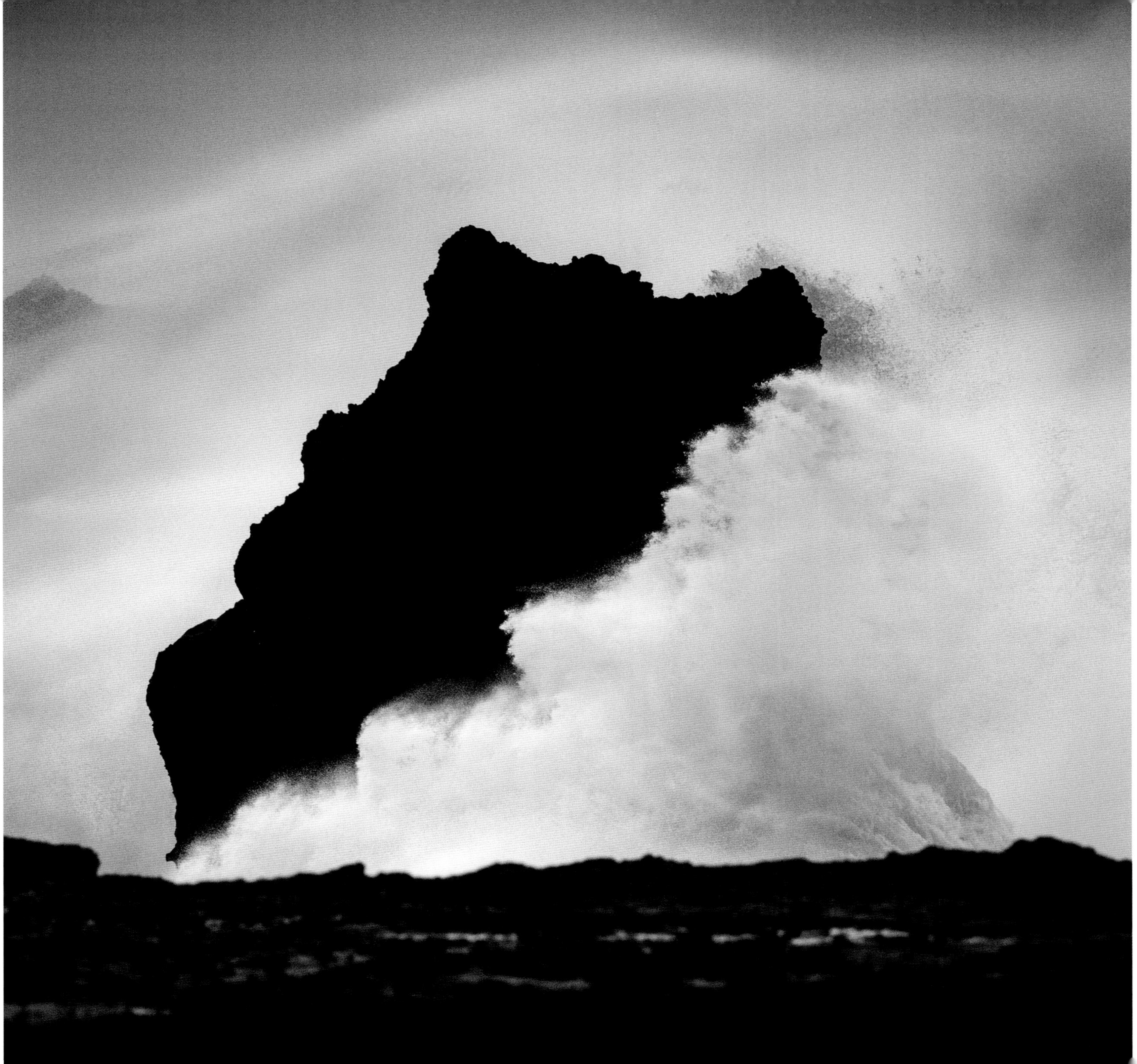

TITLE

The Fall

One thing you must train yourself as a photographer to do is not simply focus your attention on the "obvious" subject matter when you go to a place of natural beauty. The waterfall, alone, is the "star" of this area in Iceland, and I saw countless photographers setting up their tripods to capture it. I did, too (naturally). But after a short period photographing that, I decided to take a few steps back and see what I was missing. The result was an image that I cherish much more than the waterfall on its own.

Location: Seljalandsfoss, Iceland

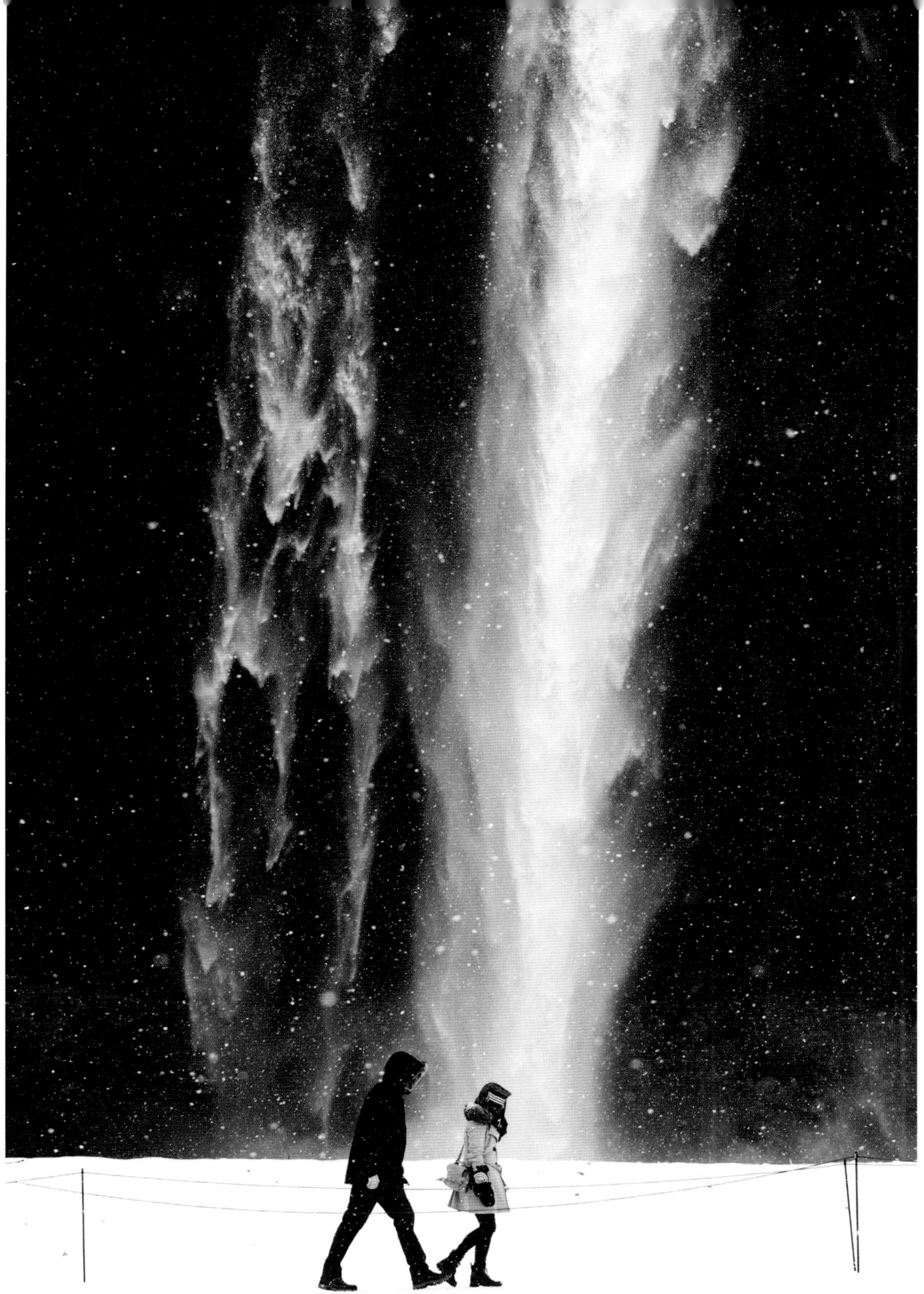

TITLE

Two

Fundy National Park is a place of stunning beauty, to be sure. Towering sea cliffs, old growth forests, and incredible coastline. I spent a week there one summer, photographing and hiking and exploring amazing vistas...but it was this simple image of two roadside trees that stood out against their peers that captured my artistic attention the most. These are the poetic scenes in nature I most enjoy.

Location: Fundy National Park, New Brunswick, Canada

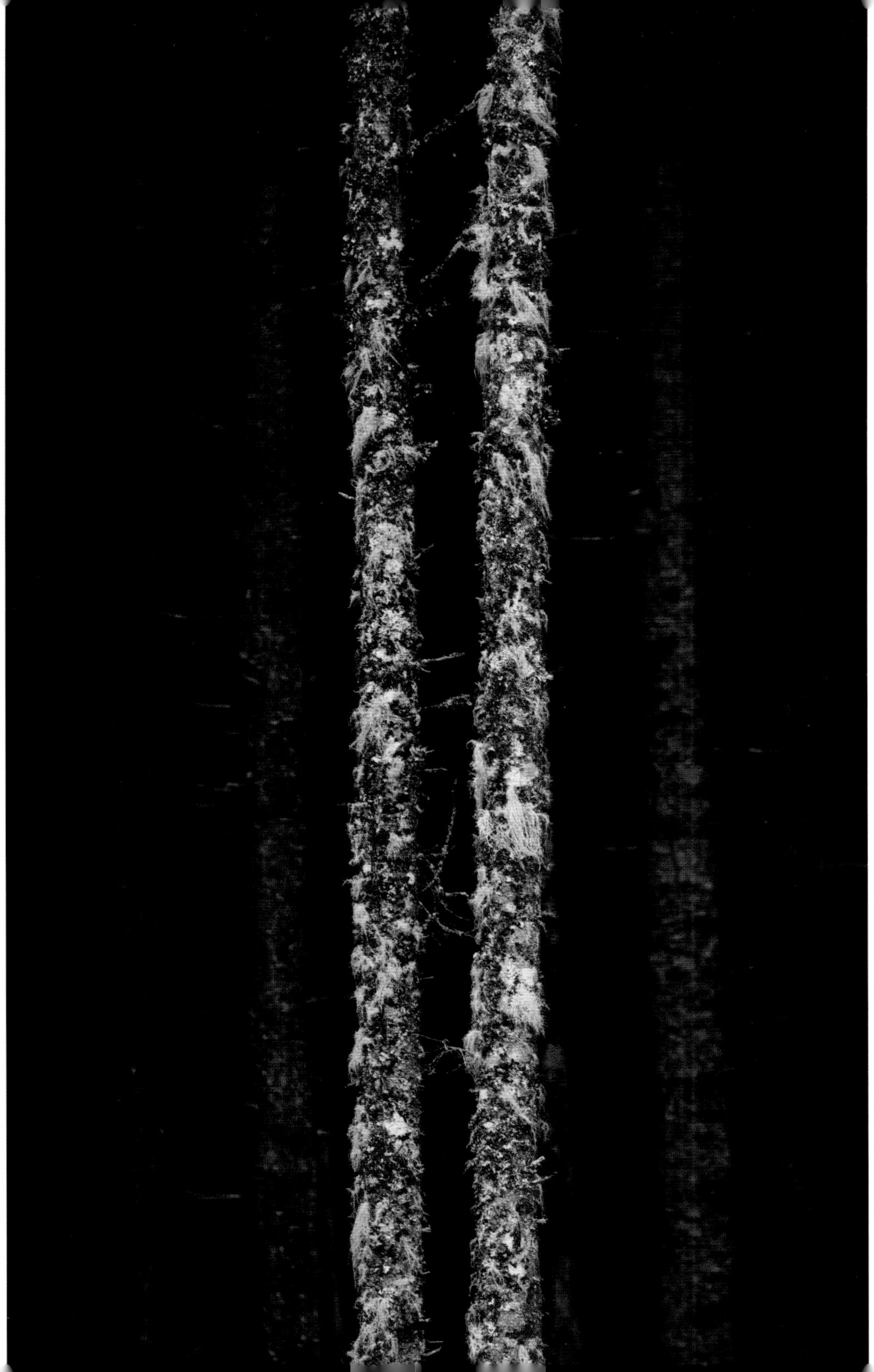

TITLE

Black Magic

A classic long-exposure scene in beautiful Bayfield, Nova Scotia, looking out over the Northumberland Strait. A storm had just broken and gave me a long enough window to capture some of its moody magic before the clouds dissipated entirely and the chaos turned to calm.

Location: Bayfield, Nova Scotia, Canada

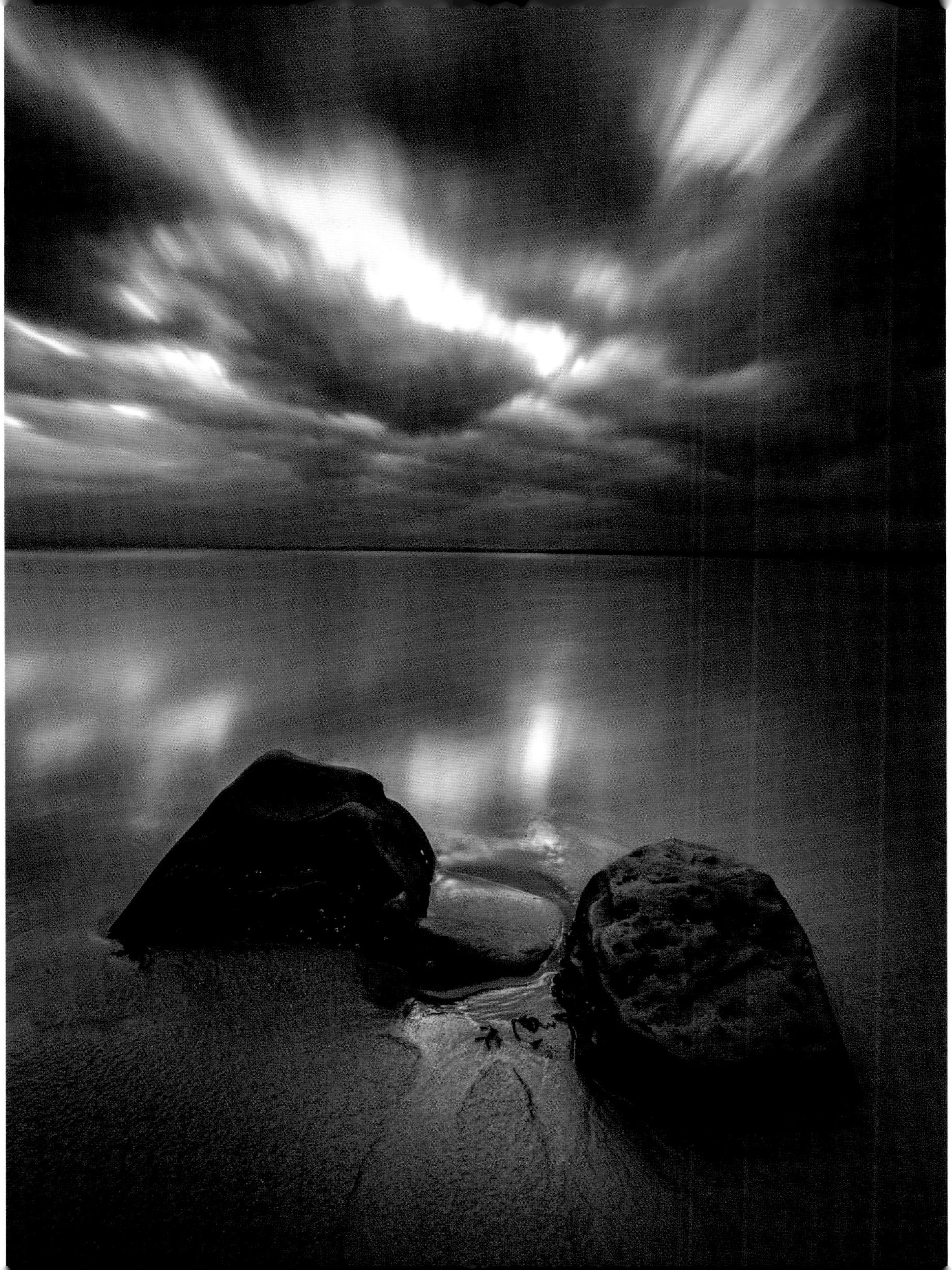

TITLE

Centre Glow

A classic photographic "superpower" in black and white photography is the power of underexposure. In the presence of the brightest of light, you can confidently underexpose an image and plunge your lighter shadows into the depths of darkness, if that's what satisfies the creative muse. On this day, blinding sun spilled an abundance of shine upon the Bow Valley Parkway, which allowed me to underexpose the scene for a moody take.

Location: Banff National Park, Alberta, Canada

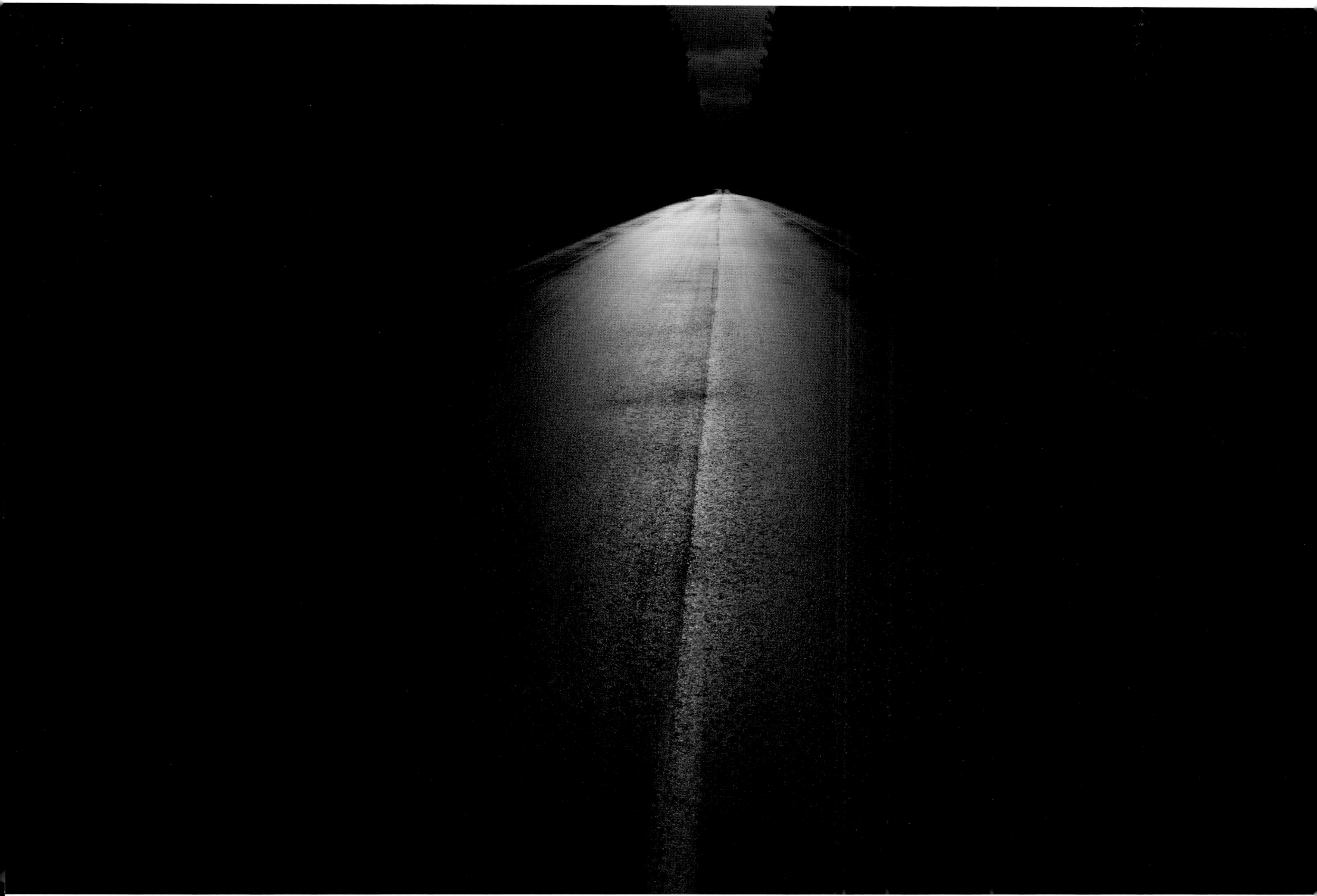

TITLE

Silent Simplicity

Again and again in my career I've been drawn to the "cusp" of weather systems. That fine line between a snowstorm, sideways rain or other inclement weather is where you'll often find unique beauty – and often, quiet calmness.

Location: Banff National Park, Alberta, Canada

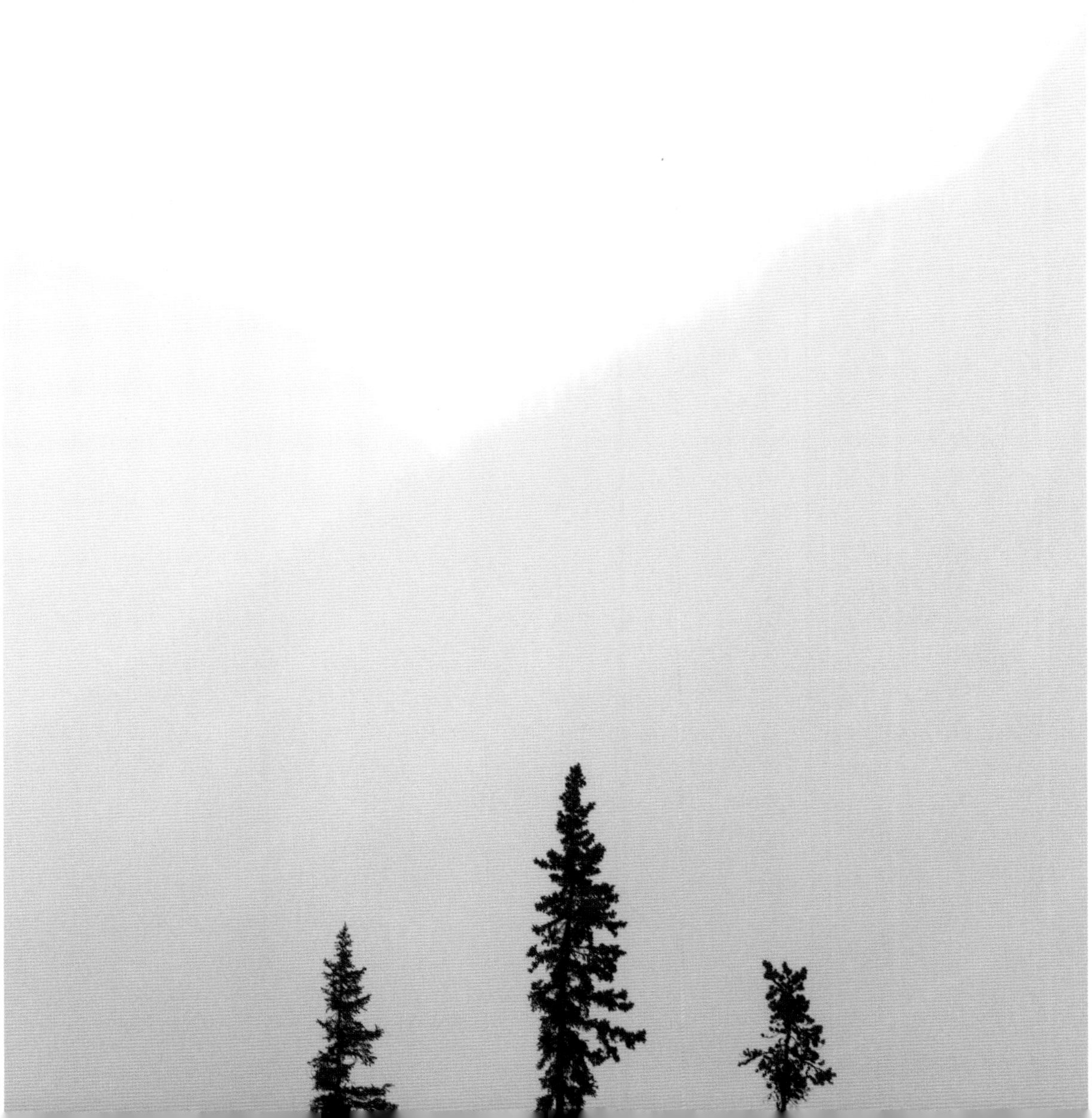

TITLE

New Year’s Day

The first light of the first day of a New Year, photographed near the New London lighthouse in my home province of Prince Edward Island. The snow is yet to come, and the moody decay of another autumn is holding on.

Location: New London, Prince Edward Island, Canada

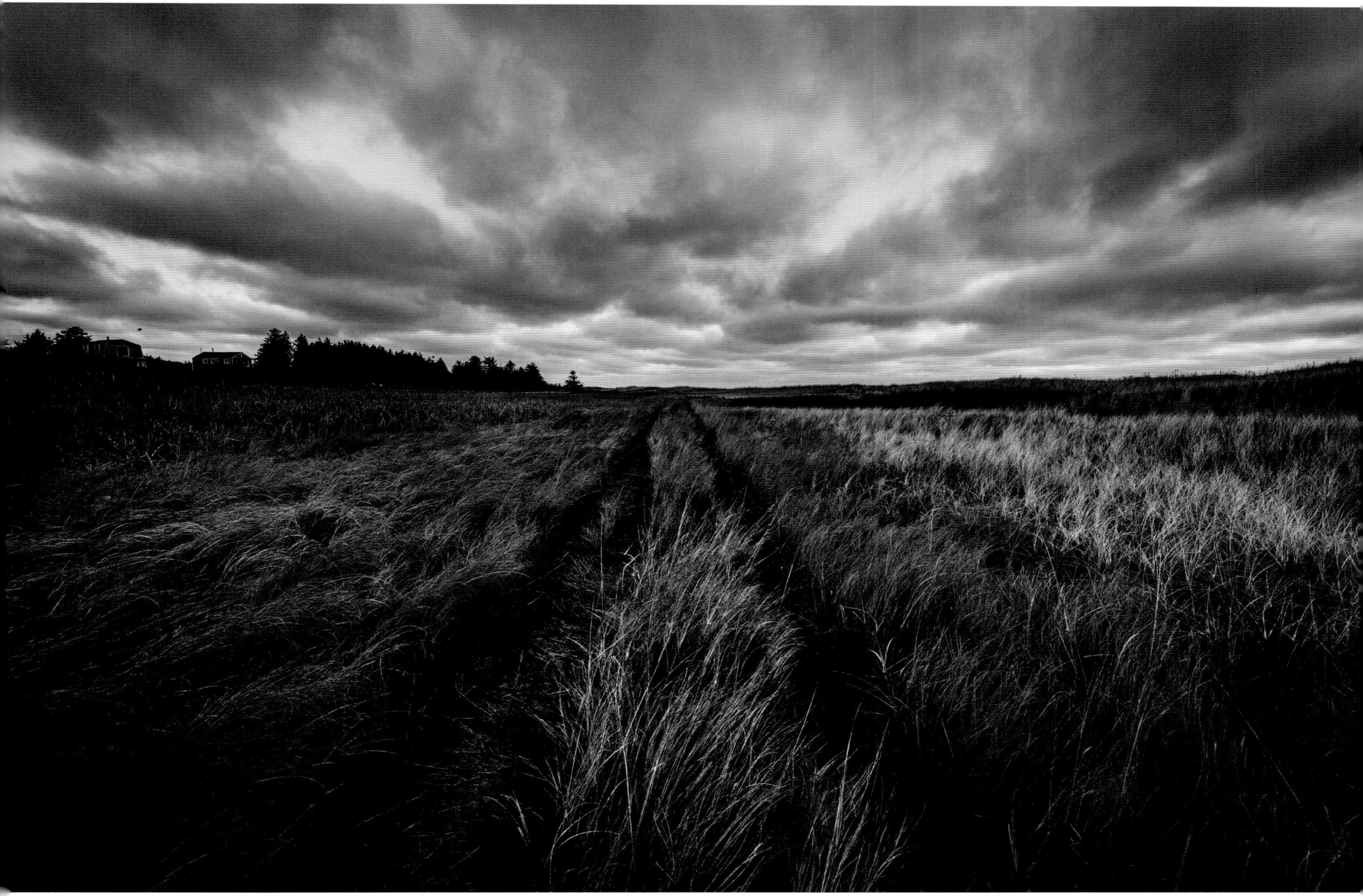

TITLE

Went Out Wandering

There's a U2 song featuring Johnny Cash on vocals, "The Wanderer," and that song was in my head when I went out to shoot this moody self-portrait here on Prince Edward Island. "I went out with nothing...."

Location: New London, Prince Edward Island, Canada

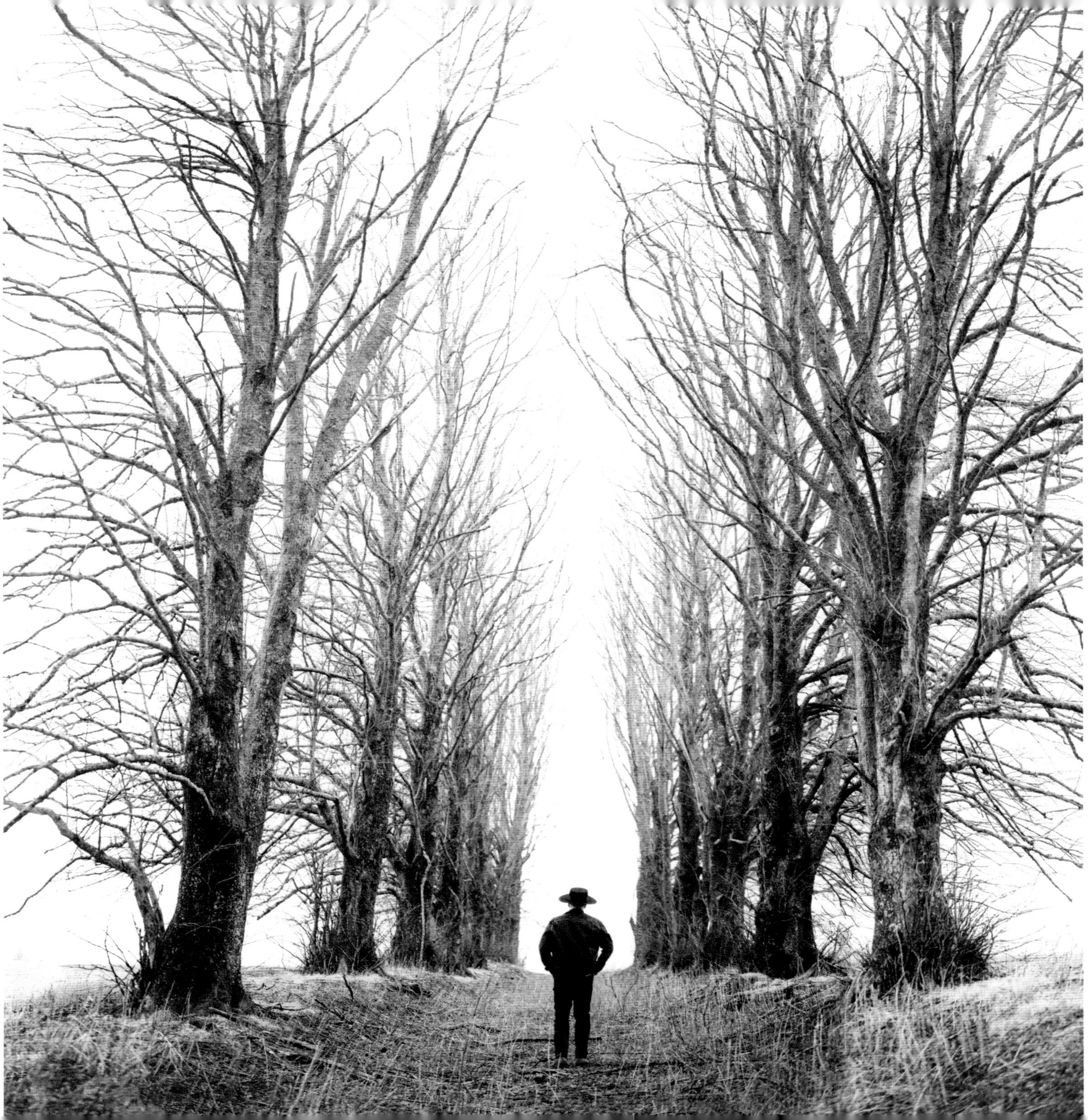

TITLE

A Spoonful of Light

A simple mountain scene of light and shadow and cloud plays amid the beauty of Banff National Park.

Location: Banff National Park, Alberta, Canada

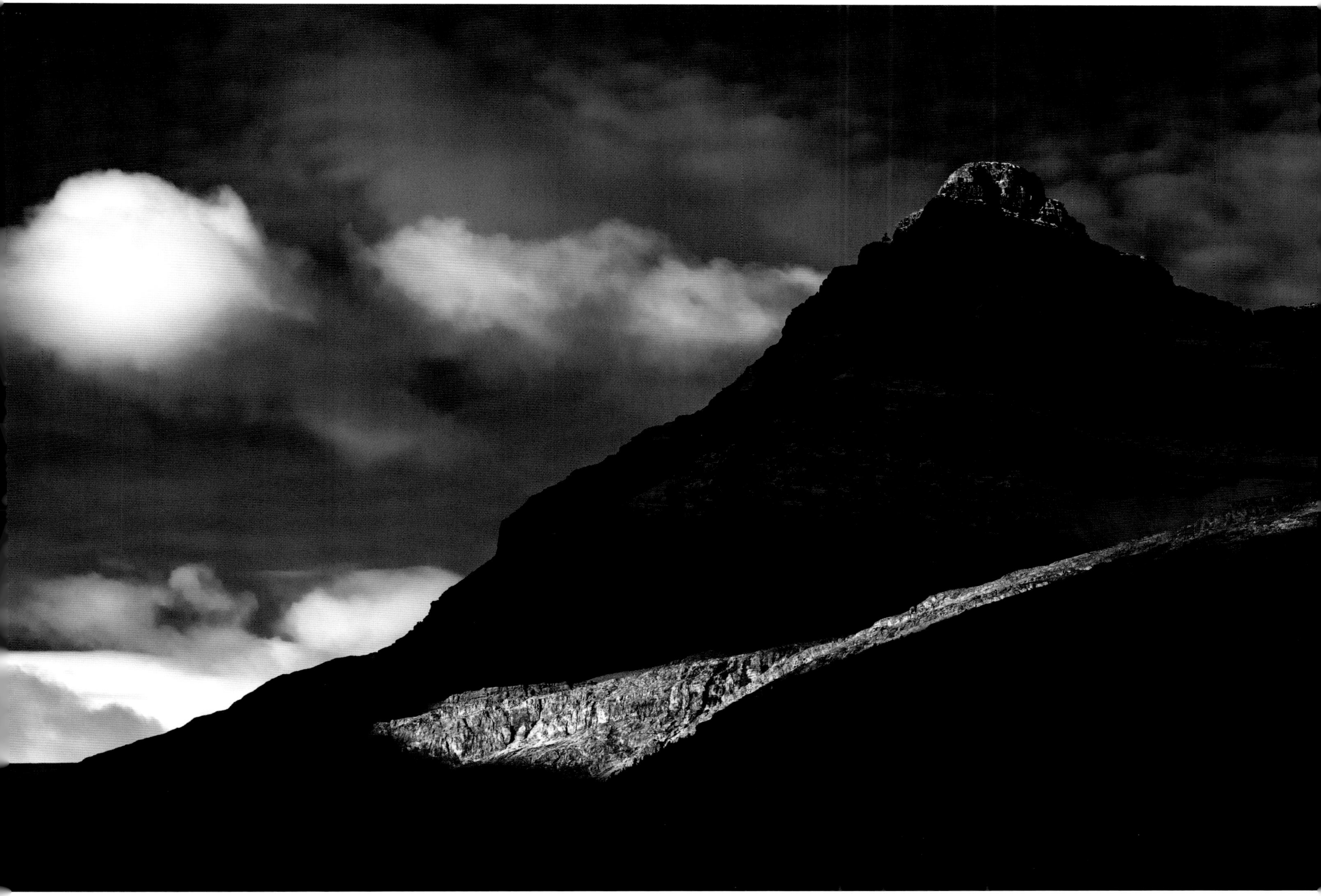

TITLE

When the Rains Came

You can't look at this scene and not feel a sense of "wet" – which is appropriate, I suppose, for an image from the Faroe Islands. I associate that place with always dancing with the threat of oncoming rains, and often losing.

Location: Saksun, Faroe Islands

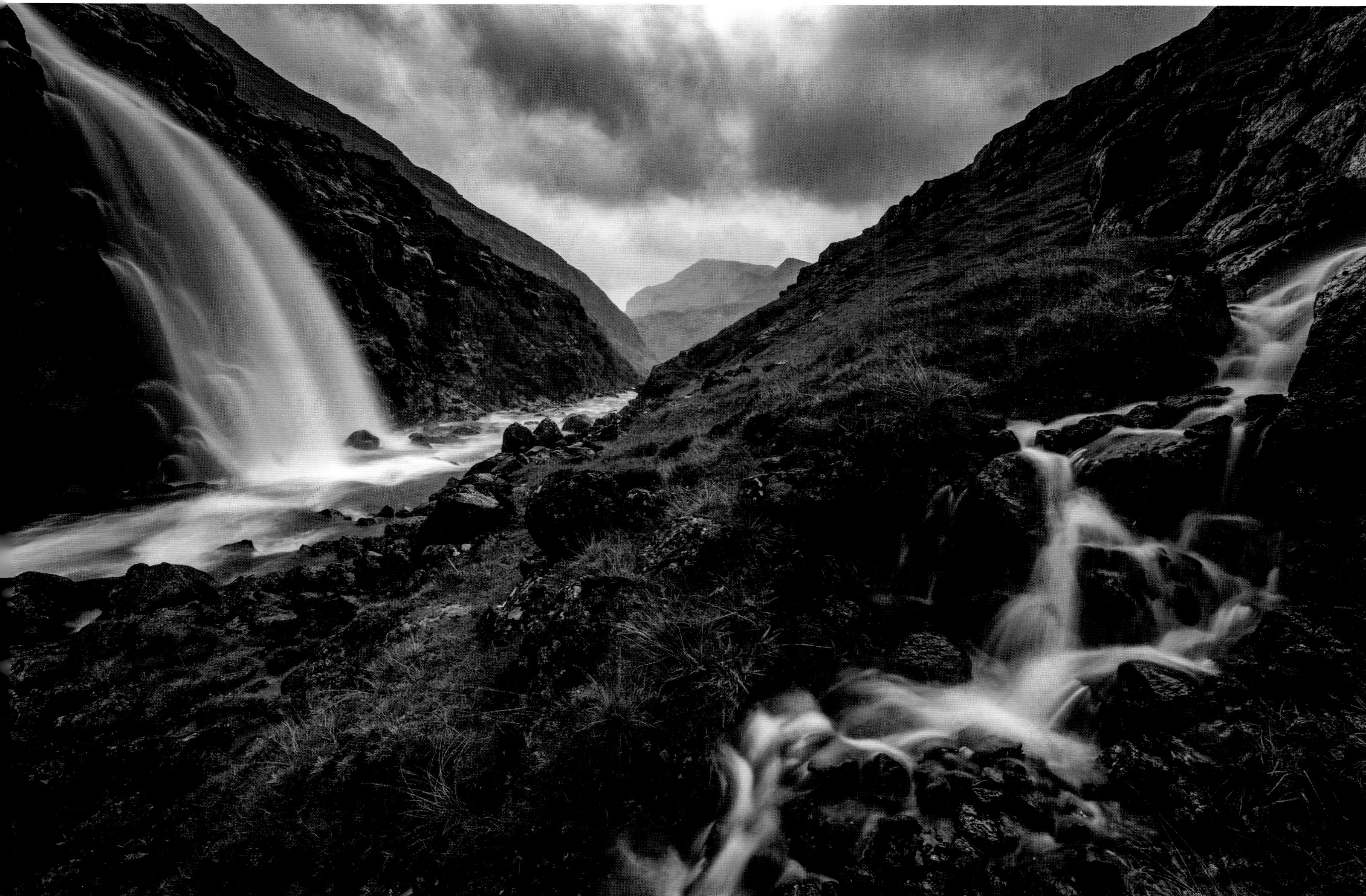

TITLE

Valley of Light

This was photographed on a ten-day trek through the Himalaya in Bhutan. When you're walking endless kilometres per day, you appreciate your rest periods immensely. When I rest, I observe and truly take in my surroundings in ways I often don't while hiking (I go into more of a meditative state while hiking). While resting I watch for light and shadow and lines and the movement of our natural world. And when I rest, I see.

Location: Chomolhari Trek, Bhutan

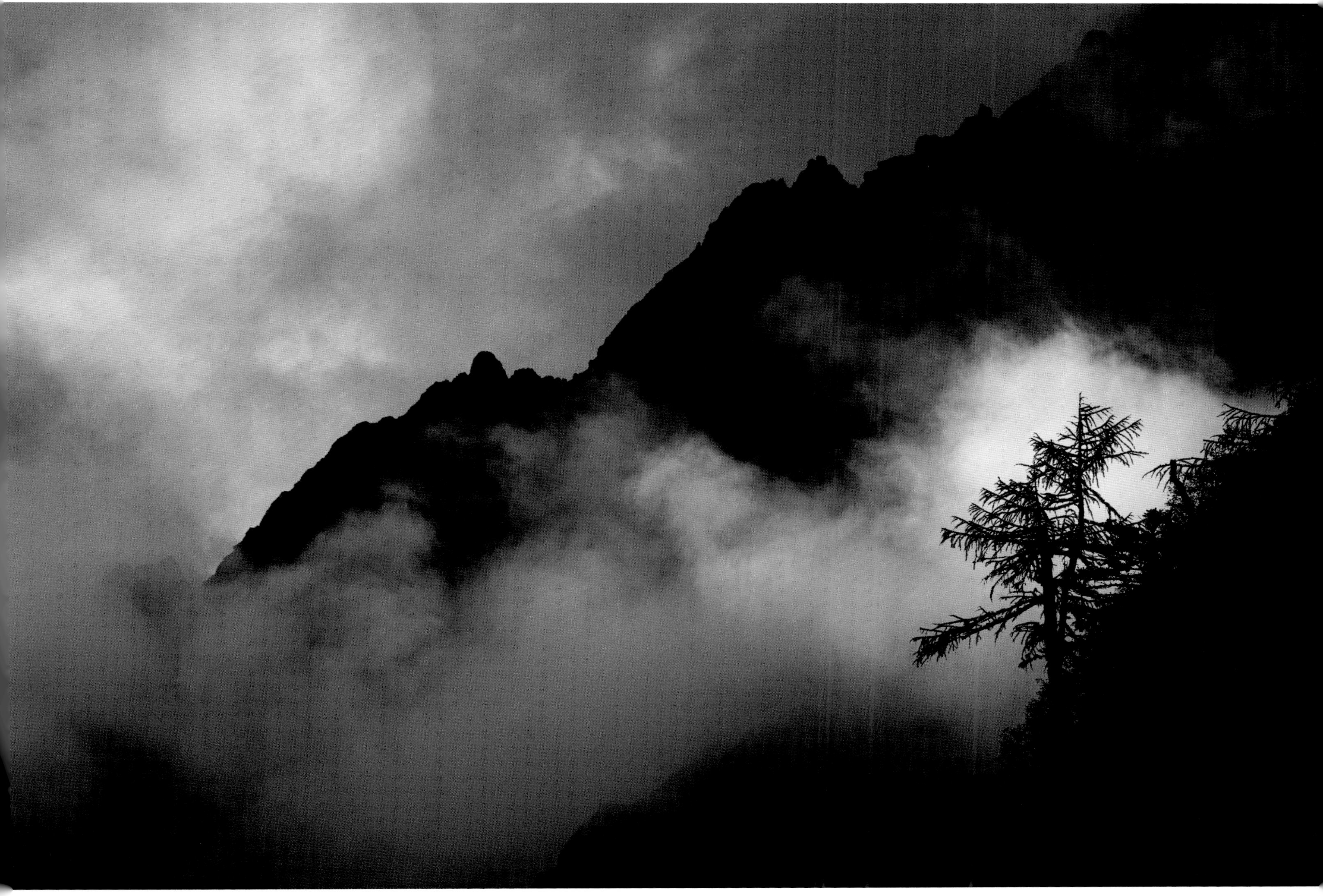

TITLE

On a Limb

A high-contrast story in the wilds of the Okavango Delta in Botswana, which is home to a dazzling array of bird life.

Location: Okavango, Botswana

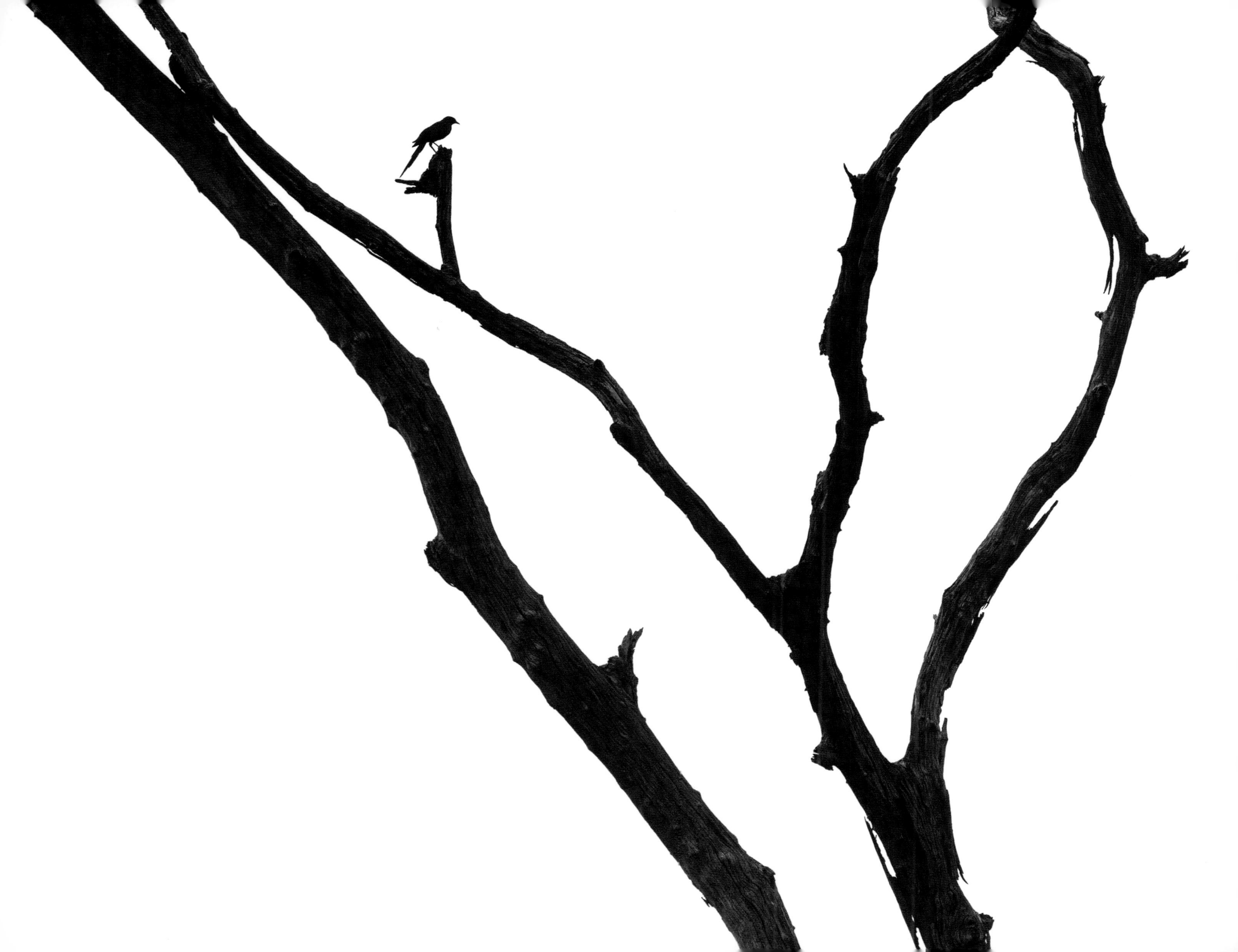

TITLE

The Tempest

February is an incredible time to be in Iceland, if you're someone who enjoys drama, uncertainty and chaos in their life. Weather systems come across the country continuously, and locations often look dramatically different from one hour to the next.

Location: Landeyjahafnarvegur, Iceland

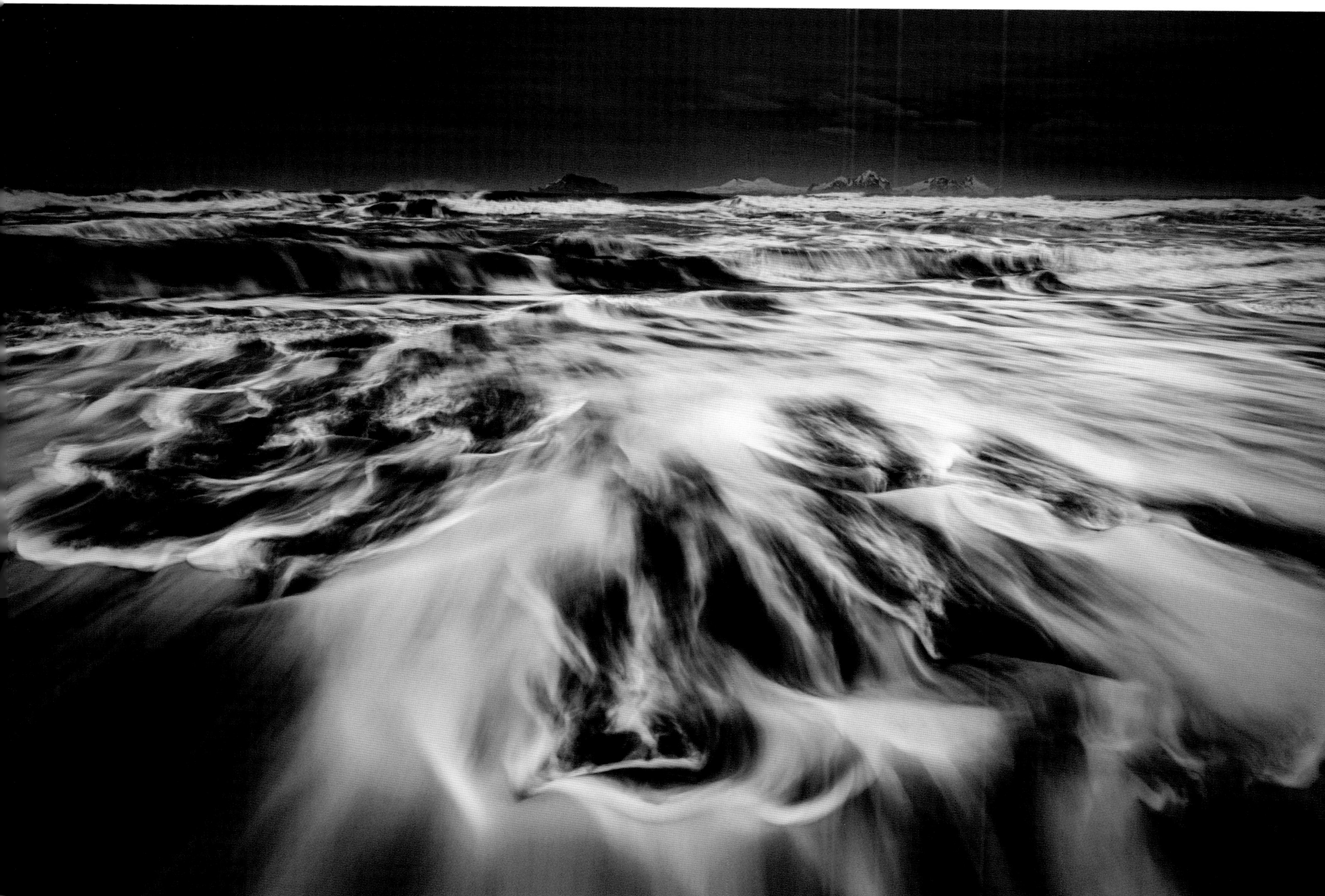

TITLE

Explore and Inspire

Photographer and friend Paul Zizka exploring the moody elements in the Faroe Islands. Paul is one of the most committed and passionate explorers I know, and it's always such a pleasure to head out exploring with him, either on one of our joint business (OFFBEAT)'s trips, or in his backyard in the Canadian Rockies.

Location: Vagar Island, Faroe Islands

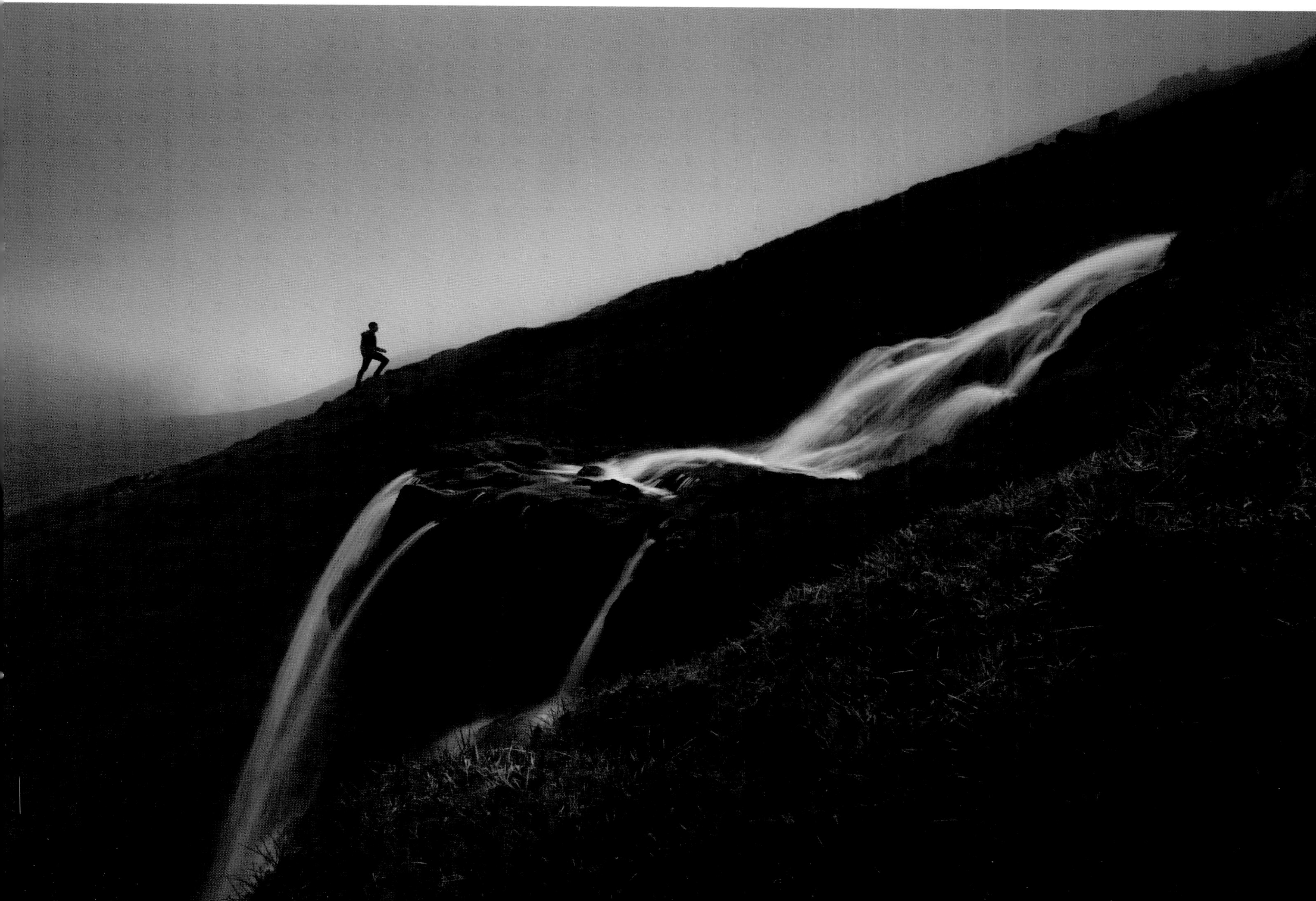

TITLE

Simple Study

Like many photographers – especially those in the nature and monochromatic genres – I have gotten a tremendous amount of inspiration from some of the pioneers of the craft, like Ansel Adams. Ansel photographed a variety of subjects, but you can tell that the mountains were one of his foremost passions. I think of Ansel every time I photograph in the mountains, and always wonder what he would think of the modern era of photography.

Location: Jasper National Park, Canada

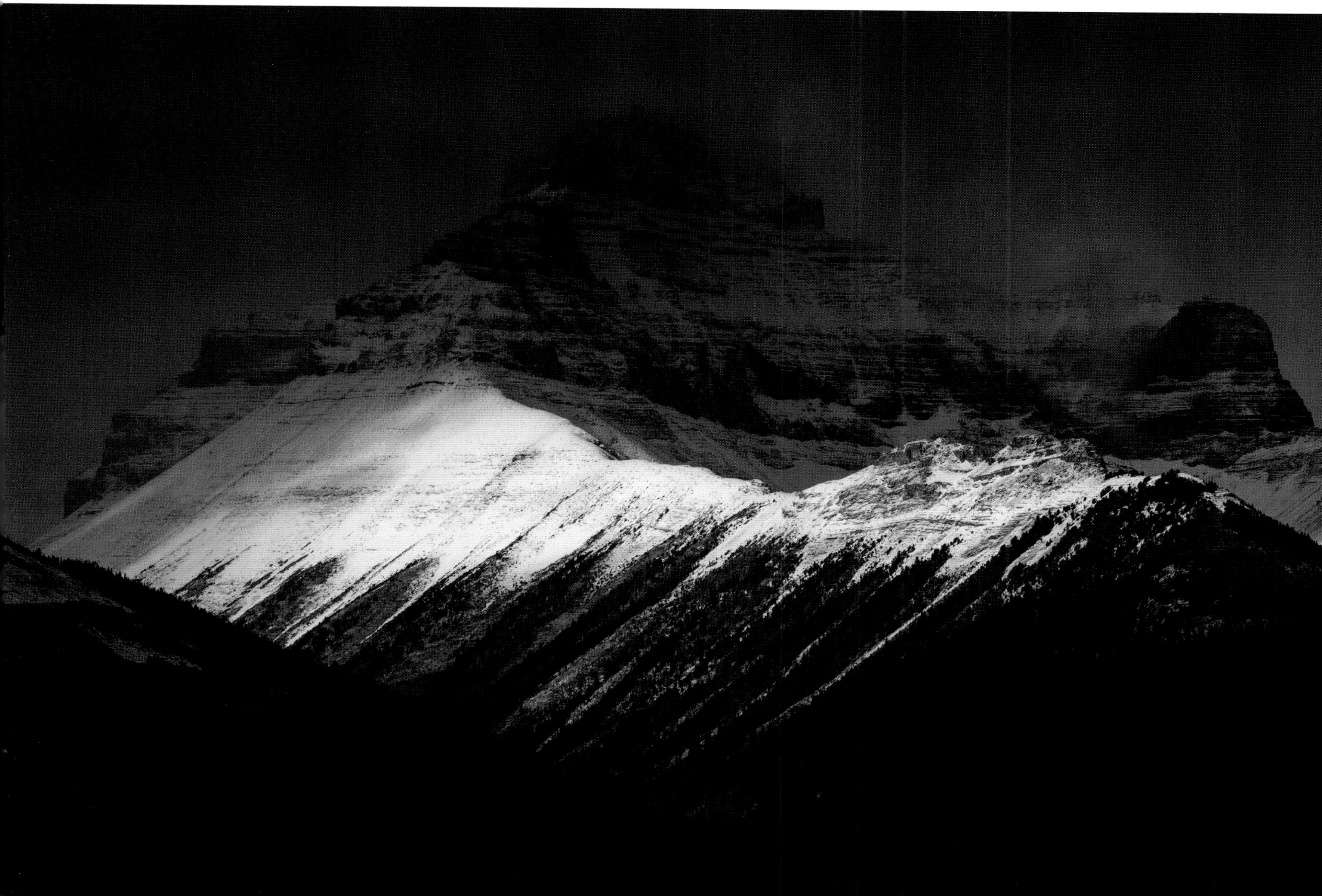

TITLE

Flowers for Your Home

An idyllic, even peaceful scene. Photographs don't tell the whole story, however. That night would be one of the worst sleeps of my life: cold, wet and miserable. A damp sleeping bag, and hours of shivering until the first light of dawn cracked high in the Himalaya. You can't win them all...but you can take a photo.

Location: Chomolhari Trek, Bhutan

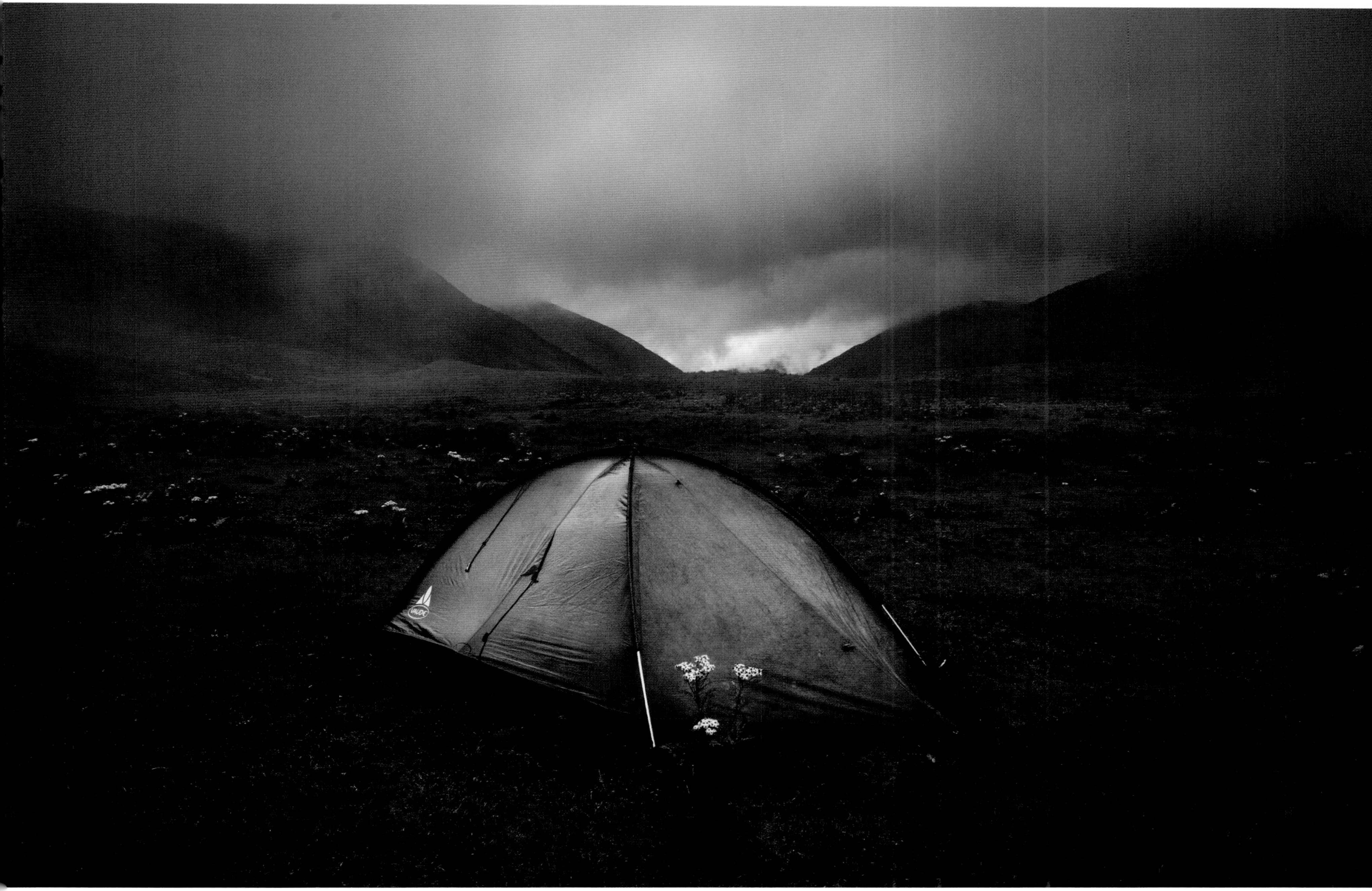

TITLE

The Space Between

From a compositional standpoint, photography is often about balance. My eternal dialogue when dealing with groups of animals (including people) is often "okay, move left...a little more. Okay, stay right there! Don't move!" You're looking for the puzzle pieces to align, for the spaces to feel right.

Location: Okavango Delta, Botswana

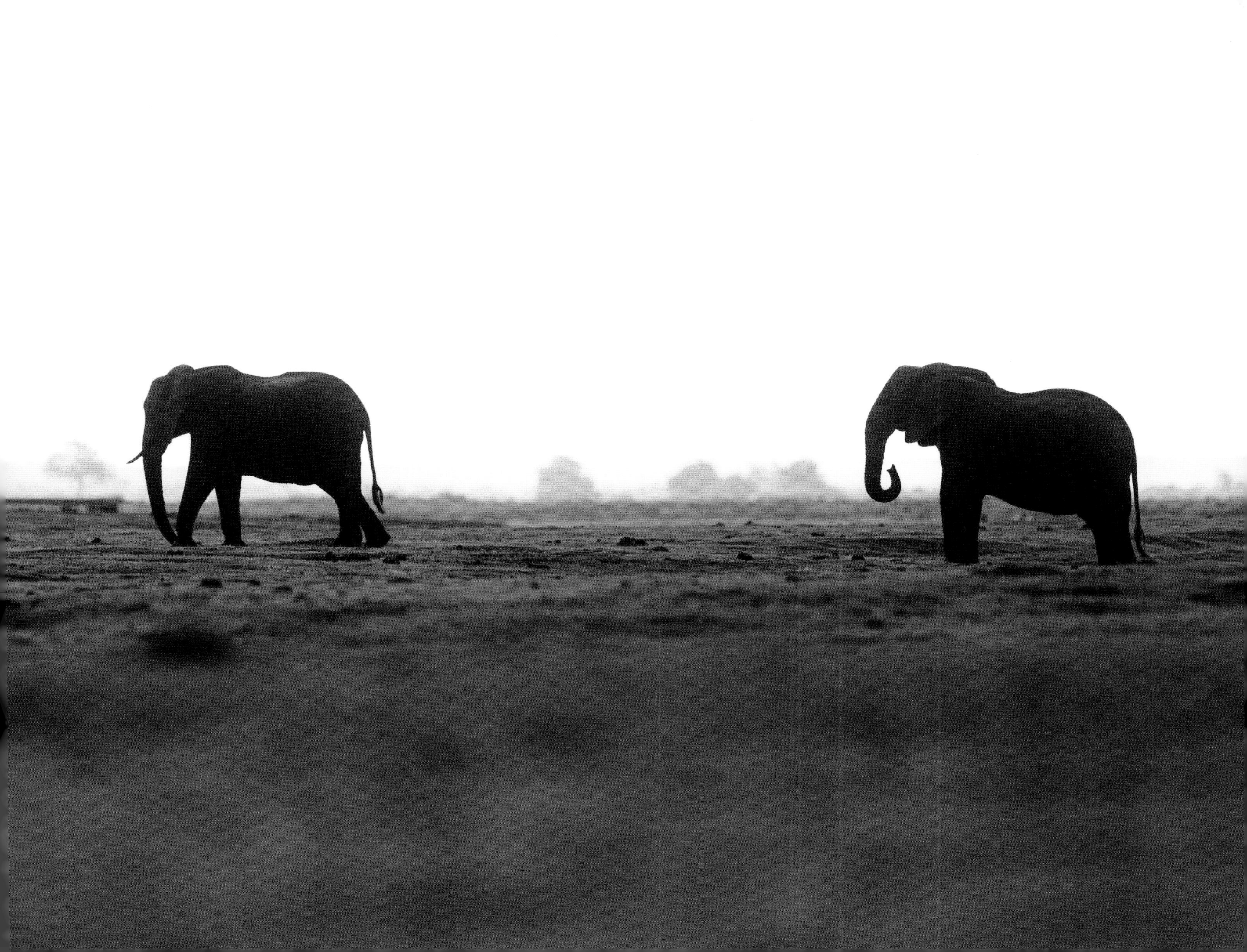

TITLE

Hear Ye

To observe hippopotami is to observe a lesson in group dynamics: the silent and strong, the loud and flashy, the wild and aggressive.

Location: Okavango Delta, Botswana

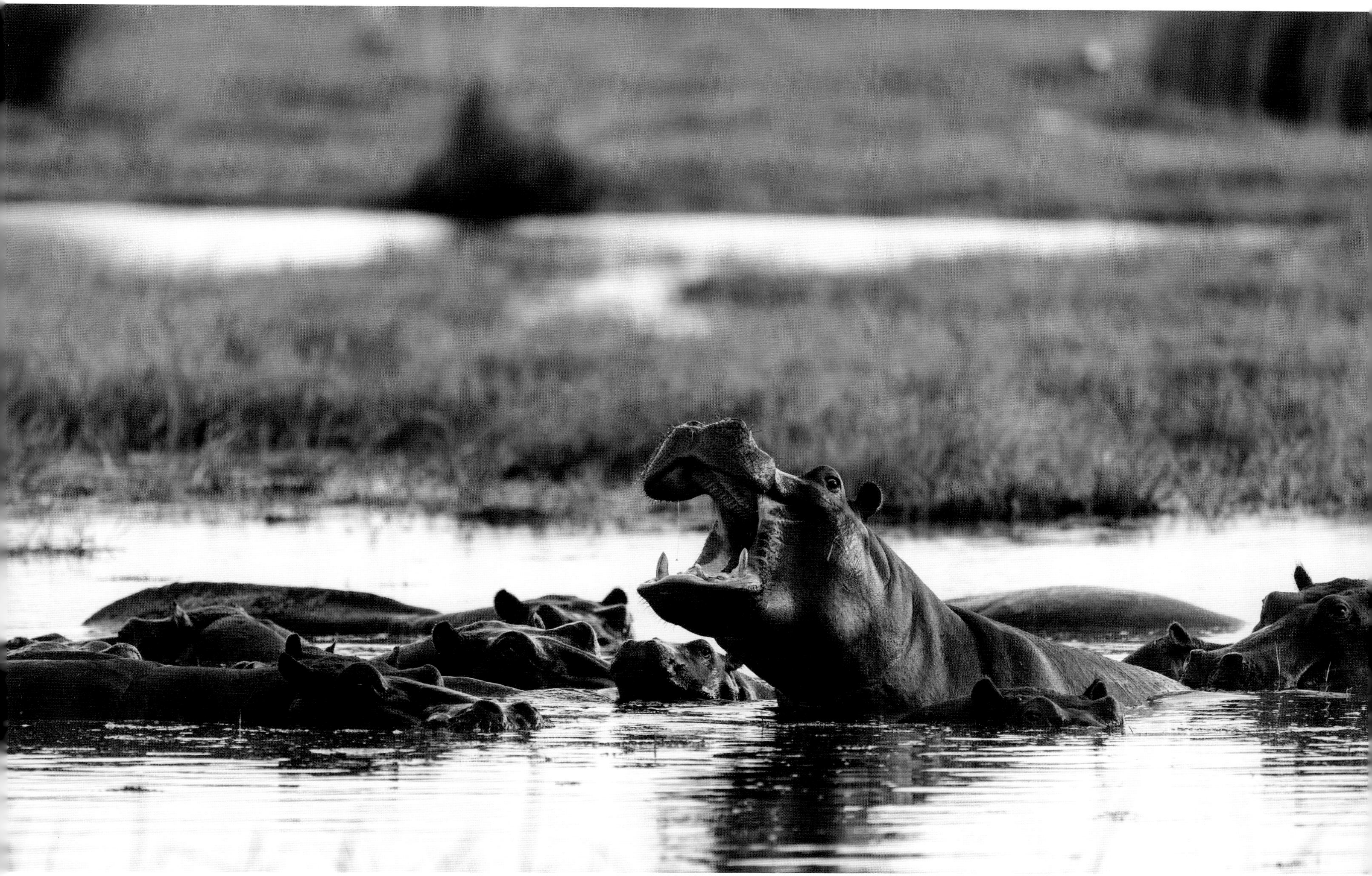

TITLE

Weathered

The camel thorn trees at Deadvlei, Namibia, are estimated to be approximately 900 years old. They are not petrified, but they haven't decomposed, due to the incredibly dry conditions in the area.

Location: Deadvlei, Namibia

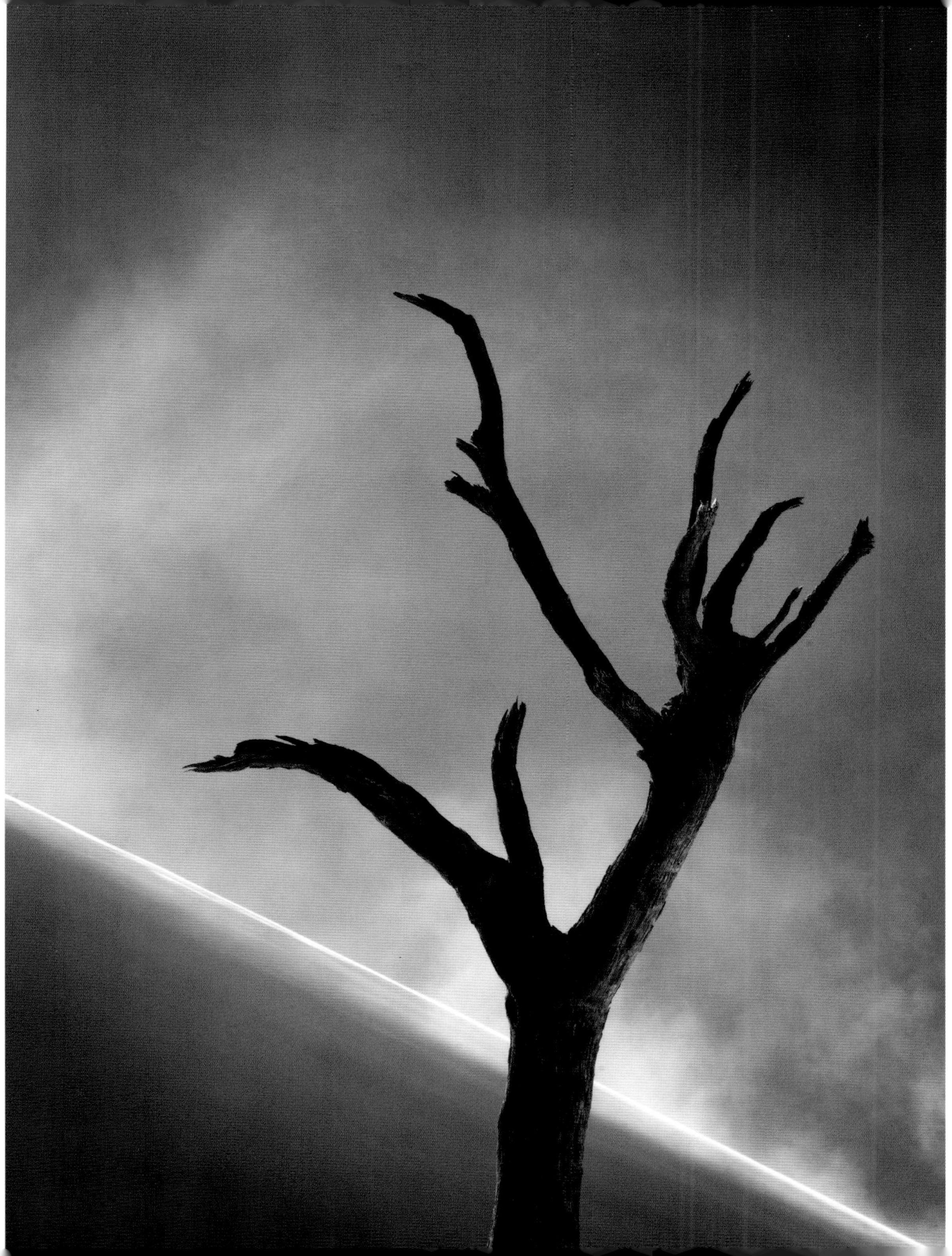

TITLE

Children of the Sea

Post-storm low tide exploration on the dramatic south shore of Prince Edward Island. One part beachcombing, one part splashing, two parts fun.

Location: Rice Point, Prince Edward Island, Canada

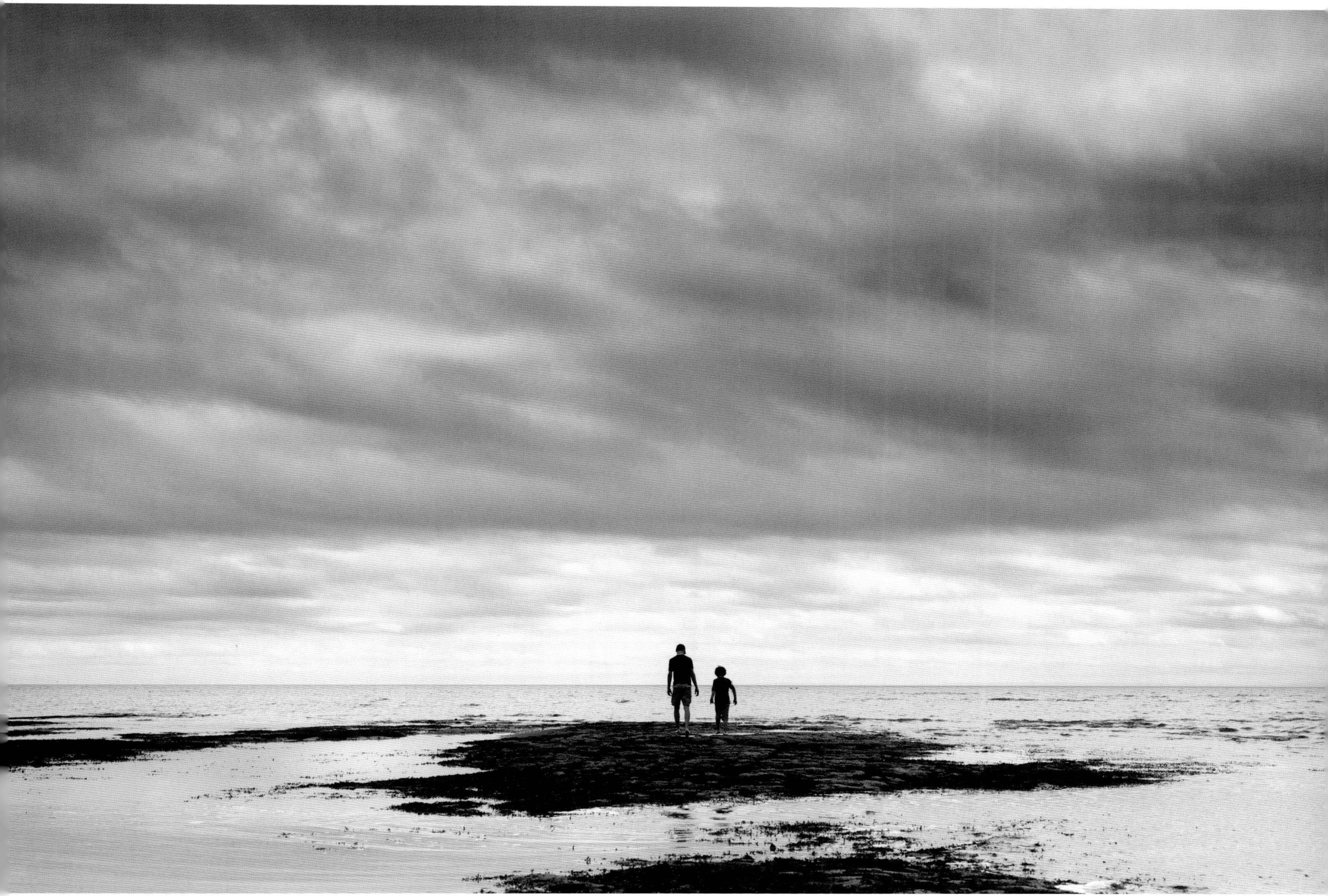

TITLE

Together until the End

The last image I photographed on my last day on a remarkable trip to Botswana. And an appropriate "end."

Location: Chobe National Park, Botswana

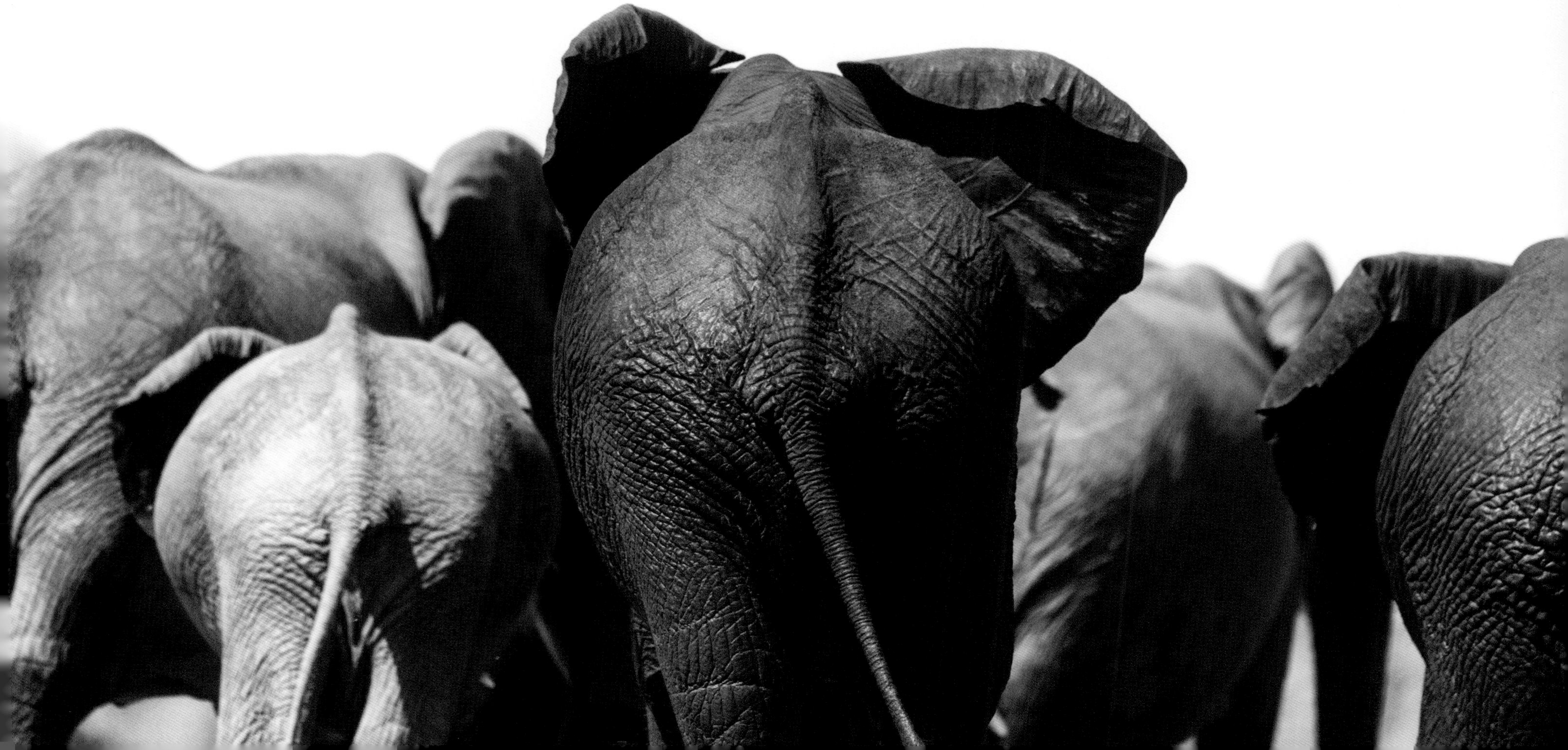

More photography books by Dave Brosha

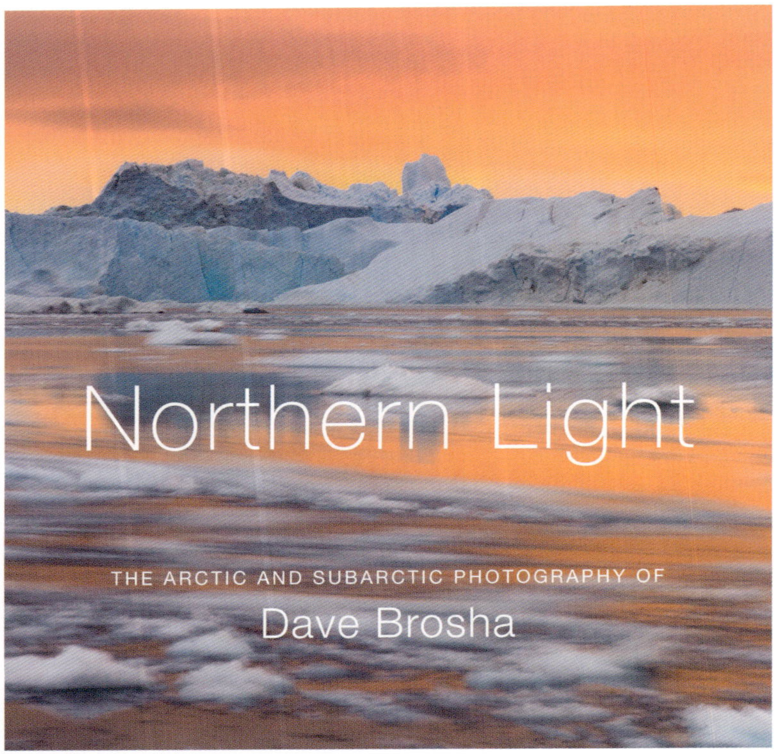

Northern Light

The Arctic and Subarctic Photography of Dave Brosha

Hardcover | 9781771602983

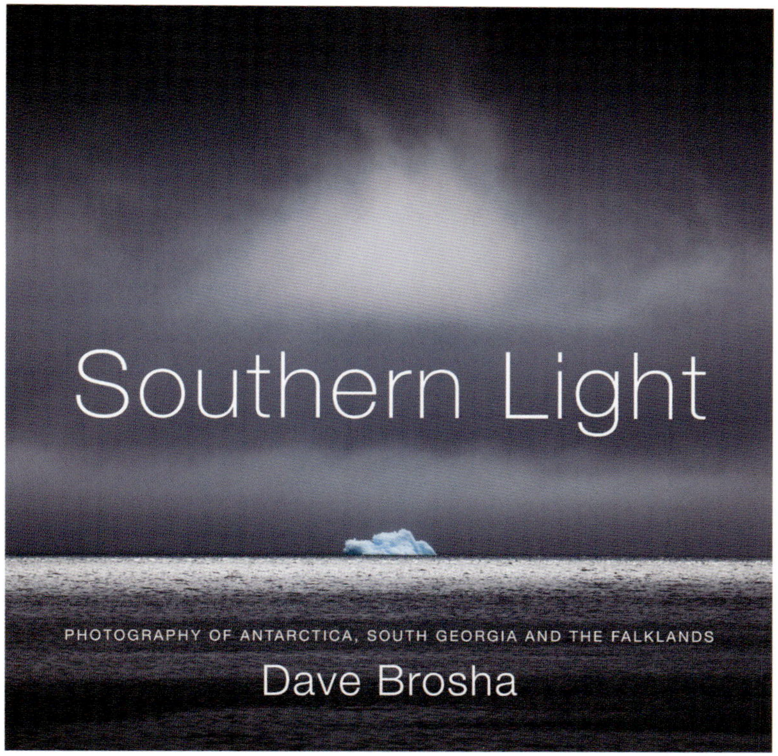

Southern Light

Photography of Antarctica, South Georgia, and the Falkland Islands

Hardcover | 9781771604253